UNDER
A COMMON SKY

UNDER A COMMON SKY

⤳

ETHNIC GROUPS
OF THE COMMONWEALTH
OF POLAND
AND LITHUANIA

—

Edited by Michał Kopczyński and Wojciech Tygielski

Translated by William F. Hoffman

—

Polish History Museum * Warsaw

PIASA Books * New York

Revised version of the book published under the title
Pod wspólnym niebem. Narody dawnej Rzeczypospolitej,
Warszawa: Muzeum Historii Polski, Bellona, 2010

Published in the United States by PIASA Books
The Polish Institute of Arts and Sciences of America
208 East 30th St., New York, NY 10016
www.piasa.org/pb.html

Published in Poland by Polish History Museum
33/35 Mokotowska Street, 00-560 Warsaw
www.muzhp.pl

Maps: Tomasz Opach
Graphic design: Syfon Studio

ISBN 978-83-65248-18-3
Library of Congress Control Number:
2017936731

Translated into English thanks to financial support
from The Lanckoroński Foundation

Fundacja
Lanckorońskich

Contents

—

National Identity before nationalism: The case of the Commonwealth of Poland and Lithuania

---

MICHAŁ KOPCZYŃSKI

"The Commonwealth of Two Nations" and "the nation without [burning at] stakes" are informal descriptions often used in connection with the pre-partition Polish-Lithuanian Commonwealth. When speaking and writing on this subject, it is customary to emphasize the Commonwealth's religious tolerance, which was unique in Europe in the 16ᵗʰ century. Further association usually leads to thoughts of the multiethnic character of the state, in which there were far more ethnic groups than just the Poles and Lithuanians to whom the designation "two nations" referred. The people who lived beneath the sky of the Commonwealth of Poland and Lithuania can be divided into three categories: "the locals," that is, the chief ethnic groups inhabiting each of the main parts of the future Commonwealth; the "assimilated ones," or immigrants who came to those lands in the Middle Ages, before the conclusion of the union between Poland and Lithuania; and "the newcomers," foreigners who came during the 16ᵗʰ and 17ᵗʰ centuries in search of living conditions and career opportunities better than those in their homelands.

This is the division we have used in this book. The first of these groups are the Poles, inhabitants of Wielkopolska (Greater Poland), Małopolska (Lesser Poland), and Mazowsze (Mazovia); the Lithuanians, inhabiting Samogitia and Lithuania proper (Aukštaitija); and the Ruthenians, who lived in modern-day Belarus and Ukraine. In the "assimilated" category we include the Germans, who arrived as settlers beginning at the end of the 12th century, in Pomerania, Silesia, and the lands of central Poland; the Jews; and, far less numerous but still very visible in the society, the Tatars, Armenians, Gypsies, and Karaites. The "newcomers," the last of the groups mentioned, were the Scots, Italians, and Dutch Mennonites, who arrived in the early modern era. The proposed categorization of ethnic groups may, obviously, arouse controversy. Is not including separate texts on Belarusians and Ukrainians in a book devoted to the early modern period a case of presentism gone too far? Yet, arguing on behalf of separate treatment of the Ruthenians who inhabited today's Belarus and Ukraine is the fact that as a result of border changes of the Crown (i.e., the Kingdom of Poland) and the Grand Duchy of Lithuania in 1569, they found themselves on both sides of a border dividing the former Commonwealth that, while internal, was nonetheless important. The fate of those lands also took separate courses. Many inhabitants of central Poland, both from the ranks of the magnates and of the nobles, moved to the territory of the Ukrainian provinces that belonged to the Kingdom of Poland from 1569. Together with the polonization of the local elite and the religious conflict between the Uniates and the Orthodox, this led to a long-lasting struggle. Begun as a civil war, it ended as a great battle between the mightiest powers of Central and Eastern Europe, and it resulted in a persistent weakening of the international position of the Commonwealth. It is to this conflict and its social and religious roots that Mirosław Nagielski has devoted his text. Although the mid-17th century conflicts did not bypass the territory of today's Belarus, then within the borders of the Grand Duchy of Lithuania, political events are not exclusively the subject of interest for Oleg Łatyszonek. He writes of a discovery that developed slowly in the early modern era, the discovery of the Belarusian character of those lands, understood as distinct not only from the Crown and Lithuania, but also from Red Ruthenia.

No less diverse are the other texts included in this volume. This diversity is only partly a result of the different writing temperaments of the indi-

8

vidual authors. One must remember that the ethnic groups of the former Commonwealth were diverse both in terms of faith and customs as well as in social composition and position in the social hierarchy. Poles, Lithuanians, and Ruthenians had their own nobility, which participated actively in the political life of their own nation and district. It was different for the Jews, Karaites, Armenians, Scots, Tatars, and Gypsies; for although they formed diverse communities and had their own elites, nonetheless, those were not treated on a par with the nobles. The Italians, on the other hand, differentiated by property, social position attained in the Commonwealth, and professions, did not create their own self-rule and inner hierarchy. Each of these groups deserves attention, however, because each made its own contribution to the cultural landscape that unfolded under the common sky of the Commonwealth.

Regarding the matter from a contemporary perspective, it is easy to view the history of Poland from the late Middle Ages to the 19th century as a multicultural experiment that lasted over 400 years, reminiscent, at least to a certain degree, of the situation of many of today's countries in western Europe. This association comes to mind as evident; but before we follow it, we must determine whether ethnic and religious differences in those times signified the same thing as today. According to Ernest Gellner and Tomasz Kizwalter, the author of the latest Polish synthesis devoted to the problem, nations understood as communities possessing a sense of ethnic distinction were formed relatively recently, during the era of the Industrial Revolution, mass media, and modern schooling. Their development was one of the elements of social modernization. In earlier times, social divisions were so sharp that it was difficult even to imagine a feeling of community reaching from the highest strata all the way down to the lowest (and this is the essence of the contemporary concept of a nation). The population's relative geographic immobility, the difficulty of communication, and the lack of mass media favored the diversity of local communities. Historians debate whether those distinctions were so strong as to overshadow the sense of community arising from a linguistic basis or by contrast with foreign immigrants. In the literature devoted to the process of nation formation, one may encounter the view that the origin of nations in the contemporary sense was a direct result of manipulation, of creating somewhat artificially—with the help of schooling and symbols preferred by the authorities (anniversaries, monuments, and the like)—a sense of community that had not previously existed. According to this opinion, in the Middle Ages or in the Early Modern Era, activities of this kind on the part of the authorities were doomed to failure in view of the poorly developed "infrastructure of coercion." By the very nature of things, the social reach of the ideas propagated by the central authorities had to be less than in the 19th and 20th centuries.

At the other end of the interpretational spectrum must be placed the traditional view, according to which nations exist objectively since time immemorial. In this sort of view, the question of the existence or non-existence of a sense of community based on ethnic grounds has no great meaning. It is language that plays the key role here, becoming a carrier of community identity. The classical argument seems to be supported by numerous examples from the history of the European languages, as from the turning point of the Renaissance, they began to be treated as a cause for pride and a means of articulating identity. "All *nations* have thought nothing more powerful to unite minds than the community of language," wrote the English globetrotter Fynes Moryson at the turn of the 16th century.

Languages were—even in those times—an element of conscious policy on the part of the authorities. Serving as evidence of this is the statute of Kilkenny (1366) that threatened the English and the Irish "living among the English" with imprisonment for using Gaelic words rather than English in their speech. Repressions were also announced by the regulation in the 1536 Act of Union between England and Wales that forbade use of the Welsh language in courts and administration, under penalty of loss of office and benefices. Language also played an essential role in Bohemia, where the estates demanded knowledge of the Czech language by the naturalized citizen and his descendants as a condition for naturalization. Less repressive, albeit firm, was the position of the nobility of the Commonwealth, which in 1696 ordered that judicial records in the Grand Dutchy of Lithuania were to be kept, not in the Ruthenian language, but in Polish. All these regulations, however, were restricted to the elite or to contact with institutions of government, and had no effect on the language used every day in the lower levels of the social hierarchy. The statute of Kilkenny speaks only of those among the Irish who were "in English surroundings." The regulations of the Act of Union between England and Wales were also limited in their scope. In 1563, Elizabeth I ordered Holy Scripture translated into Welsh in order to avoid a situation in which "prayers in church were conducted or sacraments administered in a language incomprehensible to the people." Then, too, the Reformation compelled a compromise between the state's drive for omnipotence and common sense. In Bohemia, breaking the estates' provisions on language was a political act connected with the struggles between the Habsburgs and the Czech estates, which in the final reckoning suffered a defeat in the first phase of the Thirty Years' War, a defeat that led to change in the ethnic composition of the ruling elite on a massive scale. But at the same time, hardly anyone cared what language the Czech people used. In the case of Poland, the bill rejecting Ruthenian, as well as the demand to cease using the German language in the records of Royal Prussia, were consequences of the fact that hardly anyone among the nobility could still use these two languages. It was, therefore, the expression of a victory of practical sense over bureaucratic inertia, and not a conscious purpose aimed at denationalizing. The case of Sweden seems the one exception to the rule; there the authorities consciously and consistently promoted not only legal but also cultural and linguistic swedenization of the population inhabiting the provinces acquired from Denmark by virtue of the treaty in Roskilde (1658, Scania, Halland and Blekinge). In accordance with the orders of Charles XI, services were held

—
11
—

in Swedish and religion was to be taught from Swedish psalters and Bibles (edict of Ljungby, 1678). Although the ambitious intention succeeded on that front (perhaps because of the close relationship between Danish and Swedish), the plans of swedenizing the Baltic provinces collapsed in the political phase, in the face of rebellion by the German-speaking nobility.

The extreme example of Sweden was a forerunner of the turning point that came in the mid-18th century, when the elites in many European countries realized the meaning of what Moryson spoke of in the passage cited above, and subsequently began to seek to enforce linguistic homogeneity in the regions over which their national authority extended. One may cite as an early and model example (although not the earliest, in view of the events in Sweden) the report of Henri Gregoire presented to the National Convention in 1794, postulating the standardization of the French language "so as to fuse the citizenry into a national mass." On the other side of the Atlantic, American lexicographer Noah Webster seconded him, writing: "a national language is a bond of national union, and what country needs that more than America?" Within a few decades, the first romantic nationalists, who in many regions of Europe were to clash with authorities determined to impose linguistic uniformity on their subjects by force, stepped into the historical arena.

In the early modern era, a more important factor than language in terms of distinguishing individual communities was religion. The authorities did much to bring about the unification of their inhabitants in that regard. And although they did not always succeed, they did not hesitate to build an "infrastructure of violence" to attain that goal. Religious tolerance was often regarded as a necessary evil, the consequence of inability to root out heresy by force. Religious divisions, essential in the early modern era to construct an image of the stranger and to build a sense of the separateness of one's own group, often did not coincide with ethnic divisions. It is sufficient to remember the consequences of the Reformation, which divided Poles and Lithuanians, who spoke the same language and undoubtedly had a sense of national unity and of belonging to the same state, by the faith they professed.

In the Commonwealth, where religious tolerance—at least for the nobles—was inscribed in the catalog of fundamental constitutional principles, a sense of separateness from the surrounding community based on faith could develop without major impediments and could become an essential factor cementing individual ethnic groups. This was so in the case of the Jews, Mennonites, Armenians, and Tatars. The latter accepted the Polish language as their own relatively easily and quickly, preserving their separateness, however, not only during the Commonwealth period but long afterward, into the 20th century.

The question therefore arises, what united the multiethnic and multidenominational Commonwealth into a single whole? Was it not simply an accidental conglomeration of various ethnic groups whose representatives had made their way here, lured by religious tolerance and the chance for a better life?

"What unites this nation into a single whole?" asked the Venetian envoy Lorenzo Priuli (quoted by Antoni Mączak) when telling the Senate of the *Serenissima* about 16th-century France. One of the factors mentioned by the ambassador was the king, whose will and authority counteracted any divisions of the state that might arise. This answer is obvious for each of us today who knows even a little about the history of France, but it was not at all obvious in the era of religious wars lasting over 30 years. Despite the many conflicts tearing a country apart, a common ruler as a factor uniting early modern states was of fundamental importance, both in a France threatened with Civil War and in a nobles' Commonwealth that elected its own monarch. The logic of building a dynastic state—the type of state prevalent during the era that interests us (with a few exceptions, such as Venice and the Netherlands)—differed from the logic of building 19th- and 20th-century nation-states. Rights to territory were decided by considerations of kinship, and possibly treaties that did not need to be

—
13
—

accompanied with mass resettlement called "ethnic cleansing," as happened in the 20th century. The consequence was the formation of states with a federal structure, or outright confederations, in which the king had to consult the representatives of the estates of the realm, who guarded their legal autonomy and local privileges, on all matters of importance. Where the political significance of representative institutions was great, as in the Commonwealth, the estates, on a par with the king, grew to the rank of bearers of sovereignty. Only absolutism, with its tendency to standardize those areas most important to the government, such as taxes and administration, led to gradual "conquest" of the provinces by the central government, at the same time restoring the person of the king to the rank of sole symbol of sovereignty. Absolutism in Catholic countries was supported by the religious legitimization of the ruler's authority, whereas the churches were made subordinate to the monarchs in Protestant countries.

Absolutist homogenization of the state mostly did not reach farther than imposing a more or less consistent order on differences of a legal nature. In the majority of cases, there was no requirement to renounce local culture and customs. Linguistic norms were mainly imposed on the upper strata and primarily in order to bind them strongly to the government. Even the most radical steps of the extreme representative of enlightened absolutism, Emperor Joseph II (1780–1790), who reformed all areas of life in a manner outright maniacal, seem less oppressive than French regulations during the time of the Revolution. Only religion was an exception, and that only for a time; from the moment of wide-scale acceptance of legitimization of authority based on social contract as understood by Hobbes, the significance of religion in justifying authority diminished considerably.

A natural consequence of the functioning of states with a confederate structure during the early modern era was the formation of two-track loyalty toward the state and monarch. In the Commonwealth, which did not know an absolutist "standardization" of government structures, great significance was given to identification with the state represented both by the person of the king and by the *sejm* (parliament). At the same time, the nobles, and even some of the townsmen, identified with their own province, treating its legally distinct character as their own and as a first, and sometimes the most important, point of reference.

Most strongly manifested was Lithuania's autonomy from the Kingdom of Poland, confirmed by the Act of the Union of Lublin, the wording of which was disputed, as well as by the existence of separate Lithuanian law codified in the three Lithuanian Statutes issued by Sigismund the Old, Sigismund August, and Sigismund III Vasa (written in the Ruthenian language). Some historians—and not only Lithuanians—are inclined to see this as a sign of Lithuanian patriotism, if not outright nationalism. For others, those laws are only manifestations of the egoism of the Lithuanian magnates, who feared domination by the nobles of the Crown, possessing as they did a political program attractive to the Lithuanian nobles, who wished to emancipate themselves from the influences of the magnates. Both these views are extreme in nature. The former seems exaggerated, especially in the light of Ernest Gellner's definition of "nation" cited above, to say nothing of the fact that these views were not published in Lithuanian or even in Ruthenian, but in Polish. The latter view ignores the Lithuanian elite's attachment to the living, recent tradition of the Grand Duchy of Lithuania's autonomous existence. I do not think that this was only a play of the personal interests of a handful of mighty and powerful clans, because even a minor Lithuanian noble identified with the Grand Duchy. The existence of such a strong identification gives the lie to the traditional view of Ludwik Narbutt, shared even today by some Lithuanian historians, that after the Union of Lublin, Lithuania ceased to exist as a state. Its institutions still functioned—offices, treasury, army, law—and it was on them that the sense of autonomy was focused. This sense did not stand in opposition to identification with the Commonwealth as a whole, to loyalty toward its monarchs and to its laws established by the three estates of the *sejm* (King, Senate, and Chamber of Deputies).

15

Map 1: The Crown (Korona) and Lithuania (Litwa) before the Union of Lublin.

Map 2: The Crown and Lithuania after the Union of Lublin.

The lack of separate institutions, or their preservation only in relict form, was decisive for the fact that the sense of autonomy was significantly weaker in other parts of the Commonwealth. The diversity that had existed in the Crown from the period of feudal fragmentation ($12^{th}-14^{th}$ centuries) disappeared gradually, beginning with the reign of Casimir the Great (1333–1370), up to the time of the Executionist movement in the 16th century, when the autonomy of Royal Prussia and the Duchies of Oświęcim and Siewierz was abolished. The legal and structural uniqueness of Mazovia also disappeared gradually. Although the sense of local identification, as an inhabitant of Greater Poland or Lesser Poland, a Mazovian or a Prussian, remained in the consciousness of the nobles, it was nonetheless less intense than in the case of the nobility of the Grand Duchy of Lithuania because it was not supported by separate institutions. A similar state of affairs existed with the Ruthenians. In White Ruthenia, or present-day Belarus, gradually incorporated into Lithuania from the end of the 13th century, separate institutions were not maintained. A law written in the Ruthenian language was common for all Lithuanian nobility, and thus could not play a role as a factor for concentrating a sense of autonomy from the Grand Duchy. In Red Ruthenia, the Kyiv and Halych tradition affected the consciousness of the local nobility even less. Promises of preserving the Ruthenian language in court records, or the exclusion of Ruthenian provinces from fiscal reforms pursued in the Crown, could not be the main carriers of a sense of autonomy. Consequently, the polonization of culture and customs proceeded quickly as soon as religious conversion had occurred. One cannot rule out that if the Cossacks, or at least their elite, had attained the noble status that they strove for, the history of these lands might have turned out otherwise. A similar role could have been played by autonomous institutions inherited from Ruthenian duchies, if any such had existed. The attempt to create them, in the Union of Hadiach (1658), was at least a century too late.

—

17

—

From what has been said above, it is clear that the main carrier of identification for the elite during the early modern era were local institutions, and it was on them that the feeling of autonomy was focused. It is no surprise that in nations ruled absolutely, the central authority tried to destroy or subordinate those institutions.

When speaking of factors that united the nobility on a Commonwealth--wide scale, one cannot ignore the "imagined community," or the Sarmatian myth. Renaissance scholars inscribed their nations into ancient tradition, thus seeking sources of national communities. This was a phenomenon common in all of Europe. In France, the tradition of the ancient Gauls was called upon; in Sweden the genesis of the people was sought among the Vandals and Goths. Polish historians (Jan Długosz, Marcin of Miechów, Bernard Wapowski, Marcin Bielski, Aleksander Gwagnin—the latter an Italian by descent) traced the Slavs back to the gallant Sarmatians who inhabited the regions between the Sea of Azov and the Don River in antiquity. After a certain time, only the nobles began to be recognized as descendants of the Sarmatians, independently of language or real ethnic descent. The Lithuanian version of the myth derived the Lithuanians from ancient Romans who supposedly fled the Empire during the time of Nero and gave rise to the Lithuanian magnates. This version, disseminated, among others, by Maciej Stryjkowski (who, incidentally, came from Mazovia), was not accepted, and the Lithuanian nobles, like those of the Kingdom of Poland, regarded themselves as descendants of the Sarmatians. The myth of the nobility's joint Sarmatian descent became an important foundation of the community and consolidated its bonds, at the same time determining its ideology, system of values, political culture, and even customs and artistic taste. Thus Sarmatism fulfilled similar functions to 19th- and 20th-century nationalism, with the difference, however, that it concerned only the nobility.

With this way of constructing a quasi-national "imagined community," immigrants belonging to other ethnic and religious groups were no threat as long as their arrival did not threaten the dominance of the elite. If, there-

18

fore, they could be useful to the state and its inhabitants, they were welcomed. Such was the case of the representatives of the ethnic groups described for the purposes of this book as "assimilated" or "newcomers," differing only in the time of their immigration. Jews were useful because of their knowledge of trade and financial operations; so were the Karaites and Armenians. In the case of the Tatars, and partly also of the Karaites, military considerations were decisive; in the case of Germans it was their economic expertise. It was similar in the early modern era: Mennonites had unquestioned skills in the area of land improvement; Italians in the fields of economy, diplomacy, and obviously, artistic culture; Scots were skilled in military matters and additionally filled a gap in the field of internal trade. And although conflicts arose more than once between the newcomers and the locals and manifested themselves in various ways—from slurs and accusatory characterizations to violence—these did not lead to statutory restrictions on immigration. The newcomers did not present a threat to the ruling class, and therefore no preventive measures were taken. Where a threat was perceived, the nobles were able to defend themselves, as evidenced by their taking away the right to ennoble and grant *indygenat* (recognition of foreign noble status) from the king in 1576 and transferring it to the parliament, which, obviously, was far more careful in granting it.

In summary, the multicultural experiment of the old Commonwealth, lasting several centuries, enriched Polish history, adding to it—simultaneously in the 20th century, the era of national states—a special conception of citizenship, today regarded as old-fashioned, based on historical tradition, not only on ethnic commonality. And although after Poland regained its independence in 1918, this idea proved impossible to realize, it is worth remembering warmly today.

Bibliography

Burke, P., *Languages and Communities in Early Modern Europe*, Cambridge: Cambridge University Press, 2004.

Davies, N., *God's Playground. A History of Poland*, vol. I: *The Origins to 1795*, New York: Columbia University Press, 1982.

Evans, R. J. V. "The Politics of Language in Europe, c. 1525–1697," *Przegląd Historyczny*, vol. 97 (2006): pp. 455–476.

Fedorowicz, J.K., *A Republic of Nobles*, Cambridge: Cambridge University Press, 1982.

Friedrich, K., Pendzich, B. M., *Citizenship and Identity in a Multinational Commonwealth. Poland and Lithuania in Context, 1550–1772*, Leiden–Boston: Brill, 2009.

Gellner, E., *Nations and Nationalism*, Oxford: Blackwell, 1983.

Hobsbawm, E., *Nations and Nationalism since 1780: Programme, Myth, Reality*, Cambridge: Cambridge University Press, 1990.

Hobsbawm, E., and Ranger, T. (eds.), *The Invention of Tradition*, Cambridge: Cambridge University Press, 1983.

Kizwalter, T., *O nowoczesności narodu. Przypadek polski* [On the Modernity of the Nation. The Polish Case], Warszawa: Semper, 1999.

Litwin, H., "Narody Pierwszej Rzeczypospolitej" [Nations of the First Commonwealth], in: Sucheni-Grabowska, A., and Dybkowska, A. (eds.), *Tradycje polityczne dawnej Polski* [Political Traditions of Ancient Poland], Warszawa: Editions Spotkania, 1993, pp. 168–218.

Sulima-Kamiński, A., *Historia Rzeczypospolitej wielu narodów, 1505–1795* [History of the Commonwealth of Many Nations], Lublin: Instytut Europy Środkowo-Wschodniej, 2000.

Mączak, A., Samsonowicz, H., Szwarc, A., Tomaszewski, J., *Od plemion do Rzeczypospolitej. Naród, państwo, terytorium w dziejach Polski* [From Tribes to the Commonwealth. Nation, State, Territory in the History of Poland], Warszawa: Książka i Wiedza, 1996.

Snyder, T., *The Reconstruction of Nations: Poland, Ukraine, Lithuania, Belarus, 1569–1999*, New Haven: Yale University Press, 2003.

Stone, Daniel, *The Polish-Lithuanian State, 1386–1795*, Seattle: University of Washington Press, 2001.

Taszycki, W. (ed.), *Obrońcy języka polskiego* [Defenders of the Polish Language], Wrocław: Zakład Narodowy im. Ossolińskich, 1953.

Polish-Lithuanian unions

―

A N D R Z E J   R A C H U B A

Unions joining several states (two or more) are a phenomenon seen almost since ancient times. In terms of form, we distinguish among them personal unions (by far the most frequent, based on a common ruler) and real (the union of states). A certain "fashion" for personal unions developed in the Middle Ages, due to several factors. First of all there were the family ties of rulers in various states, the dying out of those dynasties, and the agreements made between them, especially in the fairly common situation of treating a state (or a portion of it) as one's own (dynastic) property or *patrimonium*. Examples of unions of this sort were those of Aragon and Barcelona (1164), León and Castile (from 1230), France and Navarre (1285–1328 and from 1589), England and France after the extinction of the Capetian dynasty (1422–1453), Naples and Hungary (1385–1386), as well as Hungary and Poland (1370–1382).

A second factor influencing the creation of unions was that of external threats on the part of an aggressive neighbor or neighbors. The states entering into such unions thereby joined forces against the enemy, which gave them a chance of settling armed confrontations victoriously, or even avoiding a confrontation by a show of force. Sometimes a union of this sort resulted from marriage between rulers or the children of rulers. One may cite as examples the Union of Calmar (1397–1523), Hungary and Poland (1440–1444), Castile and Leon with Aragon (1474), several unions

―
21
―

between Hungary and Bohemia, such as that under the Holy Roman Empire of the Luxembourgs, and subsequently that under Austria and the Habsburgs, etc.

Finally, a union might result from the conquest, armed or peaceful, of a neighboring state and the seizure of its throne by the victorious monarch. We encounter such a situation as early as 1003–1004, when Bolesław I Chrobry, the ruler of Poland, was at the same time Duke of Bohemia, and in the years 1300–1306, when the Bohemian kings Václav II and Vacláv III were also rulers of Poland. Such phenomena also occurred in Europe due to the conquest of England by Sweyn Forkbeard, King of Denmark (union during the years 1013–1042), and later by William the Conqueror, Duke of Normandy (union in the years 1066–1250), during the construction of the single French state in the 15th century, and so on.

So the Kingdom of Poland had known unions of various kinds, their virtues and faults. In deciding on an alliance with the mighty Lithuanian state, the Polish magnates (primarily those of Lesser Poland or Małopolska) saw mainly its advantages, obviously; and the advantages were varied. Poland needed above all a powerful ally in the fight with the Teutonic Knights; and the brief alliance of Władysław Łokietek (the Elbow-high) with the Lithuanian ruler, Gediminas (1325–1330), supported by the marriage of their children, Casimir and Aldona (Anna), had shown that the two states could be victorious working together. That alliance was generally, however, an exceptional period of cooperation; far more often, there had been armed conflicts between the Polish and Lithuanian dukes, in which the Lithuanians had achieved success far more often. Their frequent raids on Polish territories (for instance, on Łęczyca in 1294, on Sandomierz district in 1295, 1296, and 1304, on Dobrzyń district in 1300, and on Kalisz in 1305 and 1306) produced enormous destruction and large population losses. In addition, during the reign of Casimir the Great (Łokietek's son), Poland engaged in a major conflict with Lithuania over Volhynia and Podolia, which at the end of the war became partially conquered by Poland with support from the Hungarian army. The matter of these lands, however, was a constant element of Lithuanian-Polish friction. For the Lithuanian state—which experienced unprecedented territorial expansion in the 14ᵗʰ century, leading to contacts and conflicts with the Duchy of Muscovy and the Golden Horde to the east and south, and Teutonic Knights in the west and north—an alliance with Poland was an attractive proposition. It offered a chance to end the conflict over Volhynia, Podolia, and Podlasie, as well as support in its struggles with the Teutonic Knights, the Tatars, and Moscow. What is more, it made possible the realization at last of repeatedly delayed plans for the Lithuanians' acceptance of baptism in the Catholic rite, and thereby Lithuania's entry into the ranks of the Catholic nations of Europe with their cultural achievements, which had long since become a condition of its survival in its national character.

All these prospects were certainly noted by the ruler of Lithuania, Jogaila (called Jagiełło by Poles), who would become an important player on the international stage through his marriage with Jadwiga, the daughter of Louis of Anjou, King of Hungary and Poland (as the son of Elżbieta Łokietek), and heiress to the throne of the latter state. In the very rich historiography regarding the so-called Union of Kreva (Polish name Krewo), there are disputes over who initiated the idea of this marriage and of the consequent union of the two states. It does not seem possible to resolve the matter unambiguously. One should assume, rather, that a portion of the influential elite of the Kingdom of Poland and Lithuania, headed by Jogaila himself, pressed for this union. The coronation of Jadwiga of Anjou as King of Poland on 16 October 1384 placed the question of marriage with Jogaila on the agenda. In the first half of 1385, this matter was finally settled; and on 14 August of that same year, in Kreva, Jogaila accepted the conditions proposed by the Poles on which with his marriage to Jadwiga could proceed. The Polish counterpart of the Kreva accord was the agreement contracted in Vaŭkavysk on 11 January 1386, by which Jogaila was given preliminary recognition as ruler of Poland in advance of his election, which

—
23
—

was expected to take place soon. The election followed in Lublin of 2 February; and it was, in fact, an unprecedented event that a pagan should be elected king of a Catholic state. It was not until 15 February that Jogaila was baptized (taking the name Władysław), and he married Jadwiga on the 18th, which allowed him to be crowned King of Poland on 4 March. It was an important event for both the states contracting this personal union.

The so-called Act of Kreva is itself a subject of Polish-Lithuanian controversy, both over its authenticity, character, and validity, as well as over a single Latin formulation, very important and not overly precise philologically—*ap[p]licare*. The authenticity of the record was questioned by some Lithuanian historians; but in the end, we can accept (following Maria Koczerska) that the document drawn up in Kreva is not an international treaty but an "authenticated protocol of negotiations" with Jogaila in the matter of the marriage, a hastily drawn up prenuptial agreement. In it, the Grand Duke undertook to accept baptism along with his pagan brothers and relatives and knights; to put up funds for regaining certain lost lands of Lithuania and the Kingdom of Poland; to contract marriage with Jadwiga; to pay Wilhelm of Habsburg very high compensation for taking away his betrothed (possibly wife?); to free prisoners of war who came from Polish lands; and finally, for all time, to *applicare* (incorporate, merge, join) his Lithuanian and Ruthenian lands to the Crown of the Kingdom of Poland. This word *applicare*, which is ambiguous and therefore unclear, has been regarded by some scholars as a term from feudal law, and by others as no more than a colloquial word.

In Polish historiography as late as the 19th century, it was accepted that Lithuania was incorporated into Poland in 1386, and therefore ceased to exist as an independent state. At the same time, from the document itself, only the intention to incorporate is clear, connected with the problem of marriage dowry—Jadwiga brought her husband Poland, and he brought her Lithuania. Jogaila made this incorporation a reality only formally, as the Lithuanian-Ruthenian dukes performed acts of homage.

Lithuania was joined to Poland in a double sense—it directly affected only the region of Vilnius, and the rest of the Lithuanian and Ruthenian duchies indirectly. In reality, however, this incorporation was not fully accomplished and the Lithuanian state did not cease to exist in 1386. If one goes along with Juliusz Bardach in assuming that the Lithuanian state was patrimonial in nature, then as a result of Jogaila's marriage to Jadwiga, it became the joint property of a new dynasty, and the legal basis of the union of these two states was the "dynastic patrimonial concept" imposed by the Lithuanians. In this context, two concepts of incorporation seem most convincing to me. The first, presented before World War II by the German scholar Josef Pfitzner and finding rather few adherents, relies on taking the word *applicare* to mean attaching the Lithuanian state to the Crown of the Kingdom of Poland (and not to Poland) with its independence and integrity retained. In the immediate vicinity, unions of this sort joined Silesia and the Lands of the Bohemian Crown (Lands of the Crown of St. Wenceslaus). The second concept was presented over thirty years ago by Karol Górski, who interpreted the word as meaning a union of two states of unequal legal personality (a kingdom and a duchy), where the legal, social and administrative peculiarities of the incorporated body remain intact. The closest example of such a union for the issue that interests us was the union of the Kingdom of Bohemia with the Margraviate of Brandenburg in 1374. It seems that both these concepts are closely related and can be treated jointly. They lead to the conclusion that Lithuania was attached to the Polish Crown while retaining almost complete independence in practice, which, for a while, suited the interests of all sides. Lithuania, under the rule (from 1395) of the Duke Vytautas (called Witold by Poles, the cousin of Jogaila, who was still formally the supreme ruler of the Grand Duchy of Lithuania), soon departed from the provisions of Kreva, and aimed at complete independence.

Queen Jadwiga's attempt to discipline her vassal by demanding , at the request of the Polish lords, payment of the dowry, led to additional conflict, and gave Vytautas and his Lithuanian supporters cause to question the union with Poland. What is more, he was already preparing the ground for accepting a royal crown. Vytautas's policy of independence ended with defeat in the battle with the Tatars' Golden Horde at the Vorskla River on 13 August 1399; and the death of Jadwiga of Anjou partially changed Władysław Jogaila's position on the Polish throne. Finally, the option of confirming him on the throne and joining Lithuania more closely with Poland won out among the Polish ruling elite. Vytautas and his retinue were compelled to swear loyalty to the Kingdom of Poland (1400); but this also led to drawing up a new agreement between the states that better protected the parties' interests. Drawn up in Vilnius (18 January 1401) and Radom (11 March 1401), the conditions of the union confirmed Poland's sovereignty in regard to Lithuania, as guaranteed by her ruling elite, to which, in return, it allowed election of a new king and promised military aid against enemies. Vytautas was proclaimed Grand Duke of Lithuania for life; but formally, Jogaila continued to rule over him as supreme prince *(princeps supremus)*. The Vilnius-Radom union was undoubtedly a compromise that finally defined clearly Lithuania's position in the union with Poland, as well as that of Vytautas himself in regard to Jogaila within the state. Poland's aid was necessary for Lithuania, because after the collapse of his eastern policy, Vytautas had to settle affairs with the Teutonic Knights. The new union passed the test during the subsequent conflict with the Knights' state. As a result of the defeat on the fields of Grunwald (15 July 1410), the Teutonic Order definitively lost its position as a military power to the enormous monarchy of Jogaila.

Only a dissolution of the Polish-Lithuanian union could change that situation, and this was what the ever ambitious Vytautas strove for, with his Lithuanian-Ruthenian retinue, in the face of the conflicting aspirations of the Polish elite, which demanded compliance with the obligations of the union. As a result, on 2 October 1413 at a conference in Horodło, a new union of the two states was formed. The agreement confirmed joining of the Lithuanian-Ruthenian lands to Poland and resulted in the Lithuanian nobility being absorbed into the community of the Kingdom of Poland, as the nobles of the two nations were now to meet together to make decisions in the most important affairs of state. Thus, while now becoming feudalized at an accelerated pace and still not playing a major political role, the society of Lithuania was drawn into the vortex of great politics by becoming a partner of the Grand Duke's rule. Nonetheless, it was deprived of the right to participate with the nobility of the Kingdom of Poland in the election of the Polish king. It had instead the right to elect future Grand Dukes, along with the King of Poland and his lords. A testament to this fraternization of the Polish knights with those of Lithuania was the adoption of 47 representatives of the latter (this was the retinue of Vytautas, and not the Lithuanian ruling elite) into the armigerous clans of the Kingdom, which was the next step in assimilating the Lithuanian boyars with the Polish nobility in terms of organization. The agreement was a success for Catholic Lithuanians in the struggle for domination within the state, because from then on, only they could be advisors of the Grand Duke and hold the highest state offices. By the Act of Horodło, Jogaila transferred his rights to part of Lithuania (his patrimony, or the Duchy of Vilnius) to the Kingdom of Poland, and thereby each ruler of Poland became the owner of that part. The Union of Horodło was an enormous success for the Polish side. The might of the states, now united, was soon demonstrated in the war with the Teutonic Knights (1422), who were quickly compelled to capitulate and finally transfer Samogitia over to Lithuania.

The death in 1430 of Vytautas, whose efforts to obtain the royal crown of Lithuania had led in the later years of his life to bitter Polish-Lithuanian conflict, placed the union of the two states on the agenda once more. The elevation of Jogaila's brother Švitrigaila (Bolesław) to the Grand Duke's throne in Vilnius evoked a hostile reaction on the part of the Polish lords. The result was a war between the two states in 1431, which Poland won militarily; but in the end, it was forced to agree to Švitrigaila's rule in Lithuania and his territorial acquisitions (Podolia). The break with Poland also evoked a negative reaction on the part of some of the Lithuanian elite, however; in 1432, in collusion with the Poles, they removed Švitrigaila from power and placed Žygimantas (whom Poles called Zygmunt), the brother of Vytautas, on the Grand Duke's throne. He swore to the Vilnius-Radom union in Hrodna.

The death of Władysław Jogaila in 1434 confirmed that Poland was interested in maintaining the union with Lithuania, because Vladislovas (Władysław III), the supreme Duke of Lithuania and the eldest son of the deceased, was placed on the throne. Žygimantas, who remained in Lithuania, tried to carry on his great brother's policy of separating from Poland, which suited the interests of the Lithuanian ruling elite, who feared an influx of Poles in Lithuania and their domination in political life. Nonetheless, when Žygimantas began to build an anti-Polish coalition of neighboring states, the Poles compelled him to confirm the Union of Hrodna, and a faction of the Lithuanian lords murdered him in 1440. Desiring neither a complete break with Poland nor a close union, these Lithuanian magnates appointed to the throne of the Grand Duke the youngest of Władysław Jogaila's sons, Kazimierz (1440)—which signified, however, a break in the personal union. Busy with its own affairs, Poland was not in a position to react to this action.

The hopes of Lithuania's political elite for loosening the union with Poland were rapidly dashed by the unexpected death of Władysław Jagiellończyk in the battle with the Turks at Varna (1444). The Polish lords offered the throne to Kazimierz, the ruler of Lithuania; and although the Lithuanians intended to take advantage of the situation to negotiate terms more favorable to themselves, they were rather quickly compelled to make concessions. In the end, therefore, as of 1447, the personal union between the two states was revived; King Kazimierz, by the so-called Great Charter of 2 May 1447, confirmed the independence and territorial in-

28

tegrity of Lithuania as a state, but one that was to remain in fraternal union with Poland. From then on until the Union of Lublin (with a brief interlude), the union of Lithuania and Poland was based on a joint ruler of the Jagiellonian dynasty, while maintaining the independence, autonomy, and collaboration of two state organisms that were distinct but were slowly becoming more alike in many areas. The new Lithuanian-Polish agreement did not eliminate the tension between interest groups of both countries, especially over the regions of Volhynia and Podolia, on which the Polish lords (mainly those of Lesser Poland) had had designs for many years. Finally, in 1452, Lithuania recognized Volhynia as part of its state, despite Polish protests. Fierce controversy between Poles and Lithuanians as to the nature of their union (a group of nobles from Lesser Poland, headed by Cardinal Zbigniew Oleśnicki, incessantly demanded the incorporation of Lithuania) constantly poisoned the atmosphere in both countries; and repeated attempts to settle those differences at joint meetings brought no results. In the end, due to the anti-Polish course of the Lithuanian elite, led by Jonas Goštautas (called Jan Gasztołd by Poles), Lithuania itself lost the most, as it was in no position to resist independently the aggressive attempts on Ruthenian lands on the part of the Muscovite state, or to participate in the partitioning of the Teutonic Knights' realm after the Knights lost the war with Poland (1454–1466).

A subsequent gravitation of Lithuania toward full independence was fully realized after the death of Kazimierz Jagiellończyk (1492), when Lithuanians chose as Grand Duke his youngest son, Aleksandras (Aleksander Jagiellończyk), but Poles elected as their king the older son, Jan Olbracht—although the former did not feel he was an independent ruler, and the latter did not resign the title emphasizing his superior right to Lithuania. The Lithuanian council of lords (an advisory body to the Grand Duke, which had, however, assumed many of his powers during the reign of Kazimierz Jagiellończyk, becoming almost an equal institution in the state, the expression of the aspirations of the new Lithuanian elite) maintained its course of isolation from Poland, however. That course brought Lithuania a series of defeats in wars with Moscow and the loss to Moscow of enormous areas of the state. The defeats of Lithuania and Poland in wars with Turkey and the Tatars, and the failures of the Jagiellonians in the international arena, finally compelled the elites of both countries to confirm the treaty of Horodło in 1499 and declare future joint election of the ruler in each of the countries. This Polish-Lithuanian agreement was necessary for both sides in view of the complicated relations with Turkey and Moscow. The latter attacked Lithuania once again in 1500, and after defeating its forces in the Battle of the Vedrosha River, seized more Ruthenian lands from the Lithuanian state, which could not organize an army that could defeat its aggressive foe. Aleksander Jagiellończyk himself, instead of going to war against Moscow, went to Poland in 1501 in order to secure for himself the royal throne after the unexpected death of his brother, Jan Olbracht. In return, to win over the Polish lords, he had to accept far-reaching concessions in the matter of Lithuania's union with Poland. The Lithuanian council of lords, terrified by the military defeats, also had to agree to concessions in order to obtain Polish aid. The agreement signed in Piotrków on 3 October of that year and confirmed by Aleksander on the 23rd of that month in Mielnik created a union of two states under a single scepter, with a jointly elected king (the election of Grand Duke was not provided for, but the new ruler was to use that title as well). There was to be one society, joined in brotherhood, and one parliament as the legislative body. Foreign policy, the army, and the currency were also to be joint. The document confirmed a leading place in the country for the senate of the Kingdom of Poland and the Lithuanian council of lords. But the latter had no desire at all for such close ties with Poland. Nor did Jagiellończyk wish to be deprived of hereditary rights to the Grand Duchy and to see the lords of the council so elevated. As a result, the Act of Mielnik was not ratified by the Lithuanian parliaments in 1502 and 1505 (and that was a condition for its implementation). The death of Aleksander in 1506 brought rule over Lithuania and subsequently over Poland to the youngest of Kazimierz Jagiellończyk's sons, Zygmunt, who was compelled to issue a grand charter on 7 December of that year in Hrodna, in which he promised to preserve the independence of Lithuania and the significance of its council of lords. Polish efforts to strengthen the union in subsequent years were rejected by that council. What is more, some of its members put forward a proposal to place Zygmunt's underage son, Zygmunt August, on the throne of Lithuania; but this was not taken up even by the monarch himself. Nonetheless, Zygmunt August was elected Grand Duke of Lithuania in 1529, while his father was still alive. After his father's death in 1548, he assumed the throne of Poland as well.

Toward the end of his life, this last male representative of the Jagiellonian dynasty tried with all his might to unite Lithuania with Poland in a real union, because he feared for the fate of his homeland, which in 1557 came into a new conflict with the Grand Duchy of Moscow over Livonia, the lands of the Teutonic Knights and the Archbishopric of Riga. The failures in this conflict, which resulted not only in the loss of parts of those lands but also of strategically situated Polotsk (in 1563), demonstrated clearly that without Poland's support, which Lithuania could not afford financially, Lithuania would lose every subsequent war with its aggressive eastern neighbor, which was striving to incorporate the territory of Ruthenia. Most likely, the next war between them would lead to occupation by Moscow's ruler, Ivan the Terrible, of all Lithuania, and therefore, the annihilation of its statehood. Poland, however, demanded in return for its assistance not only money to pay mercenary troops, but also a real union, which would give the Polish nobility the right to acquire estates in the lands of Lithuania and Ruthenia. What is more, the more ardent advocates of union among the leaders of the movement called "executionist" in Poland even demanded that after Lithuania's incorporation into Poland, the name "Lithuania" be replaced with "Nowopolska" or "New

—
31
—

Poland" (by analogy with Wielkopolska, "Great Poland," and Małopolska, "Lesser Poland," which made up the Kingdom of Poland).

In the 16th century there finally occurred a political "awakening" of the Lithuanian and Ruthenian boyars, who, to that point, had been dominated completely by lords and princes and had therefore virtually no influence on the policies of their state. This was due to constant contact with the Polish nobility, which in the 15th century had already been a powerful political force with significant influence on Poland's policies, and in the 16th century confirmed its dominance in the state. The privileges that the Polish nobility enjoyed, its freedoms, rights, liberties (political and economic), its self-rule and judiciary must surely have aroused the envy of the Lithuanian and Ruthenian nobility, and made them interested in acquiring those privileges for themselves. This was only possible, however, with closer ties to Poland, to which the Lithuanian nobility was prepared to consent. On 13 September 1562, assembled in camp at Vitsebsk for an expedition against Moscow, the nobles decided to form a confederation and asked the king to form a real union with Poland. They saw in this their only chance for obtaining military assistance in their war with Moscow, and for making their position equal to that of the Kingdom's nobles. They demanded a joint Polish-Lithuanian parliament and joint election of new kings in the future, and they threatened to make an agreement directly with the Poles, bypassing the council of lords. It was known that Zygmunt August supported this. The king actually went farther than his Lithuanian subjects, who desired a union on terms of equality of both parties and mutual agreement on goals and means; they wanted both countries to share the same laws and similar political, administrative and legal systems, while retaining exclusivity of offices for Lithuanians, and to have a common foreign and defense policiy, but to retain separate armies. Thus, there existed a very favorable aura for an alliance of the monarch with the nobility against the majority of the lords of the council headed by the Radziwiłłs. For them, the loss of their previous position in the state, being made equal before the law with the masses of the nobility, and especially the loss of *hospodar* estates (i.e., estates belonging to the ducal domain that were leased to members of the aristocracy) was a mortal danger. It is true that these demands of the nobles were rejected at the time by Zygmunt August, under pressure from the lords of the council; but the Lithuanian nobles followed through and tried to reach an agreement themselves with the Poles at the parliament in Piotrków in 1563.

The king, already resolved to compel the Lithuanians to unite with the Poles, took decisive steps in that direction during the subsequent years. Thus, in 1563 he made the Orthodox nobles (primarily Ruthenian) equal to the Catholic ones (primarily Lithuanian) in political rights; in 1564, he ceded to the Kingdom of Poland his hereditary rights to the throne of Lithuania, and equalized all citizens under the law (that is, made the nobles equal with the lords and princes), making them subject to a uniform judicial system modeled on that of Poland. Fundamental changes in the administrative division of Lithuania were also conducted during the years 1564–1566, by which self-governing military and judicial units, or *powiaty* (30), were created in 13 voivodeships. The nobles in those *powiaty* were to gather at local parliaments, at each of which they were to elect two delegates to the general parliament, and the latter (although not overly similar to that in the Kingdom of Poland) gained the right to make decisions regarding the defense of the district, with which the fundamental questions of passing taxes or making new laws were connected. These actions, which formally broke the monopoly on power of the Lithuanian magnates and made the country's system similar to Poland's, were to prepare the Grand Duchy for incorporation into the Kingdom of Poland. The Lithuanian magnates tried to delay some of these processes, in particular, they did not agree to a closer union; but they were slowly compelled to make concessions and seek agreement with the nobles. In doing so, there were influenced mainly by military defeats on the Moscow front, but also by Polish pressure and by the king himself, who had already rejected

— 33 —

an alliance with the council's lords in favor of the nobles' camp, which favored a union with the Kingdom of Poland. Finally, a portion of the Lithuanian magnates (which continued to play a major role in the public life of the country) had been won over to the idea of the union, mainly at the price of not conducting so-called executions of estates in Lithuania (that is, taking mortgaged or donated hospodar estates away from lords and princes). Their vision of the union, however, definitely differed from that of the Poles and of the king himself, who, in this situation, decided to take steps that were radical and legally controversial.

When, in early 1569, the parliaments of both states convened in Lublin with the aim of agreeing on the terms of the union—but due to the influence of Lithuanian malcontents, no agreements were reached and the Lithuanians went home—Zygmunt August decided to incorporate Podlasie and Volhynia, which were part of the Grand Duchy, into the Kingdom of Poland. Soon afterwards, he included the Kyiv region as well. The Grand Duchy lost almost half its territory and became smaller than the Kingdom of Poland; and its military potential was already completely inadequate to oppose Moscow. Weakened militarily and financially, Lithuania had to make concessions; and finally, on 1 July 1569, a real union between Poland and Lithuania was contracted. Both sides agreed that they would form for all time "a single inseparable and indistinguishable body" called the Rzeczpospolita or Commonwealth (in later years, this name also had qualifiers such as "of Poland" or "of Two Nations"—these were not official names, however), headed by a king elected jointly by Poles and Lithuanians (the lack of an election in one of the nations would not cancel the results of the election), always in Poland, crowned in Kraków, and not elevated to the Grand Duke's throne in Vilnius any more, for coronation as king simultaneously gave him the Lithuanian title. At his coronation, the king was to swear to the laws of both states.

The highest legislative body of the new state was to be the *Sejm* or parliament (always called *koronny* or "of the crown"), convened in Poland.

Despite the widespread opinion in Lithuanian historiography that a new, joint body had been created, its new form came into existence when the parliament of the Kingdom of Poland accepted a Lithuanian representation, modest and at a disadvantage in terms of numbers and in hierarchy of importance. The "Order of the Crown Council, Polish and Lithuanian," determined separately at the parliament in Lublin, allotted only 27 of 140 senatorial offices to Lithuania: two bishops, 10 voivodes and the same number of castellans, and finally five ministers—a grand marshal and a court marshal, a grand chancellor, a vice-chancellor, and a (grand) district treasurer—only because they were equivalents to their Polish colleagues, after whom they sat in order in the senate. Their position was initially uncertain, however, because the Polish ministers questioned the scope of their powers and their place in the hierarchy, particularly in regard to the offices of marshals and chancellors. The rest of the ministers, officials, and dignitaries remained outside the senate. The princes and lords (present in the Lithuanian parliament) were not part of the new parliament, and the same was true of the *powiat* marshals (in principle, counterparts of the so-called *kasztelan drążkowy* or minor castellans in Poland). The weak position of Lithuanians in the senate corresponded to their situation in the chamber of deputies, because there were 44 deputies in it after the Union, and in later times, an additional two from Smolensk, two from Starodub, and two from Livonia. In total, therefore, the Grand Duchy of Lithuania could have between 71 and 85 representatives in parliament (from 27 to 35 in the senate, and from 44 to 50 in the chamber of deputies), which, in comparison to the Kingdom of Poland—with 112–121 senators and 113–127 deputies, not counting the Prussian representation, in theory unrestricted—was not a significant force and could not tip the scales in voting at significant moments or force through its own ideas; and that surely was what the Poles had intended. Hence their unwillingness to admit the Lithuanian district marshals to the senate. It is interesting that Royal Prussia, which entered the Commonwealth parliament at the

— 35 —

same time as Lithuania, acquired a much more advantageous position in the chamber of deputies. Some historians try to downplay the disadvantage of Lithuania's representation, pointing out that it was barely relevant in a situation where the principle of unanimity prevailed; but this statement is not accurate. It assumes, as it were, negative treatment of participation in the parliament through the possibility of vetoing resolutions unfavorable for a given nation, which is what resulted.

The Act of Union preserved Lithuania's offices, its laws, administrative system, treasury, and army. The foreign policy, currency, and tariff system were all to be joint, and all legal restrictions on Poles' acquiring estates in Lithuania and Lithuanians' acquiring estates in Poland were to be eliminated. The Lithuanian oligarchs did, however, succeed in pushing through a provision prohibiting the execution of estates in their homeland, which the Polish advocates of execution had to accept reluctantly. What is more, during the first twenty years of the joint state's functioning, Lithuanians succeeded in changing its spirit to their advantage, without changing the provisions of the Act of Union. They preserved their own currency, national borders, right of citizenship, and thereby limited the chances of Poles to hold office in Lithuania; in principle, both states were to guard their own borders. It is true that Lithuania did not succeed in winning the position in political life of one of two equal members of a federal state; in the end, it had to accept being one of its three provinces (Greater Poland, Lesser Poland, and Lithuania). But its autonomy was so great that in principle, what united it with the Kingdom of Poland was only the person of the king, the parliament, and the institution of the primate as interrex. Everything else was different for the two members of this common state.

Poles and Lithuanians have differed in their evaluation of the Union of Lublin since the last decades of the 19th century. While in Poland the Union is honored with monuments and names of city streets and squares, we see nothing of the sort in Lithuania. In the struggle to transform the society in the spirit of contemporary nationalism, which had to be directed against *polskość* or "Polishness" as the greatest threat to Lithuanian identity, culture, and language, the Polish-Lithuanian union was evaluated as evil, the cause of Lithuanians' denationalization and their Polonization. Only in recent years have some Lithuanian historians (Alfredas Bumblauskas, Mečislovas Jučas) attempted to present the complex issues connected with this union, and its positive role in the survival of Lithuanian identity, objectively. Unfortunately, this view continues to find few adherents in Lithuania, especially in the popular opinion shaped by politicians and politics. One can state with utter certainty that if Lithuania had not formed a union with Poland, its existence as a state would almost certainly have ended in the 16th century, or by the first half of the 17th century at the latest, with all the consequences typical for lands conquered by Moscow (Russia)—full Russification and loss of national identity. The union extended Lithuania's existence as a state by two centuries, allowed its society to become acquainted with and accept democratic mechanisms of public life, to function in the world of Western European values, to preserve the Catholic faith as an essential element of its culture, and to deepen its own identity.

The Belarusians as well, from the early 20th century, in connection with the formation of a Belarusian national consciousness, also had to be anti-Polish and anti-Russian as a rule. As a result, it was not the fall of the Commonwealth but its creation that was considered bad for the Belarusians, for it brought Polonization and loss of national identity. The canon for appraising the union, formulated by Vatslaŭ Lastoŭski and supported by Usievalad Ihnatoŭski, was reinforced even more negatively during the times of the USSR. What was emphasized first and foremost was the oppression of the peasants by the "Polish lords," the loss of identity, the Catholicization of the populace, the separation from Mother Russia. After the collapse of the USSR and the attainment of independence by Belarus, however, the evaluation of the union changed greatly, although the agents of this change were mostly young historians and part of the reborn national intelligentsia. They recognized the objective reasons for the Polish-Lithuanian alliance, its positive cultural and national aspects (without overlooking the negative ones). Similar phenomena may be observed in recent Ukrainian historiography, which previously also had a very negative view of the Union (which the society shared).

Bibliography

Bardach, J., *Studia z ustroju i prawa Wielkiego Księstwa Litewskiego, XIV–XVII w.* [Studies on the State System and Law of the Grand Duchy of Lithuania, 14th–17th Centuries], Warszawa: PWN, 1970.

Dainauskas, J., "Autentyczność aktu krewskiego" [Authenticity of the Krevo act], *Lithuano-Slavica Posnaniesia. Studia Historica*, vol. 2 (1987), pp. 125–142.

Frost, R. I., *The Oxford History of Poland and Lithuania*, vol. I: *The Making of the Polish-Lithuanian Union, 1385–1569*, Oxford: Oxford University Press, 2015.

Koczerska, M., "Autentyczność dokumentu unii krewskiej 1385 roku" [Authenticity of the Krevo document 1385], *Kwartalnik Historyczny*, vol. 99 (1999), pp. 59–81.

Łowmiański, H., "Wcielenie Litwy do Polski" [Incorporation of Lithuania into Poland], *Lithuano-Slavica Posnaniesia Studia Historica*, vol. 2 (1987) pp. 37–123.

Rachuba, A., *Historia Litwy. Dwugłos polsko-litewski* [History of Lithuania. Polish and Lithuanian interpretation], Warszawa: DiG, 2008.

THE

LOCALS

LITHUANIANS

∽

ANDRZEJ RACHUBA

——

Lithuanians formed a common state with the Poles only after the Union
of Lublin in 1569. Before that, only small groups of Lithuanians had
lived in Poland, settled on land as prisoners of war from the period of intense raids by Lithuanian armies on Polish lands during the 13th and 14th
centuries. This was not, however, a statistically significant group, and
it remained without significance on the map of ethnic minorities. From
1569 on, Lithuanians found themselves in the Crown (i.e., the Kingdom
of Poland) as a definite minority in Podlasie, which had been annexed
to the Crown, and in the lands of southern Ruthenia. As before, this was
not a large group, and it was surely limited to families settled on the lands
of former knights and officials of the Grand Duchy (northern Podlasie).
One must remember that a large number of Lithuanians had settled in Ducal Prussia, which bordered on Lithuania proper, and there they preserved
their own language and traditions. It was there that the first printed book
in the Lithuanian language was published; and there, too, the literature
developed that would be so important in the future for Lithuanian identity and culture.

Lithuanians predominated in the territory of the Grand Duchy of Lithuania, although there, too, ethnic relations were different in native Lithuanian regions (Aukštaitija and Samogitia) and Ruthenian regions. In the former, Lithuanians definitely predominated, whereas in Ruthenia (so-called

White and Black) they were a minority, and generally one limited only to the noble class. Up until the fall of the Commonwealth, there is no complete and reliable census for the Grand Duchy of Lithuania. One can, therefore, speak of numbers and composition of the population only very approximately, based on intermediary sources of various kinds. For the 16th century, those were the so-called *popisy* or registers of the Lithuanian army (in 1528, 1565, and 1567), and for the 17th and 18th centuries, the hearth tax and poll tax registers, although the latter group has been preserved only in fragments. Of those 16th-century sources, the most eminent expert on the matter, Henryk Łowmiański, regarded the first as best because it was the most complete; however, this register is fairly remote from the year of the Union, which is the starting point for us. In 1528, according to the *popis*, the Grand Duchy of Lithuania had about 2.7 million inhabitants, of whom the Lithuanians themselves (that is, Lithuanians and Samogitians) probably made up one third. On the eve of the Union of Lublin, as a result of large territorial losses to the Polish Crown, the population of the Grand Duchy had diminished significantly; even so, it was larger than in 1528, because the state had experienced a significant demographic boom connected with changes in living conditions, colonization, and economic development. As a result, according to Łowmiański, about 2.5 million people lived in the territory of the Grand Duchy at that point, of whom Lithuanians certainly constituted more or less a half. Less than a century later, in 1650, for the first time in Lithuania, a list was drawn up of people obligated to pay the new hearth tax. One can try to calculate the Grand Duchy's population on its basis, although the data is incomplete, and the calculation involves estimating population numbers based on the number of hearths or homesteads in villages, as well as houses and townhouses in the cities. Nonetheless, the results obtained by Józef Morzy show clearly that by the mid-17th century, the population of the Grand Duchy had grown considerably and had reached about 4.7 million, with a population density of a little over 15 persons per square kilometer.

Obviously, it is still impossible to say with any certainty what part of this number consisted of Lithuanians; but about 1.65 million people lived in the regions of Samogitia and Aukštaitija (the provinces of Vilnius and Trakai). So that if one deducts the Belarusians, Poles, Germans, Tatars, Karaites, and Jews who also inhabited those lands, there were probably around 1.5 million Lithuanians, or about 35% of the population.

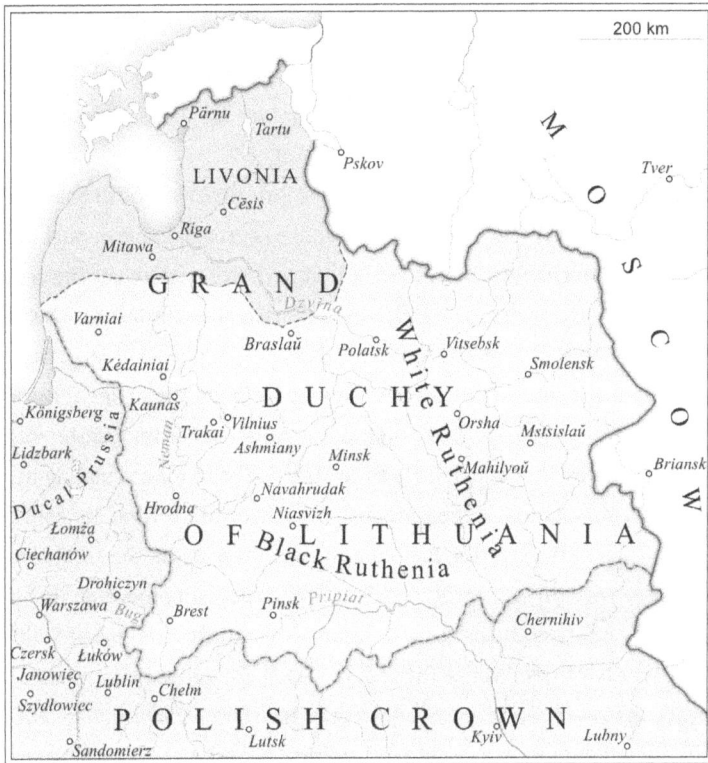

Map 3: The Grand Duchy of Lithuania
after the Union of Lublin (1569).

The wars of the mid-17th century had a catastrophic effect on the state of the Grand Duchy's population. As a result of military activities, mass deportations to Russia, plague, and horrific famine, the population diminished on average by 45%, and according to a list of hearths drawn up in 1667, it came to approximately 2.5 million (including regions lost to Russia). In the native Lithuanian lands (Samogitia and Aukštaitija), 134,178 hearths were counted, or a little over one million people, and thus 40% of the total population of the Grand Duchy. This rise in the percentage of Lithuanians was the result of the much greater devastation of the eastern lands of the Grand Duchy (the result of Moscow's occupation) than in the northwestern lands, which had been subjected to the Tsarist and Swedish rules for a much shorter period.

Forty years of peace after the Treaty of Andruszów (1667) brought a slow rebuilding of the country's economy and growth in the population of the Ground Duchy. Unfortunately, that was not registered by the next hearth tax list, drawn up in 1690, which showed only a little over 2.8 million inhabitants. This resulted from the practice—applied on a large scale by owners of estates, especially the biggest—of underreporting the size of properties in order to lower their fiscal burdens. For this reason, the 1690 list of hearths cannot serve as an effective basis for calculating the country's population, something people realized at the time. Rejecting these lists for tax purposes, they continued to make use of the 1667 *abiurata* (lord's sworn statement on the number of peasant properties on his land, which served as a basis for taxation). The cataclysm connected with the Great Northern War in the years 1700–1721 caused enormous destruction in the country and greatly reduced the number of its inhabitants. Long-lasting military activity—including a destructive civil war, years of famine, and especially the plague epidemic of 1709–1711—once more reduced the Duchy's population by about 35 to 40%, with plague affecting mainly its western regions, where the native Lithuanian population predominated. The next list, drawn up in 1717, showed only 121,000 hearths in the Grand Duchy (along with Livonia), and thus less than one million people. Once again, as before, the officials at the time recognized the scale of fraud in the list and realized that the *abiurata* compiled in 1690 corresponded more closely to reality, although it, too, aroused some doubts. It is accepted that after this catastrophe, the lands of the Grand Duchy were inhabited by about 1.85 million people, of whom native Lithuanians undoubtedly made up only about 30% of the population (some 630,000 people). More importantly, however, as a result of the two northern wars (in mid-17th century and at the beginning of the 18th century), the policies of the occupying Muscovite authorities and the plague epidemic, the ethnic border along the borderlands of Lithuania and Ruthenia had shifted. The Belarusian population had grown significantly in the districts (*powiaty*) of Ashmiany, Lida, Vilnius, and Hrodna, and an essential element of the growth was the displacement of Lithuanians from Vilnius itself. As a result, by 1737, services in the important church of St. John's in Vilnius were no longer held in the Lithuanian language because no one wanted to attend them. Obviously, this attests not only to the retreat of Lithuanian settlement, but also to the advance of linguistic Polonization.

From the end of the Great Northern War (in Lithuanian territory, this occurred definitively in 1712) up until the fall of the Commonwealth, the population of the Grand Duchy grew rather rapidly, and its economy gradually recovered. These processes were disrupted only to a small extent by the internal wars connected with the double election in 1733 and the Confederation of Bar, by the marches of the Russian army, and the policy of deportations and illegal annexation of borderlands by Russia during the rule of Stanisław August Poniatowski. These did not affect the native Lithuanian territories at all, or only partially. The state of affairs remained similar even with the first two partitions of the Commonwealth.

We have accurate statistical data on the numbers of the various ethnic groups in the Lithuanian state only from the late 18th century. The first

—
45
—

census of Lithuanian lands, as well as those of the Crown, was mandated by a 1789 *sejm* (parliament) resolution and showed the population supposedly at a level of 3.85 million. Unfortunately, it is not known whether the census in Lithuania actually took place, because a table drawn up by Fryderyk Moszyński on its basis contains much fictional data, which does not allow us to draw correct and unambiguous conclusions. And it is on the basis of these data that, more than a century ago, the theory was formulated that the largest segment of the Grand Duchy's population was made up of Belarusians (1.42 million persons, or 37% of the whole), followed by Poles (1.01 million persons, or 26%), with Lithuanians only in third place (770,000 persons, or 20%), followed by Jews (385,000 persons, or 10%), Russians (140,000 persons, or 3.6%), and finally Germans, Karaites, and Latvians (130,000, or 3.4%). Undoubtedly, many of the numerous "Poles" were Lithuanians and Belarusians who had been Polonized linguistically and culturally. This is indicated by the religious structure of the populace, of whom 1.5 million (39%) supposedly professed the Greek Catholic faith (Uniates), 1.47 million (38%) professed Catholicism, and only 250,000 (7%) professed Orthodoxy.

A relatively complete and accurate list of hearths was first produced by an inspection (*lustracja*) in 1790, according to which there were 436,856 hearths (which means about 3.5 million people) or 451,132 (about 3.6 million people), of which 182,605 hearths (about 1.5 million people) were counted in districts inhabited almost exclusively or predominantly by Lithuanians (Samogitia, part of the Vilnius region, part of Trakai district, without Hrodna). Assuming that the Ruthenian element predominated in the districts of Ashmiany (38,872 hearths), Lida (13,992 hearths), and Braslaŭ (11,161 hearths), one may surmise that in 1790, Lithuanians inhabited around 155,000 hearths (which would give a count of about 1.24 million people, or about 35% of the country's population). As 1.2 million people (including those in Livonia) came under Russian rule in 1772, the number of Lithuanians in the pre-partition borders was no higher than

25% of the total of the Grand Duchy's inhabitants. From this it is clear that only in 1790 did the country's population density exceed that of the mid-17 century, and it came to about 16 persons per square kilometer. During the period in question, the decided majority of Lithuanians were a rural populace, because outside of Vilnius and Kaunas, there were no large urban centers in Samogitia and Aukštaitija. It is calculated that in the 17th century, inhabitants of towns (not all of which had Magdeburg law) made up only 10% to 15% of the total population, and only a little more in the 18th century. Native Lithuanian lands were distinguished by larger numbers of nobility than in the Commonwealth as a whole, where the proportion of nobility is estimated at only 5% to 6%. It is accepted that nobles in Lithuania were about 10%–11% of the population, but in Ruthenian territories, only about 3%–4%. Thus, in 1777, in the whole Grand Duchy, 16,534 noble houses were registered (5.2% of the total). In 1790, the aristocracy possessed 100 palaces, and nobles with serfs owned 9,331 manors (not counting 494 town houses), while nobles without serfs inhabited 13,890 houses. These numbers result mainly from the presence of masses of petty nobles in Samogitia, in the districts of Kaunas and Upytė, concentrated in the so-called *pola, rody*, and *okolice* ("fields, clans, and neighborhoods," Lithuanian equivalents of Polish *zaścianki*). At the end of the 18th century, the hearths of nobles in that part of Kaunas district on the right bank constituted as much as 25% of the total of rural hearths! The Lithuanian society of nobles and peasants differed from that of Ruthenia, on the one hand, by its Catholic faith (although after changes during the Reformation and after the Union of Brest in 1596, the situation was not so clear-cut), and, on the other hand, by the great power and endurance of Protestantism (primarily Evangelical Reformed, or Calvinism), especially in Samogitia.

Among peasants, the Lithuanian language persisted in both its chief dialects (Aukštaitijan and Samogitian), but it passed from everyday use by the nobles rather quickly. The problem of language is a sensitive issue

—
47
—

in Polish-Lithuanian relations, and at the same time, an essential element in discussions of the process of the so-called Polonization of the Lithuanian nobility, which are not free of oversimplifications and distortions.

It is sometimes forgotten that in ancient times, before the modern formation of nations, language was not the main factor in national identification. There existed the so-called languages of culture and languages of politics, some of them with a European scope (for instance, Latin), others regional or national. In creating a state, the Lithuanians could not use their own language in documents, and they could not write down their poetry, chronicles, and tales in it, because it had no written form. The latter only appeared in the first half of the 16th century, along with the Church reform movement and the emergence of humanistic culture. Lithuanian-language works created then and in subsequent centuries had an explicitly religious and moralizing character (they were primarily catechisms, collections of sermons, primers, and church songs). The state language, however—the language of administration, law, and culture— was Ruthenian (today also called Old Ukrainian or Old Belarusian, to distinguish it from Russian),which formally retained its status until 1697, although only in the courts and district offices (of *grody* and *ziemie*), and it rather quickly came to be limited to chancellery formulas. In practice, however, language use differed: Latin was also in use in the Grand Duchy chancellery, and after union with Poland, a century's connection brought the need for constant communication in Polish in politics, social life, and culture. So Polish became first and foremost the state political language, essential for participation in public life in the territory of the Polish Crown and at the court of the Jagiellonians. It was also propagated by the numerous newcomers from Poland who settled in the Grand Duchy for good or stayed only for a time, as soldiers, Catholic and later Protestant clergy, qualified chancellery personnel, administrative personnel, merchants, and so on. As a result, as early as the 16th century, the upper strata of so-called lords and princes spoke Polish quite well; some even treated it as their everyday language, especially in families of Lithuanian descent (for instance, the Radziwiłłs), while Orthodox Ruthenians—even the magnates—were still using Ruthenian in the early 17th century.

The Reformation brought certain changes in the attitude of the Grand Duchy's population to its language. Voices arose—and, interestingly, mostly among contemporary intellectuals of Polish and foreign descent—that the national language of Lithuanians should be Latin. A result of these tendencies was the founding in 1570 of the Jesuit College in Vilnius, which was transformed in 1579 into an academy; the initiative for writing the history of Lithuania in Latin, for which Augustyn Rotundus (Mieleski) received the commission, and finally, the flowering of the theory of the Lithuanians' Roman origin. The Latinization of Lithuania was not a success, however, and the language of Cicero did not attain a position similar to the one it occupied in the Polish Crown. The Polish language triumphed completely, and in fact, to a significantly wider degree than in Poland. From the early 17th century, instructions and resolutions of local electoral and provincial assemblies (the so-called *konwokacje* and *generały*) were written in that language. Over the decade 1620–1630, Polish replaced Ruthenian in entries recording the endowment of estates and nominations for office in the *Metryka Litewska* register. We have a great deal of evidence for the use of Polish by the middle and even the minor nobility of the Grand Duchy's western lands in the first half of the 17th century the process of linguistic Polonization was fastest in the lands of Lithuania proper, and by the early 18th century, Polish was in general use even in the eastern borderlands of the state. The Polish language spread, however, not only among the nobility (Lithuanian, Ruthenian, German, Tatar), but also in the other social strata, among the clergy, townsmen, and even peasants. Practical considerations, first and foremost, demanded this. It was for the same reason that clergymen working among Lithuanian and Ruthenian peasants had to master their languages (if they did not already know them), for it guaranteed success in their field.

—
49
—

From 1697 on, Polish formally became the official language, although in the central Lithuanian chancellery, Latin had always been and would continue to be used for documents concerning the Catholic Church, towns with Magdeburg law (although more from the territory of Lithuania and not Belarus, in the contemporary understanding of those terms), Livonia, and foreigners.

One should not, however, regard the process of linguistic and cultural Polonization as a loss of political consciousness on the part of the inhabitants of the Grand Duchy of Lithuania, as their transformation into Poles in the ethnic sense. They certainly became Poles in the state sense, being accepted as members of the Polish nobility, or the privileged class, with the same rights as the nobles of the Crown, living by their ideals of freedom and equality (rather illusory in Lithuania), united in common aspirations to maintain their political position. At the same time, that same nobility zealously defended Lithuanian state autonomy within the framework of the federal state, their rights to estates and offices, their legal system as distinctly better than that of the Crown, their national symbols, and their traditions. What's more, Lithuanian autonomy, pride, and particular interests were defended also by the Poles who had been settling there permanently in rather large numbers, since the 16th century and rapidly becoming assimilated, such as the Brzostowskis, Gosiewskis, Komorowskis, Kossakowskis, Radzimińskis, Rajeckis, Wołmińskis, and Wiesołowskis, to say nothing of the Kiszkas and Ciechanowieckis, who had already come there in the 15th century. They often considered themselves Lithuanians (or citizens of the Grand Duchy) and Poles (nobility of the Commonwealth) at the same time. In tragic times for the state, the majority of both the Lithuanian and the Lithuanian-Ruthenian nobility defended their Lithuanian fatherland as well as the Commonwealth with conviction. This can be seen explicitly in the mid-17th century, when their country was freed by their joint forces from the Muscovite and Swedish occupations. Not until the beginning of the 18th century did a completely corrupted part of the generation living at the time produce people who stopped thinking in terms of responsibility for the state and, out of hatred or love of profit, were prepared to serve the interests of foreign powers (especially Russia) and even to contribute to a loss of independence. Even they, however, regarded themselves as Poles and Lithuanians simultaneously, being fully Polonized culturally. In their own fashion, they defended Lithuanian "independence," identity, and equality, which were threatened by the unification ideas of Stanisław August Poniatowski and his advisors.

The famous line, written in Polish by Adam Mickiewicz, "Lithuania! My fatherland!" was only a reflection of a sense of identity of the Lithuanian nobleman that was universal in the early 19th century, even if his roots were "Ruthenian" or his family had lived in the Ruthenian territories of the Grand Duchy for generations. Thus, it is difficult, even as early as the 17th century, to distinguish clearly ethnic Lithuanians, Ruthenians, and Poles (and there were also a few German families in Livonia), because in principle, they formed a complex conglomerate of multiethnic, multinational, multilingual, and multidenominational citizens of the Grand Duchy, with an explicitly double and even triple sense of affiliation (Lithuanian Pole, Ruthenian Pole, Livonian Pole, but also Ruthenian Lithuanian and Livonian Lithuanian). A result of this mixing was that a citizen of the Commonwealth (Polish and Lithuanian), quoted so many times in historical literature, might speak of himself as "gente Lithuanus (Ruthenus, Livo), natione Polonus," or also "eques Polonus ex Lithuania (Ruthenia, Livonia)."

Unlike many of the other peoples who made up the Commonwealth, however, Lithuanians could feel that they were co-hosts of this state, for even after the Union of Lublin, they preserved their state borders, central offices, administrative structure, laws, army, treasury, and money. They had also their representation in the parliament and the possibility of articulating their needs and defending their particular interests. And although

—
51
—

in practice the Grand Duchy rather quickly became only one of three provinces of the Commonwealth, and not one of its two states, as the Lithuanian elite had dreamed, nonetheless, in tradition and popular formulation, Lithuanians (again, in the state sense, not the ethnic) made up one of the two Nations forming that state. For the term Lithuanian designated not only a native (ethnic) inhabitant of Samogitia and Aukštaitija, but also a citizen of the Grand Duchy, and thus played a role similar to that of the term Pole for the whole Commonwealth. Essentially, therefore, the sole legitimate criterion for defining who of the nobility was a Lithuanian should be self-description by the citizens of the Grand Duchy. Neither place of birth, nor language, nor faith was an impediment to this. For if, by way of example, the Courland noble Georg Wilhelm Wibers, enrolling in 1679 as a student of the lyceum in Riga (Swedish), signed as "Russia-Polonus," then what kind of national and ethnic consciousness did he possess? Similar cases are those of the princes Dymitr and Aleksandr Ogiński, raised in the Eastern Orthodox faith and Ruthenian culture, who in 1600 enrolled at the University in Königsberg with the Latin annotation "nobiles Poloni," and their fellow countrymen, princes Jan, Paweł, Eliasz, and Daniel Puzyna (who were Calvinists), who in 1611 signed their names as "nobiles Lithuani." One also encounters in sources of this type the self-descriptions "Polonus-Lithuanus" and "Lithuano-Polonus," "Vilnensis-Polonus" and "Polonus-Vilnensis" (townsmen and nobles), but most often, and in enormous numbers, "nobilis Polonus," and that with surnames obviously coming from the Grand Duchy with Lithuanian and Ruthenian roots. The Lithuanian nobility and townsmen (the latter often of German and Polish descent) introduced to the culture (high culture as well as political) and history of the Commonwealth their own imperishable contribution in the form of regulatory and legislative activity, science and literature, and developments in the art of war, as attested to by handbooks, monographs of various fields of science and the arts, and even installments of the *Polish Biographical Dictionary*. Very often, as a result of this "appropriation" of Lithuanians to the numbers of Poles, there is a lack in the social consciousness of the proper distinction of the two nations, as well as a lack of realization of the duality of the Commonwealth, the Grand Duchy of Lithuania's place in it, with the wealth of its different culture, specific development, and social structures. Such surnames as Dauksza, Kojałowicz, Chyliński, Narbutt, Norwid, Siemionowicz, Lauxmin, Naruszewicz, Poczobut Odlanicki, Rekuć, Rymsza, Szyrwid, Woysznarowicz, Smuglewicz, Wołodkiewicz, to say nothing of the Radziwiłłs, meant a great deal for the development of science, culture, and art.

Selected bibliography

Błaszczyk, G., *Żmudź w XVII i XVIII w. Zaludnienie i struktura społeczna* [Samogitiat in the 17th and 18th Centuries. Population and Social Structure], Poznań: Wydawnictwo Naukowe UAM, 1985.

Jakubowski, J., *Studya nad stosunkami narodowościowemi na Litwie przed unią lubelską* [Studies on Ethnic Relations in Lithuania Before the Union of Lublin], Warszawa: Towarzystwo Naukowe Warszawskie, 1912.

Jurkiewicz, J., "Osadnictwo polskie w Wielkim Księstwie Litewskim w świetle badań historycznych" [Polish Settlement in the Grand Duchy of Lithuania in the Light of Historical Research], *Acta Baltico-Slavica*, Vol. 22 (1994), pp. 237–255.

Łowmiański, H., "Popisy wojska Wielkiego Księstwa Litewskiego w XVI w. jako źródło do dziejów zaludnienia" [Army Conscription Lists of the Grand Duchy of Lithuanian in the 16th Century as a Source for the History of Its Population], in: *Mediaevalia. W 50. rocznicę pracy naukowej Jana Dąbrowskiego* [Mediaevalia. On the 50th Anniversary of the Scholarly Work of Jan Dąbrowski], Warszawa: PWN, 1960, pp. 425–435.

Łowmiański, H., *Studia nad dziejami Wielkiego Księstwa Litewskiego* [Studies on the History of the Grand Duchy of Lithuania], Poznań: Wydawnictwo Naukowe UAM, 1983.

Łowmiański, H., *Studja nad początkami społeczeństwa i państwa litewskiego* [Studies on the Beginnings of Society and the Lithuanian State], Vol. 1–2, Wilno: Towarzystwo Przyjaciół Nauk, 1931–1932.

—
53
—

Łowmiański, H., *Zaludnienie państwa litewskiego w xvi w. Zaludnienie w roku 1528* [Population of the Lithuanian State in the 16ᵗʰ Century. The Population in 1528], edited by A. Kijas, and K. Pietkiewicz, Poznań: Wydawnictwo Poznańskie, 1998.

Morzy, J., *Kryzys demograficzny na Litwie i Białorusi w ii połowie xvii wieku* [The Demographic Crisis in Lithuania and Belarus in the Second Half of the 17ᵗʰ Century], Poznań: UAM, 1965.

Ochmański, J., "Zaludnienie Litwy w roku 1790" [The Population of Lithuania in 1790], *Zeszyty Naukowe Uniwersytetu im. A. Mickiewicza w Poznaniu. Historia*, no. 7 (1967).

Topolska, M. B., "Polacy w Wielkim Księstwie Litewskim w xvi–xviii w. (Przyczynek do dziejów polskiej emigracji na wschód w okresie staropolskim)" [Poles in the Grand Duchy of Lithuania in the 16ᵗʰ–18ᵗʰ Centuries (A Contribution to the History of Polish Emigration to the East in the Old Polish Period)], *Lituano-Slavica Posnaniensia. Studia Historica*, Vol. 2 (1987), pp. 147–166.

Topolska, M. B., *Społeczeństwo i kultura w Wielkim Księstwie Litewskim od xv do xviii wieku* [Society and Culture in the Grand Duchy of Lithuania from the 15ᵗʰ to the 18ᵗʰ Centuries], Poznań–Zielona Góra: Bogucki Wydawnictwo Naukowe, 2002.

Wielhorski, W., "Stosunki językowe, wyznaniowe i etniczne w wkl pomiędzy xiii a xviii w." [Linguistic, Religious, and Ethnic Relations in the Grand Duchy of Lithuania between the 13ᵗʰ and 18ᵗʰ Centuries], *Teki Historyczne*, Vol. 13 (1964–1965), pp. 17–40.

Wiśniewski, J., "Dzieje osadnictwa w powiecie sejneńskim od xv do xix wieku" [History of Settlement in Sejny District from the 15ᵗʰ to the 19ᵗʰ Centuries], in Antoniewicz, J. (ed.), *Materiały do dziejów ziemi sejneńskiej*, Białystok: PWN 1963.

Wiśniewski, J., "Dzieje osadnictwa w powiecie suwalskim od xv do połowy xvii wieku" [History of Settlement in Suwałki District from the 15ᵗʰ to the Mid-17ᵗʰ Centuries], in Antoniewicz, J. (ed.), *Studia i materiały do dziejów Suwalszczyzny*, Białystok: PWN, 1965, pp. 51–138.

Wiśniewski, J., "Osadnictwo wschodniej Białostocczyzny" [The Settlement of the Eastern Białystok Area], *Acta Baltico-Slavica*, Vol. 11 (1977), pp. 7–79.

BELARUSIANS

～

OLEG ŁATYSZONEK

———

"The fields here are completely covered with snow longer than elsewhere, everything looks white to the observer, and the white seems to spread even to the natural color of the animals: white wolves can be seen there in various areas, as well as bears, hares, foxes, and other animals, both of the forest and of the household, which, living anywhere else, are usually another color." That is how the Polish scholar Szymon Starowolski explained the meaning of the name Biała Ruś, "White Ruthenia," in his *Polonia*, published in 1632. Judging by this description, this was for him an exotic country, although he described its borders in an almost contemporary manner. This description is all the more surprising because Starowolski was a Belarusian by today's ethnic categories, since he was born in Stara Wola near Pruzhany in Brest voivodeship, and therefore in territory that he himself—although inconsistently—named "White Ruthenia." Even if one assumes that his White Ruthenia commences only from the southern border of Navahrudak voivodeship, the writer's birthplace lies close to it. Another Polish writer, Rev. Piotr Skarga, described "the region of Navahrudak in White Ruthenia" as "a Lithuanian Lombardy, fertile and populous." It is difficult to understand what Starowolski was going by in creating his fantastic description of White Ruthenia. And he himself was not miserly in his compliments for White Ruthenia: "This country abounds in all things necessary for life, such

LIVONIA

Ryga

Birže

BALTIC SEA

SAMOGITIA

Brasław

Połock

Ukn

W

Głębokie

R

Kowno

Wilno

Oszmiana

Orss

Szklów

POMERANIA

Gdańsk

P R U S S I A

Troki

L I T H U A N I A

Lida

Grodno

Borysów

Minsk

Kojdanowo

Nowogródek

Mir

WHITE

Bycho

Knyszyn

Suprasl

Mysz

Słuck

MAZOVIA

Białystok

Wołkowysk

Lachowicze

RUTHEN

Tykocin

Różana

Słonim

GREATER POLAND

Poznań

Drohiczyn

PODLASIE

Bielsk

R U T H E N

Warszawa

Mielnik

Kobryń

Pińsk

Mużyrz

Włodawa

Brześć

Osrucz

Chełm

Z

LESSER POLAND

Bełz

Krzemieniec

R U T I

R E D

Kraków

(ROKSOLAN

Lwów

A

Kamieniec

Bracła

borders of the Commonwealth
borders of "provinces"
borders of voivodeships
borders of powiaty

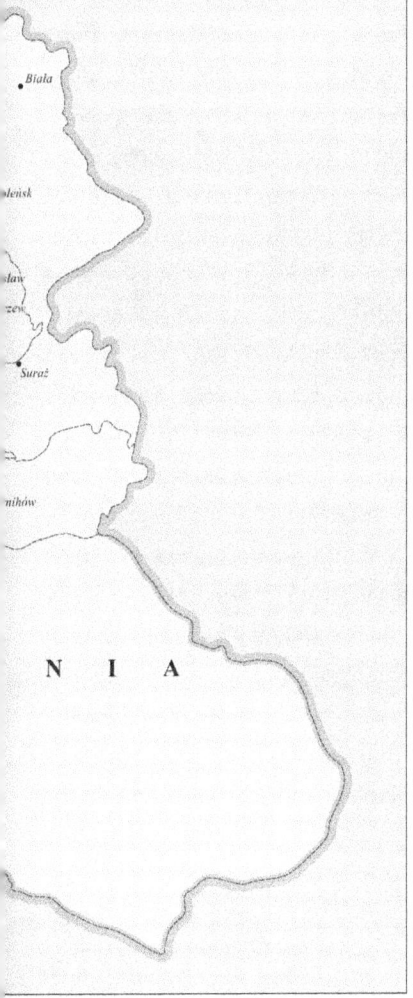

BLACK RUTHENIA
(MOSCOW)

Biała

leńsk

ław

żew

Suraż

nihów

N I A

200 km

Map 4: The Commonwealth
according to Szymon
Starowolski (1632).

as rye, barley, oats, wheat, peas, hemp, flax, lupines, wax, cattle, fish, birds, and game."

In Starowolski's time, "White Ruthenia" in the imaginations of Polish writers had borders very close to today's Belarus. This occurred as a result of a long process. The name "White Ruthenia" appears in Polish literature for the first time in the *Polish Chronicle* of Janko of Czarnków, who writes in connection with the battles among Lithuanian dukes about the imprisonment in 1382 of Jogaila (Jagiełło) by his uncle, Kęstutis (Kiejstut), "in a certain fortress of White Ruthenia, which is called Polatsk" *(in quodam castro Albae Russiae, Poloczk dicto)*. After a long pause, the name White Ruthenia was introduced once more to Polish literature around 1490 by the Italian Kallimach (Filippo Buonaccorsi). In his oration to Pope Innocent VIII, he mentioned the Slavs, of whom some had headed toward the Black Sea and settled "Podolia and White Ruthenia." Kallimach's reference is so general that by his "White Ruthenia" one can even understand all the lands of Ruthenia except Podolia. Kallimach's idea was developed further by the Kraków geographer, Jan of Stobnica, for whom "White Ruthenia" meant all the Ruthenian lands of the Grand Duchy of Lithuania along the Niemen River, as well as the Republic of Velikiy Novgorod. Marcin Kromer gave White Ruthenia (*Russia Alba*) its final form in his work *Polonia*, published in 1575. Kromer wrote its basic outline long before the Union of Lublin. Initially he diminished Jan of Stobnica's White Ruthenia, not only by subtracting Velikiy Novgorod, but also Volhynia and Podlasie, and after the Union of Lublin, also the Kyiv region. His "White Ruthenia" thus took on the contours of today's Belarus. Kromer mentions "Lithuania along with regions belonging to it, Samogitia and White Ruthenia *(Russia Alba)*, which in turn borders on the Muscovite state."

Kromer was followed by other European authors who placed White Ruthenia on the borders of the Commonwealth and Muscovy. The names "White Ruthenia" and "White Ruthenians" as descriptions of the eastern reaches of the Commonwealth and its inhabitants were spread in Europe by the Italian Alessandro Guagnini (in Poland called Gwagnin), who in 1578 published *Sarmatiae Europeae descriptio* [Description of European Sarmatia] in Kraków.

Thus, over the course of the 16th century, Polish scholars, most often connected with the University of Kraków, gradually formulated the concept of White Ruthenia. Its inhabitants, the ancestors of today's Belarusians, not only did not use that name earlier, they did not even know of it. In the 16th century, inhabitants of today's Belarus had their own system of regional divisions of the Grand Duchy of Lithuania. To the east of that country, on the rivers Dnieper and Dvina, was "Ruthenia," with such towns as Polatsk, Vitsebsk, Orsha, Mahilyoŭ, Mstislav, and Homel. To the south, "Ruthenia" bordered on the Kyiv region, "Ukraina." To the northwest, "Ruthenia" bordered on "Lithuania," which covered parts of today's Lithuanian territory with Vilnius and Kaunas (but without Samogitia) as well as part of the lands of today's Belarus, with Hrodna, Navahrudak, and Minsk. To the southwest, "Ruthenia" bordered on "Polesie," the land around Pinsk and Mazyr, as well as Ovruch in today's Ukraine. To the west lay "Podlasie" (more properly, "Podlasze"), which was still seen at the beginning of the 17th century in borders from before 1569, along with Brest. Soon, however, Brest was incorporated into "Polesie."

Inhabitants of the lands on the rivers Dvina and Dnieper began to use the name "White Ruthenia" as their own after the liberation of Polatsk from Muscovite occupation by Stefan Batory in 1579. The exact contours of White Ruthenia as identified by its inhabitants can be outlined for the early 17th century. Belonging to it then were Polatsk, Dzisna, Vitsebsk, Orsha, and Mahilyoŭ, as well as Smolensk, acquired in 1611. In the mid-17th century, so-called "Ponizowie," along with Homel and Rechytsa, became part of White Ruthenia. The western border of White Ruthenia ran more or less from its border with the Kingdom of Poland to the Dnieper and Berezyna. In time, Braslaŭ, to the north, became part of White Ruthenia,

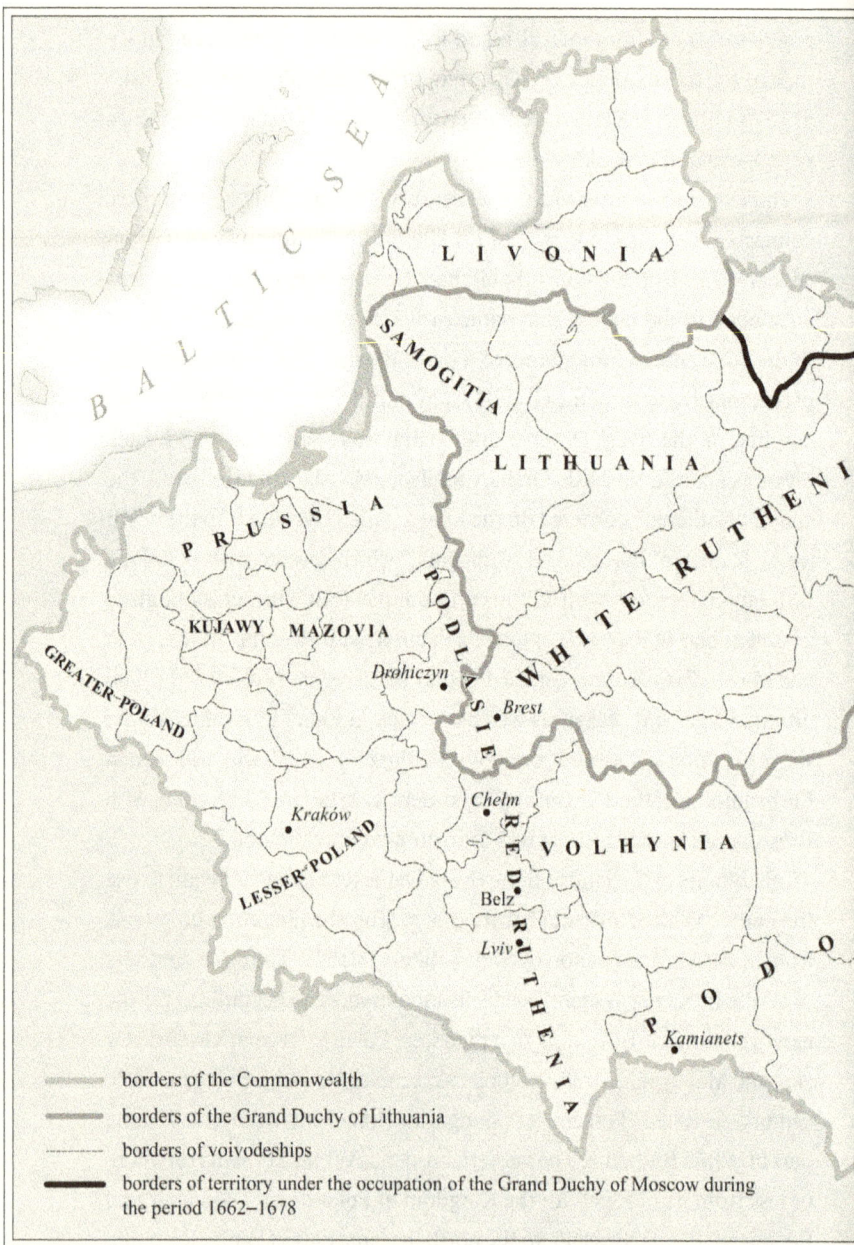

BALTIC SEA

LIVONIA

SAMOGITIA

LITHUANIA

PRUSSIA

WHITE RUTHENI

PODLASIE

KUJAWY MAZOVIA

GREATER-POLAND

Drohiczyn

Brest

Kraków

Chełm

LESSER-POLAND

VOLHYNIA

Belz

RED

Lviv

RUTHENIA

PODO

Kamianets

borders of the Commonwealth

borders of the Grand Duchy of Lithuania

borders of voivodeships

borders of territory under the occupation of the Grand Duchy of Moscow during the period 1662–1678

S C O W

ᴧ
Kaniv
• Cherkasy

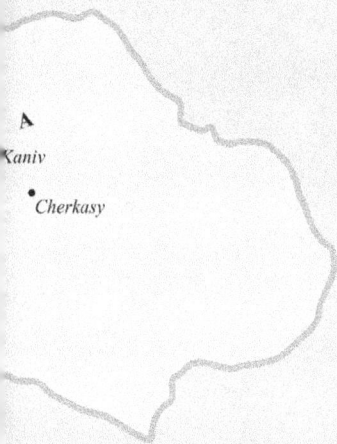

Map 5: The Commonwealth
after the Union of Lublin (1569)
according to Marcin Kromer.

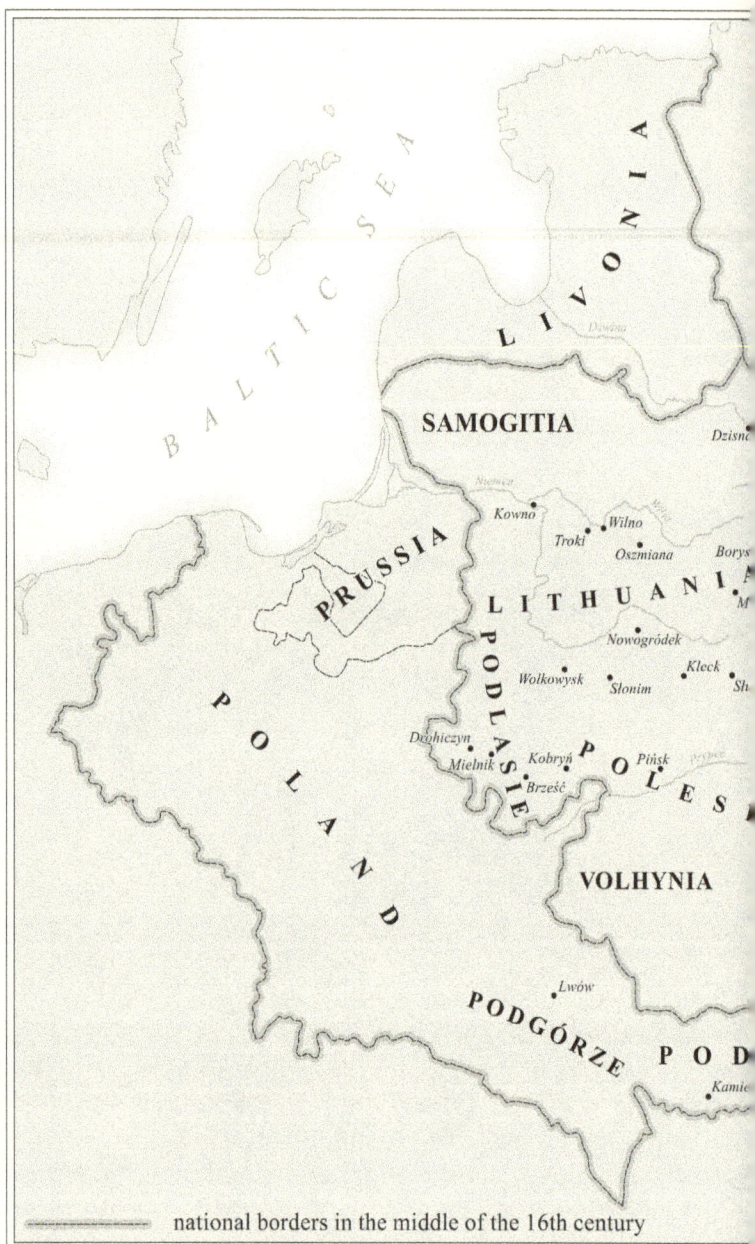

BALTIC SEA

LIVONIA

Dźwina

SAMOGITIA

Dzisn

Niemen

Kowno

Troki Wilno
Oszmiana Borys
M

LITHUANIA

PRUSSIA

Nowogródek

PODLASIE

Wołkowysk Kleck Sh
Słonim

POLAND

Drohiczyn
Kobryń Pińsk POLES
Mielnik Brześć

VOLHYNIA

Lwów

PODGÓRZE POD

Kamie

national borders in the middle of the 16th century

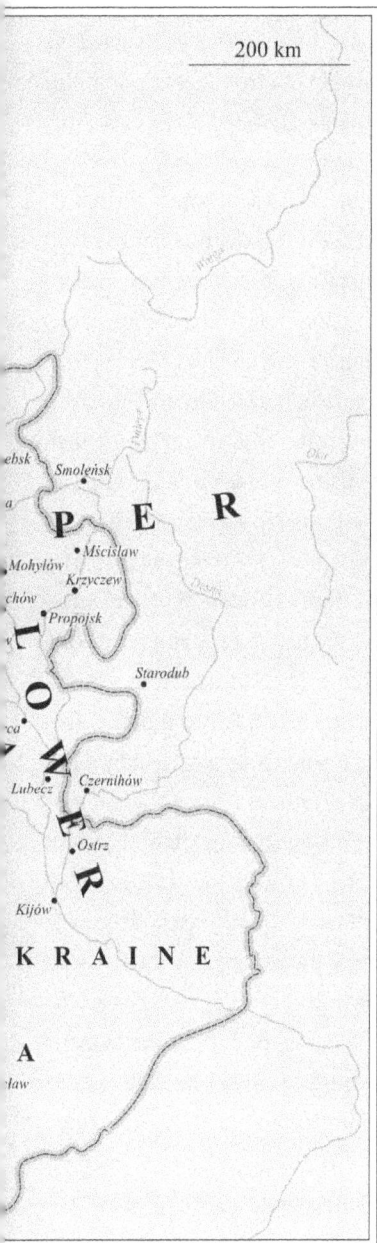

200 km

ebsk Smoleńsk

a

P E R

Mohylów Mścisław
Krzyczew
chów
Propojsk

L
O
W

Staródub

ca

E
Lubecz Czernihów
R
Ostrz

Kijów

K R A I N E

A
law

—

Map 6: Regional divisions
of the Grand Duchy of Lithuania
as conceived by 16th-century
inhabitants of today's Belarus.

and to the south, the region of Mazyr. Thus, White Ruthenia occupied the whole territory of 16th-century "Ruthenia" in the Grand Duchy of Lithuania. This territorial form of White Ruthenia persisted to the end of the Commonwealth's existence.

In the eyes of its inhabitants, White Ruthenia was not only a geographic region, but also a sort of state unit, because it was distinct not so much from "Lithuania" as from the Grand Duchy of Lithuania. One wrote not only of "Lithuania and White Ruthenia," but also of "the Grand Duchy of Lithuania and White Ruthenia." Of course, this applies only to vernacular conceptions of White Ruthenia's place in the Commonwealth, and not its actual legal status as a state. The way the description "Ruthenian people" is used in sources in which the name White Ruthenia appears leaves not the slightest doubt that White Ruthenia was inhabited by the Ruthenian people, the same in Polatsk, Vitsebsk, and Mahilyoŭ as in Kyiv, Lviv, and Przemyśl. Officially, the state bore the name "Grand Duchy of Lithuania, Ruthenia, and Samogitia," and its "state" nations were the Lithuanians, Ruthenians, and Samogitians. The Third Statute of Lithuania, in 1588, sanctioned this legally; article 12 explained that the right to receive any sort of conferral from the Grand Duke was held by representatives of three nations: "Lithuania," "Ruthenia," and "Samogitia." The statute was published in the Ruthenian language, and its author, Vice Chancellor Lev Sapieha, remained a patriot of Ruthenia as it was then understood, although he converted from Orthodoxy to Catholicism. He wrote with pride in the introduction: "And if any nation might be ashamed not to know its laws, then that is all the more true of us, since we have laws written, not in a foreign language, but in our own..." It is hard to avoid the impression that the words cited above are an implicit polemic against the earlier statement by Michalon the Lithuanian that "The Ruthenian language is foreign to us Lithuanians."

Although there can be no doubt that Samogitians existed in the 16th century alongside ethnic Lithuanians, in the sphere of ideas, the Lithuanian people included the Samogitians. Such a conception can be clearly seen in the *Kronika Wielkiego Księstwa Litewskiego i Żmudzkiego* [Chronicle of the Grand Duchy of Lithuania and Samogitia], written in the early 16th century, and later in the works of Michalon the Lithuanian, Martynas Mažvydas, Mikalojus Daukša, and others. The conviction that the Lithuanian political nation consists only of two peoples, the Lithuanian and the Ruthenian, was also expressed in state documents during this time. A 1563 charter that abolished those articles of the Union of Horodło (1413) which discriminated against Orthodox nobles was addressed to the nobles "of both nations, both the Lithuanian and the Ruthenian" to "Lithuania and Ruthenia."

A separate problem is the diversity of Ruthenians in terms of faith in the 16th century as a result of early conversions from Orthodoxy to Catholicism, and from the midpoint of that century, to Protestantism. An archetypal figure in this regard is Francysk Skaryna, translator and publisher of the *Biblia ruska* [Ruthenian Bible] as well as other religious works in the Ruthenian language in the first quarter of the 16th century. Skaryna came from an Orthodox merchant family of Polatsk, but most likely was baptized only in the Roman rite. In Skaryna's views and actions, one can see influences of Hussitism and the Reformation. Young Skaryna registered at the University of Kraków as a "Lithuanian" *(Litphanus)*, but he later appeared in Padua as a "Ruthenian" *(Ruthenus)*, and in Prague as a "Ruthenian" *(Rus)*. As he was a Catholic, the description "Ruthenian" could be treated as an ethnic term, whereas "Lithuanian" was political and state-related. Although he had great fondness for his home, "the renowned city of Polatsk," all Ruthenia was the field of his activity, perhaps even including Moscow. Although national terminology does not distinguish him from his Ruthenian surroundings, his relationship to the Ruthenian language already bears the stamp of modern times. For him, language, and not faith, was a mark of *ruskość* (Ruthenianism). He says of himself that he was "born in the Ruthenian language," and of his

—
65
—

countrymen he writes, "My brothers, Ruś." He explains that he prints holy books "in Ruthenian words but the Slavic tongue," because "a merciful God released them on this earth from that language." He states in the afterword that he published the books "for the common people of the Ruthenian language." Skaryna never says anything about the "Ruthenian" or "Roman" faith, or about Orthodox Christians or Catholics; he speaks only of Christianity. Thus, his Ruthenian Bible was a Bible for all Ruthenians, regardless of faith.

In the mid-16th century, the arrangement of ethnic and religious forces in the society of the Grand Duchy of Lithuania underwent an important change with the expansion of Protestantism, and above all, Calvinism. The majority of magnates, both Catholic and Orthodox, converted to Calvinism, as did a significant number of nobles of both faiths. Protestant Ruthenians became polonized more rapidly than their countrymen of other confessions because they mixed within the Commonwealth's Polish-language environment of dissenters. Even those polonized linguistically, however, steadfastly retained their Ruthenian identity, and were more ready to reflect on their ethnic affiliation than their compatriots of other faiths. This is attested to by the example of the Calvinist Salomon Rysiński, the first native to describe himself as a "Belarusian."

Salomon Rysiński matriculated at the University of Altdorf on 2 December 1586 as *"Salomon Pantherus Leucorussus."* Two years later, he named his fatherland as Belarus *(Leucorussia)*. It is worthwhile to note that the descriptions used by Rysiński correspond to modern Belarusian terms: *Leucorussus* is "Belarusian," and not "White Ruthenian" *(Albus Ruthenus)*, the usual term used in writing at the time. As Rysiński's self-description was a sort of intellectual invention, establishing what he had in mind when he called his country Belarus and himself a Belarusian demands a broader presentation of his profile.

The Rysiński family came from Rysin in the vicinity of Polatsk; Rysiński himself, however, was born in Kobylniki, in Vitsebsk province.

The Rysińskis were probably refugees from the Polatsk area, occupied in 1563 by Tsar Ivan the Terrible. Salomon studied abroad, and also traveled a great deal. It is likely that around 1596 he entered the service of Vilnius voivode and hetman (field commander) of the Grand Duchy Krzysztof Radziwiłł, known as "the Thunderbolt," as the tutor of his son, Krzysztof II. After the death of Krzysztof "the Thunderbolt," Rysiński held the position of councilor at the court of Krzysztof II, and at the same time was pedagogue to the latter's son, Janusz. He participated actively in the life of the Calvinist *Jednota Litewska* [Union of the Provincial Church of Lithuania, or Lithuanian Brethren]. He wrote and published many occasional Latin compositions dedicated to the Radziwiłłs and persons connected with them. His crowning achievement, however, was a volume of 1,800 Polish proverbs, published first in 1618 and later reprinted several times under the title *Przypowieści polskie* [Polish Proverbs]. The work was based on Belarusian proverbs written down by Rysiński in the area of Lubcha on the Neman.

As a "Belarusian," Rysiński was also a "Sarmatian." For Rysiński, the term "Sarmatian" means "Slavic." He wrote with delight that one could make oneself understood in the "Sarmatian" language from the Adriatic to the Caspian Sea. And so Rysiński regarded himself as a Slav *(Sarmata)* and a Belarusian *(Leucorussus)*. He regarded Belarus *(Leucorussia)* as his homeland, although in terms of state, he considered the Grand Duchy of Lithuania his fatherland *(patria)*. On the other hand, he did not consider himself a Lithuanian in the ethnic sense, because he treated Lithuanians as a nation separate from Belarusians. A Polish-Belarusian type of man of letters and lover of folklore such as Rysiński did not form explicitly until the 19th century. Salmon Rysiński is, therefore, the second archetypal figure, after Francysk Skaryna, in the history of the development of the Belarusian national identity.

The period of relative ethnic-religious equilibrium came to an end in the late 16th century. Protestantism was losing out in all of "European Sarmatia"; it still held on most powerfully in Lithuania. The Protestants did not

—
67
—

succeed in drawing the king to their side, and their camp was torn apart by endless disputes over doctrine, especially between the Calvinists and Arians. Toward the end of the century, the vision of uniting Sarmatians through Protestantism gave way to a vision of Catholic reforms following the Council of Trent.

At the same time, Orthodox brotherhoods in cities, while firm in their attachment to doctrinal orthodoxy, reformed not only city life in the Western European manner, breaking with medieval tradition, but also proceeded to reform the life of their own Church and even its rites, with the intention of simplifying them. And so, besides Protestantism in the strict sense, a unique Orthodox reformation appeared in Ruthenian lands. The role of an Orthodox Counterreformation was played by the Union of Brest, in the year 1596. Even if we interpret favorably the intentions of the Orthodox hierarchs who contracted this union, assuming that they wanted to preserve a maximum of Orthodoxy under conditions of a Catholic offensive and to contribute to the integration of the nation, the results of their measures turned out to be the opposite. Within the Ruthenian ethnos of the Commonwealth, already weakened by the conversion of the elite to Protestantism and Catholicism, there arose a long-lasting and devastating split.

In Belarus, in view of a majority of the nobles' entering into the Union, their role was taken over, at least to a certain degree, by the burghers. In the 16th century, Mahilyoŭ on the Dnieper grew to be the largest city of White Ruthenia. The Orthodox bishop in residence there was called (at that time, still unofficially) "the bishop of Belarus." The people of Mahilyoŭ considered themselves Ruthenians, subjects of the Polish king (there is not even any mention of the Grand Dukes of Lithuania in the chronicles of Mahilyoŭ). Their Ruthenian consciousness did not differ in any way from the alleged "Ukrainian" national consciousness artificially constructed by some Polish and Ukrainian historians. The Mahilyoŭ townsman Tomasz Jewlewicz, educated in Kraków, took his thinking of Ruthenian statehood to an extreme to which none of the "Ukrainian" writers had gone. In his poem *Labyrinth*, published in 1625, he recognized Ruthenia as a republic in its own right. He saw the Zaporizhian Cossacks as the defenders of this state.

The last battle of the Ruthenian nation for equal status in the Commonwealth was the uprising of Bohdan Khmelnytsky in 1648. It spread not only over the lands of today's Ukraine, but also over about half the territory of modern Belarus. Not only the townsmen and peasants joined in the insurrection, but also the Orthodox nobles, and even some magnates. However, hetman Janusz Radziwiłł (let us remember, Rysiński's pupil) suppressed the rebellion ruthlessly. As the war continued, the Lithuanian army occupied Kyiv in 1651, and the army of the Crown defeated the Cossacks at Beres-techko. That finally persuaded Khmelnytsky to ask Moscow for help. After long hesitation, the Muscovites decided to intervene, taking the Zaporizhian Cossacks under their scepter as a result of the Treaty of Pereyaslav in 1654. Tsar Alexei Mikhailovich took the title "lord and autocrat of all Great and Little Russia." The second part of the title referred to the entirety of the Ruthenian lands of the Commonwealth.

In the summer of 1654, 80,000 troops of the Moscow army and 20,000 Zaporizhian Cossacks invaded the Grand Duchy of Lithuania. Resistance was feeble. The defenders of Mahilyoŭ were persuaded to capitulate by a local noble, Konstanty Pokłoński, who went over to Moscow's side during the preparations for the invasion. Pokłoński accepted the title of "Colonel of Belarus" and obtained permission from the Tsar to form a Cossack regiment. Pokłoński's ambitions undoubtedly extended much further, both in terms of territory and the authority he aspired to. He tried to create a center of his own political and military power, but had to maneuver between the Muscovites and the Zaporizhian Cossacks, because Khmelnytsky also intended to gain control of a sizable part, if not the entirety, of Ruthenia within the Grand Duchy's borders. Pokłoński demanded of Tsar Alexei Mikhailovich that Ivan Zolotarenko, the assistant

—
69
—

commander of the Zaporizhian Cossacks in White Ruthenia, not take command in Mahilyoŭ, "for these are no longer Ukrainians but subjects of Your Imperial Majesty." By the end of 1654, Pokłoński's Belarusian regiment numbered 4,000 well-armed and trained Cossacks. Pokłoński could not endure Muscovite ways, however, and went over to Radziwiłł's side at the moment when the Lithuanian army approached Mahilyoŭ. In numerous letters sent to the people of Mahilyoŭ, Cossacks, Muscovite dignitaries, and Ukrainian leaders, Pokłoński explained the reasons for his action: "I understood that this war was to be [conducted] for the purpose of liberating oppressed Ruthenia, that is, accepting solace, as from a Christian sovereign." Instead, he writes, there was "looting of the houses of God, as the Tatars used to do," and he enumerates the misfortunes visited upon the population of the country. Pokłoński decided to return to the embrace of his "dear and golden Fatherland."

Pokłoński's Cossacks, however, did not follow him. Along with the Muscovite garrison and the townsmen, they defended Mahilyoŭ against Radziwiłł, despite enormous losses; due to hunger and plague, the majority of the city's inhabitants died, more than 10,000. About 2,000 Belarusian Cossacks and 800 Muscovite soldiers were killed, wounded, or died. The Lithuanian forces, in turn, were almost completely destroyed. This was the beginning of the end both for Radziwiłł and for Pokłoński, to whom the commander had given "unequalled colonelcy over all the lands of Belarus." Few of his countrymen followed Pokłoński, however, and he was defeated not long after, at Barysaŭ, by the Muscovites. Zolotarenko became the master of the situation on the Dnieper. In summer 1655, he led 20,000 Belarusian Cossacks in an attack on Vilnius. Among the Cossack commanders was, supposedly, the ancestor of the great Polish poet Adam Mickiewicz, leading the Novgorod Cossacks. The Muscovite and Cossack armies took Vilnius, burning the city and murdering its inhabitants. After formal entry into the captured Lithuanian capital, Alexei Mikhailovich issued an *ukase*, or decree, in which he proclaimed himself "lord of the

Grand Duchy of Lithuania and White Russia, and Volhynia, and Podolia." From that point until the end of their existence, the Muscovite Tsars bore the title "Lord of Great, Little, and White Ruthenia," or today's Russia, Ukraine, and Belarus. In reply, John Casimir changed his traditional title to "King of Poland, Grand Duke of Lithuania and Belarus."

Some of the nobility recognized Alexei as their Grand Duke when he promised to confirm all rights and freedoms for all nations of the Grand Duchy of Lithuania. Some, led by Janusz Radziwiłł, made a treaty with Sweden, whose army invaded the Kingdom of Poland and the Grand Duchy of Lithuania. Among those who signed the Kėdainiai act of union was Konstanty Pokłoński. Some of the nobles remained loyal to the Polish king, John Casimir. A struggle of each against all began.

In 1656, after the death of Zolotarenko, Khmelnytsky appointed a new commander for the area on the Dnieper, "Colonel of Belarus" Ivan Nechaya (a native Belarusian), who sabotaged all the Muscovites' orders. In addition, a self-proclaimed "Colonel of Belarus," a native of Mahilyoŭ, Dzianis Murashka, broke away from Nechaya and conducted a partisan war in the districts of Minsk and Navahrudak. Moscow directed its forces against Nechaya, while in 1658, the latter, along with Murashka, supported a new Zaporizhian commander, Ivan Vyhovsky, who made a treaty with the Commonwealth in Hadiach. The colonels of Belarus did not, however, play a major role in the rest of the war.

The colonel of Belarus, Konstanty Pokłoński, should be recognized as the first Belarusian politician, because he was the first who tried to act as a politician explicitly in the name of White Ruthenia, and not Lithuania and Ruthenia. In his activity, one can see an attempt to create an autonomous state unit in the territory of White Ruthenia, modeled after that of the Zaporizhian Cossacks. Konstanty Pokłoński was a traitor many times over. He betrayed the King of Poland and Grand Duke of Lithuania, John Casimir, for the commander of the Zaporizhian Cossacks, Bohdan Khmelnytsky, and then betrayed the latter for the Tsar of Great

—

71

—

and Little Russia, Alexei Mikhailovich. He betrayed the Tsar, in turn, returning to the Polish-Lithuanian side. Then he betrayed John Casimir once more, swearing loyalty to the King of Sweden, Charles X Gustav, whom he abandoned in favor of service with the Elector of Brandenburg, Friedrich Wilhelm, until finally he returned to the rule of John Casimir. The times were hard, but even against the background of general decline in attachment to monarchs, Pokłoński's twists and turns are extraordinary. There is, however, no reason to doubt that Pokłoński acted out of ideological motives. Undoubtedly, what mattered to him was "the liberation of oppressed Ruthenia." If considered from the viewpoint of loyalty to a national ideology, rather than to monarchs or even states, Pokłoński's activities take on a dimension other than ordinary self-interest. In the years 1654–1658, White Ruthenia was where the sabre of the colonel of Belarus reached—at Mahilyoǔ, Homel, Minsk, Navahrudak, and Ashmiany. This struggle had no support in any state tradition, and the difference in the development of state-building tendencies in Belarus as compared with Ukraine was more or less the same as the difference between the ranks of the Belarusian colonel and the commander of the Zaporozhian Cossacks. Pokłoński was defeated because he did not gain broad support among the Belarusian population, and none on the part of the nobles. The direct cause of his defeat, however, was the greatest of all his treacheries: the Belarusian colonel betrayed his own army, and that army was, at the time, the embryonic Belarusian state.

Khmelnytsky's Uprising and the war with Moscow were a total catastrophe for Belarus. In 1648, there were 2.9 million people living in the territory of today's Belarus; in 1667, the number was not even half of that: 1.4 million. Polatsk province lost almost three quarters (!) of its population. Undoubtedly, Belarus before these wars had a higher level of material culture and was significantly wealthier than it was even one hundred years later. It was the townspeople, jealously guarding their privileges, who constituted the main support of Ruthenian culture in Lithuania and

White Ruthenia at that time. Mahilyoŭ boasted of its noble rights and felt powerful enough to resist the whole army of the Grand Duchy, and a few years later, to slaughter the whole Muscovite garrison. But the town was badly damaged, and other towns and villages were simply wiped off the face of the earth. The nobles converted to Roman Catholicism and accepted as their own the Lithuanian national myth, as well as Polish culture. White Ruthenia became only a geographical concept for a whole century.

In summary, one may state that up to the end of the Commonwealth's existence, there existed neither a Belarusian nation nor a Ukrainian one. Educated ancestors of today's Belarusians and Ukrainians saw the Commonwealth as consisting of three nations: Polish, Lithuanian, and Ruthenian. The population of today's Belarus was divided, therefore, into Ruthenians and Lithuanians. In contrast to today's Belarusians, for the Ruthenians of that era, the Grand Duchy of Lithuania was not a valuable entity in and of itself. The fundamental point of reference for their loyalty was the King of Poland, and the border of 1569 was treated as non-existent. Those among the Ruthenians who identified with the Grand Duchy of Lithuania, as a rule, converted to Catholicism and made up Lithuanian descent for themselves, such as the Chodkiewiczes and Sapiehas. The Belarusian nation as a conscious community of people was not to form until the second half of the 19th century and the beginning of the 20th century, from descendants of Lithuanian Ruthenians and Slavicized Lithuanians. In the early modern era, there arose only the basic elements of an idea of Belarusian nationality: the name of the country and nation, and the germs of state-building thoughts and activities. From the end of the 16th century, there existed a country named White Ruthenia, which toward the end of that period was beginning to be called Belarus. This country was smaller than today's Belarus; but at times its borders were similar to the contemporary ones. Its educated inhabitants believed that they belonged to a broader "Sarmatian" community. The basis of the Belarusian national ideal is therefore rooted in the Sarmatian culture of the Commonwealth.

—
73
—

Selected bibliography

Bobiatyński, K., *Od Smoleńska do Wilna. Wojna Rzeczypospolitej z Moskwą 1654–1655* [From Smolensk to Vilnius: The Commonwealth's War with Moscow, 1654–1655], Zabrze: Inforteditions, 2004.

Kromer, M., *Polska, czyli o położeniu, ludności, obyczajach, urzędach i sprawach publicznych Królestwa Polskiego księgi dwie* [Poland, or about the Location, Peoples, Customs, Offices, and Public Affairs of the Kingdom of Poland, Two Books], translated by S. Kazikowski, compiled and with an introduction by R. Marchwiński, Olsztyn: Pojezierze, 1984.

Liedke, M., *Od prawosławia do katolicyzmu. Ruscy możni i szlachta Wielkiego Księstwa Litewskiego wobec wyznań reformacyjnych* [From Orthodoxy to Catholicism. Ruthenian Magnates and the Nobility of the Grand Duchy of Lithuania In the Face of Reform Religions], Białystok: Wydawnictwo Uniwersytetu w Białymstoku, 2004.

Lulewicz, H., "Salomon Rysiński," *Polski Słownik Biograficzny* [Polish Biographical Dictionary], Vol. XXXIII/4, No. 139, pp. 553–557.

Łatyszonek, O., *Od Rusinów Białych do Białorusinów. U źródeł białoruskiej idei narodowej* [From White Ruthenians to Belarusians. Among the Sources of the Belarusian National Idea], Białystok: Wydawnictwo Uniwersytetu w Białymstoku, 2006.

Morzy, J., *Kryzys demograficzny na Litwie i Białorusi w drugiej połowie XVII wieku* [The Demographic Crisis in Lithuania and Belarus in the Second Half of the 17th Century], Poznań: UAM, 1965.

Rachuba, A., "Pokłoński (Wodzgir-Pokłoński) Konstanty Wacław," *Polski Słownik Biograficzny* [Polish Biographical Dictionary], Vol. XXVII, pp. 234–235.

Sahanowicz, H., *Historia Białorusi. Od czasów najdawniejszych do końca XVIII wieku* [The History of Belarus. From Ancient Times to the End of the 18th Century], translated by H. Łaszkiewicz, Lublin: Instytut Europy Środkowo-Wschodniej, 2001.

Starowolski, S., *Polska albo opisanie położenia Królestwa Polskiego* [Poland, or a Description of the Location of the Kingdom of Poland], translated, with an introduction and commentary by A. Piskadło, Kraków: Wydawnictwo Literackie, 1976.

UKRAINIANS

∽

MIROSŁAW NAGIELSKI

—

The appearance of Ruthenians within the borders of Piast Poland was a consequence of the death of Duke Bolesław Jerzy II of Mazovia, son of Trojden I, in 1340. At that time, King Casimir the Great set out to defend with arms his inheritance from his relative who had ruled Galician-Lodomerian Ruthenia. The battles for control of the region, which Hungary and Lithuania also claimed, did not end until 1366, when Lodomerian Ruthenia was divided by virtue of a treaty written in the Ruthenian language. Volodymyr-Volynskyi along with Belz and Chełm, went to Casimir the Great. Thus the territory of the state ruled by the last of the Piasts increased by almost a third. At the same time, the Polish Crown (i.e., the Kingdom of Poland) acquired a Ruthenian population professing Orthodoxy, as well as Armenians, who received a separate episcopate in Lviv (1363).

The inclusion of more Ruthenian territory under the Polish Crown was a consequence of the Union of Lublin in 1569, or, more precisely, of the resistance of the Lithuanian magnates, who, opposed to the demands of the Crown M.P.'s and King Sigismund Augustus, left Lublin. By a royal decision, in addition to Podlasie and Volhynia, so-called Southern Ruthenia—that is, the later provinces of Bratslav and Kyiv—was incorporated into the lands of the Crown. The view that the nobility of the lands incorporated into the Crown supported this decision, as they looked forward to the prospect of gaining privileges equal to those of nobles of the Crown, does not fully reflect reality. As research by Karol Mazur shows, the nobles of both Volhynia and Bratslav hung back from sending a delegation, asking for a delay in order to consult with Lithuanian dignitaries. Despite their initial fears, however, the delegates did recognize the incorporation of their provinces into the Crown and took the oath required by law. This resulted from the fact that the elite of the southern Ruthenian lands succeeded in confirming their autonomy in the charters of incorporation, and their rights were made equal to those of the Crown. And thus the Ruthenians were accepted as citizens of the Crown as "equals among equals" and were granted the application of the Second Statute of Lithuania, the use of the Ruthenian language in offices and the royal chancellery, and permission for the princes to retain their ancient titles. What was especially important for the Ruthenian elite at the time was the guarantee that the execution of royal domain would not be conducted in the incorporated provinces. A major factor in the lack of opposition to the idea of union was the fact that the Ruthenian nobility did not change rulers, for they continued to identify their bond with the Crown (and in reality, with the Commonwealth as well) with Sigismund August, the last Jagiellonian.

The majority of historians rightly consider the Union of Lublin a turning point for Volhynia and the Ukrainian territories, although the Ruthenian nobility did not fully recognize all the consequences at the time. This is shown by the fact that they did not aim to create a tripartite state that would secure the rights of Ruthenians in the new circumstances. A long-term consequence of this inaction turned out to be the increasing influence of Polish and Latin culture, not only on the elite of Ruthenian nobility.

The incorporation began a slow but noticeable influx of Polish Catholic nobles into Ukraine, although planned colonization activity did not begin until the 1580s and 1590s. According to Henryk Litwin, who analyzed tax registers with regard to the descent of the noble families named in them, the Bratslav voivodeship was the area more subject to Polish influences, although both in the Bratslav region as well as in that of Kyiv, the Polish element played the largest role among the wealthiest inhabitants. Ruthenians still clearly predominated in the group of small and medium-sized properties. In the Kyiv voivodeship, the influx of Polish nobles was already noticeable after 1581, but did not become strong until the 1620s, and subsequently in the 1630s. According to that same author, as of 1640, Ruthenian nobles still held over 75 percent of properties in Kyiv voivodeship, although Poles already predominated among holders of liens and leases. The distribution of offices and leases in Ukrainian territory by Sigismund III to Polish magnates, veteran officers, and soldiers of the regular army increased the settlement movement to this area, which by the mid-17th century led to the creation of enormous magnate fortunes in the Bratslav and Kyiv voivodeships and in also Volhynia, although in the latter the phenomenon appeared to a lesser degree. The constant need for ready money compelled the Ukrainian elite of the time to resort to short-term leases and liens; due to this, colonized estates came into the hands of incoming "entrepreneurs" from the Crown, who swelled the ranks of new property owners in the Ukrainian lands. Another means by which arrivals from the Crown took over new territories was inheriting property from Orthodox Ruthenian families that had died out, such as the Ostrogskis. In time, the local royal properties became the basis of existence for both the Ukrainian elite and for the multitude of small property owners. Many senior officers of the regular army received rich lease properties, for example the lieutenant of the Hussar regiment of Władysław IV, the crown quartermaster Mikołaj Stogniew, *starosta* of Khmilnyk. In Kyiv voivodeship, unlike in the Bratslav region, magnates did not attain such predominance over medium-sized property owners, and the ethnic and religious structure took a different form than in Volhynia and in Bratslav region. It is noteworthy that in the last years of the "golden peace" in Ukraine (1638–1648), up to 30 percent of private property was in the hands of lease-holders, among whom arrivals from the native lands of the Crown played the leading role. This is relevant to the genesis of the largest of the Cossack uprisings in the 17th century, led by Bohdan Khmelnytsky.

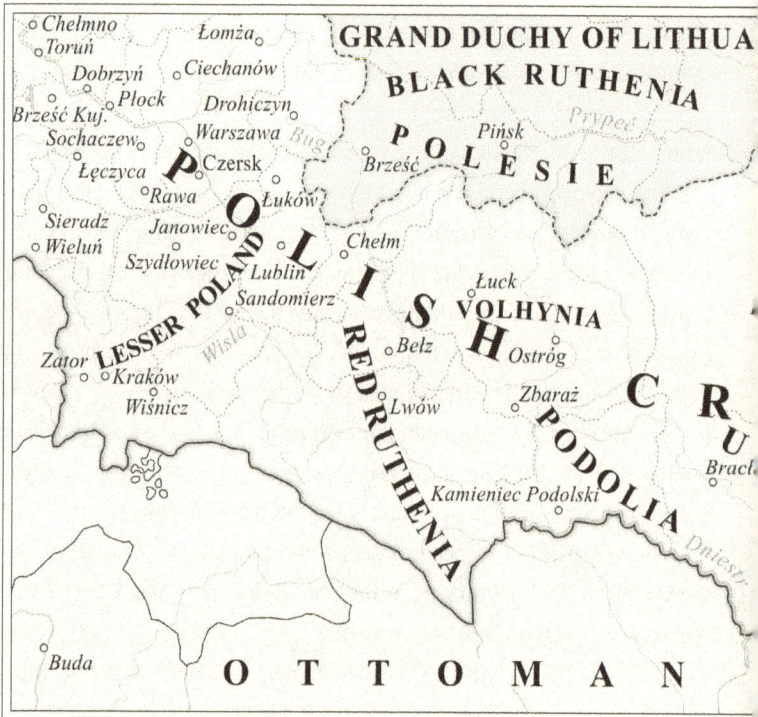

Chełmno
Toruń
Łomża
Ciechanów
GRAND DUCHY OF LITHUA
BLACK RUTHENIA
Dobrzyń
Płock
Drohiczyn
Brześć Kuj.
Warszawa *Bug*
Prypeć
Pińsk
Sochaczew
P
Brześć
O L E S I E
Łęczyca
Czersk
Sieradz
Rawa
Łuków
Wieluń
Janowiec
Chełm
O
Szydłowiec
Lublin
L
Łuck
VOLHYNIA
Sandomierz
I
Zator
LESSER POLAND
Wisła
Bełz
S
Ostróg
Kraków
RED RUTHENIA
Lwów
Zbaraż
H
C
Wiśnicz
R U
PODOLIA
Bracł.
Kamieniec Podolski
R
Dniestr
Buda
O T T O M A N

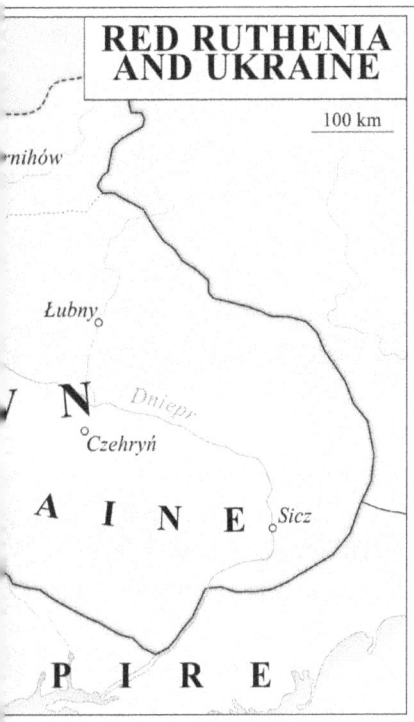

RED RUTHENIA AND UKRAINE

100 km

•nihów

Łubny

N

Dniepr

Czehryń

A I N E

Sicz

P I R E

Map 7: Red Ruthenia
and Ukraine after 1569.

A separate problem, one unsolved by the Commonwealth, was the question of religion in the Ukrainian lands, which led to many conflicts in Ruthenian society. In 1596, a synod in Brest-Litovsk, with the support of Sigismund III Vasa, approved the union of the Catholic Church with the Orthodox Church in the Commonwealth. In the face of opposition by Prince Konstanty Ostrogski, the option of the Union's opponents won out in Ukraine: a decisive factor was the attitude of the majority of the Orthodox nobles, who did not support the Union, defending "the Greek religion" in local assemblies, often invoking the Act of the Warsaw Confederation of 1573, which guaranteed peace "to those of different faiths," and the Union of Lublin, the idea of which, in the opinion of the protestors, was violated by the resolutions of the Brest synod. During the Zebrzydowski Rebellion (1606–1607), also, the nobles of the Ukrainian provinces demanded the annulment of the synod's resolutions, demanding that Orthodox church offices be conferred only on people "of the Greek faith and patriarchal obedience, through free election." In view of Sigismund III's religious policy of supporting the Uniates and Catholics, the Ruthenian nobles at local assemblies and in parliament did not hesitate to enter into alliances with Protestants. It should be noted that conversions to Catholicism by representatives of the Ukrainian power elite (the Wiśniowieckis and Rożyńskis) did not bring the Orthodox nobles and middle class with them, which inevitably sharpened disputes between Uniates and non-Uniates. The dissolution of the Orthodox hierarchy resulting from the Union of Brest caused a situation best described by Zbigniew Wójcik, who wrote that after the Union of Brest "we have a hierarchy with no congregation on the one hand, and on the other, a congregation without a hierarchy." In 1620, the situation became even more complicated when the Patriarch Teophanes of Jerusalem, returning from Moscow, ordained a new Orthodox hierarchy, headed by Kyiv metropolitan Iov Boretsky, without the permission of Commonwealth authorities. Without the support of the Zaporizhian Cossacks and their commander, Petro Konashevych-Sahaidachny, who gave Teophanes an armed guard, they certainly would not have succeeded in rebuilding an Orthodox hierarchy in the course of a few months. The Commonwealth's war with Turkey (1620–1621) and the need for assistance from the Zaporizhian Cossacks contributed to it being preserved. Thus, to the end of Sigismund III's reign, the battle continued in Ukraine over the administration of souls between two hierarchies: the Uniate supported by the king and the newly-created "disuniate" one supported by the Zaporizhian Cossacks.

At this point, one must emphasize the role of the Cossacks in the Ukrainian provinces. Tatar raids on the southeastern provinces of the Commonwealth required the organization of a system of defense of those regions, both by the Grand Duchy of Lithuania (before the Union of Lublin) and by the Crown. Neither units of the standard border defense force nor the regular army, reinforced by lords' divisions and volunteers, succeeded in the task of providing a satisfactory guard for the borders and citizens. In this situation, the idea was born of using the Cossacks who lived on the outskirts of Ukrainian towns and cities, as well as those residing in some royal estates (*starostwa*); initially, those of Cherkasy and Kaniv. Sigismund August initiated the use of Cossacks' serving for compensation "at our castles" with a decree dated 20 November 1568. The King stipulated as a condition, however, that the Cossacks had to relinquish their independent *chadzki* [expeditions, raids] to the Black Sea coast. The first units of Cossacks registered in the service of the Commonwealth were formed in 1572, and the nobleman Jan Badowski was named their superior, who was subordinate to the Crown *hetman* [field commander], Jerzy Jazłowiecki.

From the construction of the first *Sich* on the island of Khortytsia, on the Dnieper, by the forces of Prince Dmytro Vyshnevetsky, to the time of Stefan Batory's reign, the number of Cossacks grew steadily. They took part in battles with Tatars, defending the borderlands, and in the Commonwealth's military expeditions (Batory's war with Moscow in the years

—
81
—

1579–1581). Appearing alongside the Polish-Lithuanian armies, the Cossacks made an essential contribution in the battles against Sweden (Jan Zamoyski's Livonian campaign of 1601–1602), Moscow (the expedition of prince Władysław in 1618, the Smolensk war 1632–1634), Turkey and the Crimean Khanate (Khotyn 1621, Kamianets Podilskyi 1633, Okhmativ 1644). What is worse, however, is that the Cossacks took part in expeditions organized by Ukrainian magnates against the Tatars and to Moldavia, and later began to organize by themselves, thus violating the law and complicating the Commonwealth's relations with Turkey. Their uncontrolled raids on the Black Sea coast and robberies in the Ukrainian provinces led to the first serious clashes with Commonwealth authorities. The uprisings in the 1590s under the leadership of Kryshtof Kosynsky and Semen Nalyvaiko should have demonstrated the danger connected with the growth of both the Sich Cossacks and those remaining as registered soldiers in the state's service. It must be remembered that numerous uprisings of Sich Cossacks were often reinforced by registered units of the Zaporizhian Cossacks (1625, 1630, 1637–1638).

A particularly beautiful chapter in the collaboration of Zaporizhian Cossacks and the Commonwealth is the Khotyn campaign of 1621, when alongside the Polish-Lithuanian forces under the command of *hetman* Jan Karol Chodkiewicz, there was in the Polish camp a Cossack army of several tens of thousands, headed by *hetman* Petro Konashevych-Sahaidachny. Without this assistance, the army could never have driven sultan Osman II from the borders of the Commonwealth. In a petition to the king, the Zaporizhians asked not only for the pay due them, but also for freedom for the Orthodox religion and for recognition of the recently consecrated disuniate clergy. Demands of a religious nature would appear from then on, more and more often, in the petitions of the Zaporizhian Cossacks addressed to the king and *hetmans*. And thus the Cossacks joined with the Ruthenian nobility, which in its local assembly instructions demanded respect for the Greek religion. More and more often, the population of the

Ukrainian provinces saw in them their defenders, not only in questions of religion but also in disputes caused by increased exploitation by magnate administration in the great estates (*latifundia*) that sprang up during the reign of the first two Vasas.

The Zaporizhian Cossacks registered in the service of the Commonwealth, numbering six thousand people, could not satisfy the Cossack side, the more so because the more than ten thousand Cossacks discharged from the register after the end of hostilities were a potential source for fomenting subsequent rebellious outbreaks. It was difficult to imagine that having experienced freedom and tasted Cossack liberties, those people would once more submit without protest to the control of *starosta* law and go out to work on their lords' fields without resistance.

A turning point in the Commonwealth's relations with Ruthenia was heralded by the initial period of Władysław IV Vasa's reign, which coincided with struggles with Moscow and Turkey. Once more, as in 1621, Cossack reinforcements proved to be indispensable. To assure they would continue in the future, it was necessary to respond to Cossack ambitions and demands, which were not at all easy to satisfy under the conditions of the nobles' Commonwealth. They appeared already during the convocation in 1632, when the Cossack delegation sent by the Zaporozhian *hetman*, Ivan Petrazhytsky-Kulaha, demanded from the parliament rights similar to those enjoyed by the noble class. The Cossacks stated that they were citizens of the Commonwealth with full rights, "because we bear its health on ourselves, risking our necks against every enemy for the safety of the fatherland." In return, the Cossacks demanded the right to participate in the elections of the Polish monarch. In the lower chamber of parliament, when presenting their instruction on 28 June 1632, they claimed that they were "members of that same Commonwealth and therefore have the right to take part in the election, and that they give their vote to His Majesty, Władysław." In one of the main points of their instruction, they demanded that "the Greek schismatic religion enjoy peace and not be

—

83

—

violated by the Uniates." The Grand Chancellor of Lithuania, Albrycht Stanisław Radziwiłł, reacted with unambiguous negativity to the Cossack demands, and the senators rebuked the delegation for "calling themselves members of the Commonwealth (perhaps like the hair and nails are for the body, which, although they are necessary, if they grow too much, the former is too heavy for the head, and the latter cause sore wounds, both must be trimmed rather often"). The Cossacks' usefulness in the battles with the Turks, Tatars, and with Moscow was not denied; but it was pointed out that too large a number of them could lead to the Commonwealth's ruin. Although the Cossacks' demands were not met, nonetheless, despite protests from the Catholic clergy, during the election, Władysław IV signed the so-called *Punkty uspokojenia* [Points of reassurance], which heralded future equal rights for the two branches of the Greek religion. In the *pacta conventa* prepared for Władysław IV, the monarch took on the obligation of reassuring both Greek religions in the interests of a Commonwealth threatened by war with Moscow. It was not until the parliament of 1635, however, that the conditions of the compromise were confirmed, the Metropolis of Kyiv was returned to the Orthodox faith, along with several bishoprics, and a selected commission was to proceed with a new division of the churches in Ukrainian cities and in Volhynia.

Part of Polish historiography sees in these initial years of Władysław IV's reign not only the ruler's new policy toward the Orthodox religion, but also toward the Zaporizhian Cossacks as such. This is connected with the question of whether (and if so, when) it was possible to rebuild the Commonwealth of two nations into a tripartite arrangement, including the inhabitants of the lands that make up today's Ukraine. Zbigniew Wójcik took the position that the work of the 1658 Treaty of Hadiach had certain chances of succeeding in the 1630s, after the suppression of the bloody uprisings of Pavluk, Skidan, Ostrianin, and Hunia (1637–1638). It seems, however, that the suppression of the 1637–1638 revolts by the regular army was not auspicious for recognizing broad autonomy for the Ruthenian nation, including the Zaporizhian Cossacks. The events of those years led, rather, to decisions in precisely the opposite direction. In 1636—a year after the destruction of Fort Kudak by Sulyma—a royal committee whose aim was to divide Uniate and disuniate churches finished its work, and in addition, a restrictive regulation for the Zaporizhian Cosssacks, authored by Grand Crown *Hetman* Stanisław Koniecpolski, was put into effect. It put the Cossacks under the control of the nobles and the regular forces. Intoxicated by military success, the Commonwealth's authorities seemed to treat the Cossack problem the same way as at the turn of the 16ᵗʰ century, which meant disregarding the Cossacks' growth in numbers, their growing national consciousness, their social composition, and their close connection with the Orthodox clergy. Large numbers of Cossacks who had participated in the battles on the Moscow and Podolian fronts were stricken from the register and, as "dischargees," were ordered to surrender once more to the authority of the *starostas*. Some of these dischargees, unwilling to accept that prospect, ran away to the Zaporizhia, reinforcing the Sich in the estuaries of the Dnieper. Others, scattered throughout the outskirts of Ukrainian cities, awaited the next rebellion of the Zaporizhian Cossacks. The collapse of Władysław IV's plans for the Turkish war, which awoke aspirations of regaining lost privileges among some of the Cossack elite, led to the outbreak of the greatest uprising in the history of Ukraine, in which not only the Zaporizhian Cossacks but also masses of Ruthenian peasants, townsmen, and nobles took part.

Obviously, the causes of the 1648 Uprising are many, and they are connected with social, religious, and economic contradictions that existed in the southeastern provinces of the Commonwealth. Taking advantage of the conflicts between the administration of the Ukrainian lands and the local population professing Orthodoxy, and spreading the watchword of ejecting the Poles back to beyond the San River, Khmelnytsky gained widespread support in Ruthenian society during the first phase of the uprising, 1648–1649. The Cossack *hetman* skillfully emphasized

—
85
—

the ties between the Orthodox Church and the Cossacks. In discussing the origin of Khmelnytsky's uprising, one should not overestimate the influence of immigrants from the Crown, who—as Henryk Litwin emphasizes—played a large role only in the highest sphere (the magnates) and the lowest (the masses of lease-holders of small properties, both private and royal). Litwin is right in stating that the period of the "golden peace" in Ukraine (1638–1648) was an era of Polish lease-holders, who contributed to the exacerbation of social conflicts in that area. The same research, however, shows that in the 1630s and 1640s, only 10 percent of the land-owners in the Borderlands were middle and minor nobles native to the Crown. Although Poles were promoted more often than Ruthenians to district offices (about 35 percent of the nominations), it was not only they who contributed to deteriorating social relations in that area. In the Kyiv voivodeship, as of 1648, immigrants from the Crown made up only 13 percent of land-owners.

Determining the size of Ukraine's population and its structure before 1648 is very difficult in view of the incomplete source material, that is, registers of hearth taxes and poll taxes. The data is divergent to such an extent that the numbers inspire no confidence. There is also no way to define the ethnic and religious composition of the population on the basis of tax registers. For example, the population of Volhynia voivodeship in the light of tax registers from the mid-16th century is estimated at 293,800 people, whereas if one takes as a basis hearth tax registers from 1629, one can calculate 655,700 people. The situation in Belz voivodeship appears similar, where, according to the 1630 hearth tax register, we get 170,500 inhabitants, but according to tax registers from the second half of the 16th century, we have only 56,100 inhabitants. Even greater divergences affect Kyiv voivodeship, where Polish, Ukrainian, and Russian historians have undertaken research. The estimates for the first quarter of the 17th century vary between 234,000 people and 818,000. In this situation, nothing remains but to refer to the classic determinations of Aleksander

Jabłonowski, who estimated the whole community inhabiting the Ukrainian provinces in the mid-16th century at 937,000, and gave for the mid-17th century a figure of 2,179,000 inhabitants, which signifies a population growth of about 157 percent, and that despite demographic losses caused by wars, Cossack uprisings, and above all, raids by the Crimean Tatars.

The Cossacks represented only a fraction of a percent of Ukraine's population. For example, before 1648, the Zaporizhian Cossacks in the service of the Commonwealth numbered only 6,000 soldiers, not including the small forces of Sich Cossacks. With the outbreak of the insurrection and the successes of Bohdan Khmelnytsky in 1648–1649, the Cossacks' potential grew more than tenfold. This is attested to by the Treaty of Zboriv in 1649, on the basis of which the number of registered Cossacks was limited to 40,000, and the Cossack *hetman* had to discharge from the register many thousands of the Cossack rabble. A similar situation arose in 1651, when by virtue of the Treaty of Bila Tserkva, the number of registered Cossacks was limited to 20,000. The apogee of the Cossack army's growth in numbers came in the first two years of the Uprising, when their number was estimated as high as 100,000 Cossacks active in several theaters of operations. Losses in war and the enormous number of the rabble taken away by its allied Tatars in the years 1648–1654 led in the closing years of *hetman* Khmelnytsky's rule to a serious decline in the population of the Ukrainian provinces, which was reflected in the numbers of the Zaporizhian Cossacks as well. The forces available to Khmelnytsky's successor, Ivan Vyhovsky, in the victory against Moscow at Konotop (28 June 1659) are estimated at about 20,000 Cossacks. The losses borne by all social groups in Ukraine as a result of hostilities during Khmelnytsky's Uprising are hard to estimate, but in many parts of West-Bank Ukraine (that is, the part of the country on the west bank of the Dnieper), the population numbers fell almost by half as compared with those before 1648.

In view of these losses and the prospect of unending war, in 1658, the Ukrainian elite, headed by Yuri Nemyrych and *hetman* Ivan Vyhovsky, made an attempt to transform the Commonwealth of Two Nations into a state of three nations. By virtue of the Treaty of Hadiach, a Duchy of Ruthenia was to be created, limited territorially to the former provinces of Kyiv, Chernihiv, and Bratslav, where all the senatorial offices were to be distributed to nobles of the Greek rite. In the document, not only the question of freedom for the Orthodox religion and its adherents was emphasized, but the dissolution of the Uniate Church was agreed to. The Duchy of Ruthenia was to have its own judiciary, administration, and army, although Ivan Vyhovsky had to compromise and accept limiting its numbers from 60,000 to 30,000 Cossacks and a *hetman*'s guard of 10,000. The Kyiv metropolitan was guaranteed a place in the Commonwealth's senate, and the Kyiv-Mohyla Academy was elevated to the role of a university educating the Ruthenian youth. The stationing of Crown forces was to be prohibited in the Duchy, although nobles were assured the right of return to lost estates they had owned before the war. This point was dangerous for the *hetman* and the Cossack elders supporting him because of opposition among the rabble, who did not relish the prospect of returning to serfdom under their former owners. The *hetman*, along with the Zaporizhian Cossacks and those provinces torn from the Commonwealth, would voluntarily "return as free men to free men, equals to equals, and noble-minded to noble-minded," the document stated. The Cossacks strove to include in the borders of the Duchy of Ruthenia the voivodeships of Podolia, Volhynia, and Ruthenia as well, but pressure from the Muscovite army and an opposition growing in power compelled Ivan Vyhovski to accept the Treaty of Hadiach and concentrate on defending it against Moscow.

Obviously, the Treaty of Hadiach required time to gain the acceptance of the societies on both sides. Lack of support from the Polish side for the Cossacks in the 1659 campaign, the change of some of the points of the Treaty in parliament that same year, and growing resistance on the part of the pro-Moscow opposition among the Cossacks finally led to the fall of *hetman* Vyhovsky and the idea of transforming the Commonwealth into a state of three legally equal nations. The Commonwealth, embroiled in heavy battles in 1658–1659 with the Swedes in Royal Prussia and at grips with a confederation of part of the army, was in no condition to help out at this moment so important for the *hetman*, the more so because it was known that Moscow was preparing for a decisive blow against the Commonwealth. Support for the idea of the Treaty of Hadiach on the part of the Polish-Lithuanian elite rose and fell, and only a few dignitaries were ready to accept without reservation such broad autonomy for Ukraine. The work of 1658 was treated as a temporary concession dictated by the military situation. Lithuanians, who were interested in ending the war with Moscow and returning to their own lands, were unwilling to accept the conditions of the treaty, because it would prolong the struggle between the two states for dominance in Central and Eastern Europe. Few officials understood that in 1659, an opportunity was lost that would never come again, an opportunity not only for an essential modernization of the political system of the Commonwealth but also for winning the competition with Moscow for Ukraine. Among the few who understood the importance of the moment was an expert on negotiating with the Cossacks, Volhynian castellan Stanisław Kazimierz Bieniewski. In a letter to the Bishop of Kraków, Andrzej Trzebicki (28 October 1659), he wrote, "The paralyzed fatherland, when it needed hands the most, did not have them. And thus we destroyed Vyhovsky, drove the Commonwealth back to the sea again, and comforted our enemy, that is, the Tsar of Moscow."

That epoch-making solution in the annals of Polish-Ukrainians relations, the Treaty of Hadiach, was born not as the result of far-reaching political calculation but as the result of shock caused by defeats during the Insurrection of Bohdan Khmelnytsky, the collapse of the state's structures in struggles with the Swedish aggression, and the occupation of the Grand Duchy of Lithuania by Moscow. All those events strengthened the belief that without the support of the Zaporizhian Cossacks, the Commonwealth

—
89
—

could not be successfully rebuilt in the borders from before the war with Moscow, which had began in 1654. As we saw, however, that belief was not strong enough to induce the Commonwealth's elite to summon up the determination necessary for decisive action. At the same time, divisions among the Cossacks themselves and the military presence of Moscow on the left bank of the Dnieper determined the effective division of Ukraine into two parts: Right-Bank Ukraine (on the western bank of the Dnieper), where the Commonwealth preserved its influence, and Left-Bank Ukraine (on the eastern bank), where the Moscow faction began to rebuild its influence under Ivan Briukhovetsky as *hetman*. Neither the Polish-Lithuanian victories of 1660–1661 nor the activity of the pro-Polish *hetman* of the Cossack forces on the Right Bank, Pavlo Teteria, led to a return of the state of affairs before 1648. Also working against such a possibility were significant changes in the social and ownership structure that had taken place at the time in Ukraine. The Cossack elders on both sides of the Dnieper had received many grants, both from John Casimir and from Tsar Alexei Mikhailovich, and the Cossack rabble, if not gone in chains to Crimea, were compelled to do corveé labor even heavier than before, due to the grave losses in population resulting from devastating wars. There was also no more talk of the nobles returning to their estates in the Ukrainian provinces, as provided by the Treaty of Hadiach. New agreements with the Zaporizhian Cossacks such as those made after the 1660 victory at Chudniv, although they confirmed the protection of the Orthodox Church in the Commonwealth, did not renew the idea of union that had been buried when Ivan Vyhovky relinquished the *bulava* [mace] of *hetman* of the Zaporizhian Cossacks in 1659. The consequences of the failure of the Commonwealth's new policy toward the Cossacks are demonstrated by the ups and downs of John Casimir's unsuccessful campaign on the Dnieper at the turn of 1663, which not only failed to drive Moscow from the Dnieper, but finally buried for good the idea of cooperating with the Cossack elite of Right-Bank Ukraine, who were receptive

90

to calls for rebellion coming from the Sich (Ivan Sirko) and Left-Bank Ukraine (Ivan Briukhovetsky).

In view of the spread of rebellion to Right-Bank Ukraine and of Ivan Vy-hovsky and Ivan Bohun entering into talks with the opposition, the deputy *hetman* of the Polish army in Ukraine, Colonel Sebastian Machowski, or-dered both Cossack leaders to be executed at the camp at Vilkhovets. Ob-viously, this did not make things easier for the Polish forces and Cossacks commanded by Stefan Czarniecki and Pavlo Teteria, who were contending with rebels supported by the forces of Ivan Briukhovetsky.

As a result of military action in Right-Bank Ukraine, an increasing num-ber of people from those areas fled to Left-Bank Ukraine. The situation was not altered by the conquering of Kyivan Polissia in January 1665 by Stefan Stanisław Czarniecki, the *hetman's* nephew. A lack of support from the Tatars and the recall of Polish forces to the Crown's heartland due to Jerzy Lubomirski's rebellion caused the downfall of Pavlo Teteria, and along with him the Commonwealth's control of Right-Bank Ukraine. Fol-lowing a struggle for succession after Teteria, Petro Doroshenko became *hetman*, and he decided to rely on the Ottoman Porte and the Crimean Khanate. The Polish-Muscovite armistice talks caused further complica-tions in Ukraine. Fearing a Polish-Muscovite alliance, Doroshenko, with Tatar support, defeated Machowski's division at Stina and Brayiliv, taking its commander prisoner. The southeastern wall of the Commonwealth was left effectively defenseless.

The Tatars' going over to the side of Doroshenko's Cossacks hastened the Polish-Lithuanian commissars' negotiations with the Tsar's commis-sars at Andrusovo. On 30 January 1667, a treaty was signed, ending the Polish-Russian war of almost 13 years; the treaty divided Ukraine into a right-bank part, belonging to the Commonwealth, and a left-bank part, given to Moscow. Kyiv was to be under Russian rule only temporarily, but in effect remained outside the Commonwealth's borders for good. The Truce of Andrusovo produced much dissatisfaction in Right-Bank

Ukraine, where there were fears that the nobles would return to their estates, and also on the part of *hetman* Doroshenko, who had counted on rebuilding the Cossacks under his own leadership, and on both sides of the Dnieper. The Sich Cossacks, whose raids on the Black Sea coast were the basis of their existence, regarded the alliance of Doroshenko with the Tatars as unacceptable. In the Ukrainian crucible, where everyone was fighting everyone else, the highest price for the different attitudes of the Cossack elders was paid by the Ruthenian people, whom the Crimean Tatars, allies of the changing Cossack leaders, took prisoner in massive numbers. The period of Doroshenko's *hetmanate* brought further devastation and demographic losses in the provinces of Kyiv and Bratslav. The execution of Left-Bank *hetman* Ivan Briukhovetsky in June 1668 left authority over the left-bank regiments in Doroshenko's hands for only a short time, for the counteraction of Moscow and opposition of the Sich Cossacks forced him to surrender finally to Turkey.

Doroshenko had no opponent worthy of him in Right-Bank Ukraine, for the new *hetman*, Colonel Mykhailo Khanenko, appointed by King Michał Korybut Wiśniowiecki against the advice of John Sobieski, did not enjoy the support of the Cossacks. Doroshenko's surrender to Turkey, especially after the fall of Kamianets-Podilsky (1672), caused a further mass exodus of the populace from Podolia and Right-Brank Ukraine to the Left-Bank section. And thus, Doroshenko was universally accused of "having sold Ukraine into Turkish slavery." After Chyhyryn was occupied by Muscovite forces in September 1676, the *hetman* was taken to Moscow, and his *hetman's* insignia made their way to the Kremlin treasury. Doroshenko wanted to unite Cossack Ukraine on both sides of the Dnieper under his rule, contrary to the international conditions imposed by the division of Ukrainian territory by the 1667 Truce of Andrusovo. The price he paid was the complete depopulation of a strip of land between Kyiv and Chyhyrn, as far as the Southern Buh River. During the 1677–1681 war between Turkey and Moscow, the lands on the Dnieper were completely devastated, and the population was resettled in Left-Bank Ukraine, under the supervision of Cossacks loyal to the *hetman* of Left-Bank Ukraine, Ivan Samoilovych. Chyhyryn itself was taken in 1678 by the Turkish army and leveled to the ground. The territory between Kyiv and Chyhyryn as far as the Southern Buh was recognized as uninhabitable, both in the treaty ending Turkey's war with Moscow in 1681 and in the "eternal peace" between the Commonwealth and Moscow in 1686.

The decline of the Zaporizhian Cossacks as a military force is illustrated by the poor contribution of Cossack regiments in the Vienna campaign of John III Sobieski in 1683. As a result of belated recruitment, only the *sotnia* of Paul Apostol (150 men) took part in the expedition; the rest of the Cossack regiments, under the command of *hetman* Stefan Kunytsky, fought in the winter campaign in Moldavia. Despite the efforts of John III Sobieski, the use of Right-Bank Cossacks in operations against Turkey and the Khanate during the Holy League was small and limited to a few thousand soldiers. It is, therefore, not surprising that the Polish monarch desired the restoration of the Cossacks in the service of the Commonwealth. The results, however, turned out to be modest, despite parliament's having adopted the bill "Protection of the Zaporizhian Cossacks" in 1685, guaranteeing Cossack liberties and privileges. *Hetman* Andriy Mohyla took only about 3,000 Cossacks on the 1685 Moldavian expedition. The next year, under the personal command of John III Sobieski, 6,000 Cossacks set out, and were disbanded after the campaign's end. The final episode in the period of wars with Turkey was the participation of Cossacks under the command of the commissar for Cossack affairs, Stanisław Zygmunt Druszkiewicz, in an expedition to Moldavia in 1691. Up until the Treaty of Karlowitz with Turkey (1699), small Cossack forces appeared in the theater of operations around Kamianets and in Moldavia, but they did not play a major role in the war.

Although they were not numerous, the Cossack regiments were a thorn in the side of the nobles, who had suffered numerous wrongs inflicted by Cossack colonels, both in Kyivan Polissia and in the Ukrainian provinces. With the end of the Turkish war, parliament decided to disband the Right-Bank Cossack regiments. In a bill titled "Dissolution of the Cossack hosts in Kyiv and Bratslav voivodeships," we read: "that His Excellency the castellan of Kraków and Grand Crown *Hetman* [Stanisław Jabłonowski] two weeks after the closing of parliament dismiss all the Cossack host from the service of the Commonwealth and effect the dissolution of that host." The nobles may have thought that they would increase their estates at the expense of those of the Cossack elders, and the released soldiers would become laborers on their estates. The Commonwealth's weakness, the war plans of Augustus II, and the efforts of Fastiv colonel Semen Paliy, however, prevented the implementation of parliament's decision.

Peace did not last long on the Cossack side. A direct cause of their rebellion in 1702 was the activity of the *starosta* of Bohuslav, Stanisław K. Jabłonowski, who required the assistant *hetman* of Right-Bank Ukraine, Samus, to hand over military insignia and cannons, and introduced economic constraints for Cossacks in the territory he administered. The rebels, headed by Samus and Paliy, controlled the majority of towns in the provinces of Kyiv and Bratslav by the end of 1702 and exterminated the local Poles and Jews. The contraction of Crown forces under the command of *hetman* Adam Sieniawski led to the ejection of the rebels from Podolia and Bratslav provinces; but in March 1703, operations were interrupted, thereby forgoing an attack on Semen Paliy's headquarters in Bila Tserkva. The year 1704 brought new complications, when *hetman* Ivan Mazepa, leading an army of 25,000 Cossacks, crossed over into Right-Bank Ukraine, occupying Bila Tserkva. Thus, with the Tsar's consent and contrary to the Treaty of Narva dated 30 July 1704, the Right-Bank Cossacks came under the command of Mazepa. Bila Tserkva remained in Russian hands until 1714. The Commonwealth's rule over part of Kyiv province was restored formally after Mazepa's downfall as a result of the Swedish defeat at Poltava in 1709—but in fact, this happened only after the finish of the

Great Northern War, when the last Russian forces left Ukraine. In the 18th century, besides the Cossack uprisings of 1702–1704, *haidamak* riots took place in Right-Bank Ukraine under minor Cossack leaders such as Perebyinis (1714), or a certain Verlan (1734), whose *haidamak* rebellion in the Bratslav region was suppressed by Polish and Russian forces. The fall of Ivan Mazepa brought the final unification of Ukraine with Russia subsequent to the reforms of Peter I. After a brief period of increased significance for the *Hetmanate* during the rule of Empress Elizabeth I, Catherine II abolished the office of *hetman* in 1764 and transferred authority over the Cossacks to the Little Russian Collegium. The last step in the destruction of the former Cossack state was the abolishment in 1775 of the New Sich. Cossack lands went to the Empress's favorites (until 1784, over four million dessiatines in Zaporizhia were given out).

The best known and, at the same time, bloodiest *haidamak* uprising of the 18th century was the Koliyivshchyna of the 1760s, the origin of which remains controversial among historians who argue over the roles of the Orthodox clergy, Russia, and the Commonwealth in it. According to Wiesław Majewski, the nucleus of this revolt was the Zaporizhians, joined by the local populace. Władysław Serczyk, on the other hand, emphasizes that the rebellion on the Right Bank was provoked by Russian operations in the region beyond the Dnieper and the behavior of the Commonwealth's authorities. The abolition of the office of Cossack *hetman* by Catherine II in 1764 caused an uproar among the Cossacks. Serving as pretext for the uprising were attacks on the Holy Trinity Church of the Motryn monastery that took place in April and May 1768. At first, only a few units made up of Zaporizhian Cossacks under the command of Maksym Zalizniak began to occupy Ukrainian towns, including Cherkasy, Korsun, and Bohuslav. Soon after, following the treason of Ivan Gonta, *setnik* from the Cossack regiment, rebels seized Uman and massacred the populace. Mainly Jews, Poles, and Ruthenian Uniates were murdered. The number of victims of the Uman massacre is estimated

—
95
—

at 12,000 to 20,000. Despite the counter-activities of the Russian corps of General Rumiantsev, the peasant rebels controlled a large area of the Kyiv and Bratslav voivodeships. Only the defeat of Maksym Zalizniak's group in Uman at the hands of Russian forces, as well as decisive operations of Crown forces under *hetman* Franciszek Ksawery Branicki, brought peace back to these regions. Moscow's reaction was connected not only with the need for rapidly suppressing the Koliyivshchyna in view of preparations for war with Turkey, but also with the intention of keeping the Confederation of Bar from seizing the Ukrainian provinces. Another concern certainly was isolating a rebellion that broke out in the Sich and was crushed in January 1769. The Cossack uprisings on the Right Bank and in the region beyond the Dnieper had no chance of succeeding, especially as from 1734 (or from the Verlan's rebellion), Russian forces participated in suppressing them, along with Polish units, which revealed the military weakness of the Commonwealth.

The constant unrest that beset Ukraine in the 18th century also caused economic reconstruction to proceed very slowly. Tadeusz Korzon in *Dzieje Polski za Stanisława Augusta* [History of Poland under Stanisław August] documented the meager population of these regions and the small number of people inhabiting the largest cities. It is enough to say that in the second half of the 18th century, under conditions of slow economic growth, the largest cities in Ukraine had only a few thousand inhabitants each (Kamianets-Podilskyi around 6,000; Lubar 4,800; Ostroh 4,600; Konstantyniv 4,000; Bila Tserkva, Lutsk, and Labun 3,600 each; Berdychiv 2,700; Tulchyn and Ostroh 2,500 each). Among the inhabitants of towns and cities, Poles and Ruthenians were now minorities. The Jewish population predominated, and its numbers grew steadily and rapidly, especially in the regions of former Halych Ruthenia, where around 30 percent of all the Commonwealth's Jews lived. Typical for settlement of these lands were the numerous magnate residences and noble manors. In rural areas, on the other hand, Ruthenians formed a decisive majority of the population.

From the end of the 16th century, the Commonwealth was never able to solve the Cossack problem and work out a consistent policy toward the Zaporizhian Cossacks. Plans for military colonization of the Ukrainian borderland, put into place after use of the Don Cossacks by Moscow to put an end to Tatar raids in the second half of the 17th century, did not succeed. Ukrainian magnates and a large part of the nobility were opposed to these solutions; they objected to the building of the Zaporizhian army in the service of the Commonwealth, and even more to granting the Ruthenian nation the same rights enjoyed by Poles and Lithuanians. The fate of the Treaty of Hadiach in 1658–1659 showed that chances of forming a tripartite Commonwealth were limited in view of the ever stronger position of Moscow in that part of central and eastern Europe.

Along with dissolution of the nobles' Commonwealth and final settlement of the New Sich question, the majority of Ukrainian lands—around 80 percent of their territory—fell into Russia's hands. Right-Bank Ukraine, like southern Ukraine, remained ethnically and religiously diverse. Alongside the numerically dominant Ruthenian element, at the end of the 18th century over a quarter million Poles continued to live in these regions, among them tens of thousands of nobles, who constituted the most rebellious element in the western provinces of Russia. It was the presence of the Polish nobility, alongside the rapidly growing numbers of Jews (110,000 by the end of the 18th century in Right-Bank Ukraine) that presented the greatest obstacle to the Tsarist authorities' policy of unifying the Ukrainian lands with Russia. The 19th-century national uprisings, which covered the western regions of former Right-Bank Ukraine as well, proved this.

Selected bibliography

Borek P. (ed.), *W kręgu Hadziacza A.D. 1658. Od historii do literatury* [In the Circle of Hadiach A.D. 1658. From History to Literature], Kraków: Collegium Columbinum, 2008.

The Locals

Chynczewska-Hennel, T., *Świadomość narodowa szlachty ukraińskiej i Kozaczyzny od schyłku xvi do połowy xvii wieku* [National Consciousness of the Ukrainian Nobility and Cossacks from the Late 16th to the Mid-17th Century], Warszawa: PWN, 1985.

Franz, M., *Idea państwa kozackiego na ziemiach ukrainnych w xvi–xviii wieku* [The Idea of Cossack State in the Ukrainian Lands in the 16th–18th Centuries], Toruń: Wydawnictwo Adam Marszałek, 2006.

Jakowenko, N., *Historia Ukrainy od czasów najdawniejszych do końca xviii wieku* [The History of Ukraine from Ancient Times to the End of the 18th Century], translated by O. Hnatiuk, K. Kotyńska, Lublin: Instytut Europy Środkowo-Wschodniej, 2000.

Jakowenko, N., *Naris istorii serednovicnoi ta rannomodernoi Ukraini* [Sketch of the History of Medieval and Modern Ukraine], Kyiv: Kritika, 2005.

Korzon, T., *Wewnętrzne dzieje Polski za Stanisława Augusta* [Internal History of Poland under Stanisław August], Vol. 1, Kraków–Warszawa: Księgarnia L. Zwolińskiego, Księgarnia Teodora Paprockiego, 1897.

Kroll, P., *Od ugody hadziackiej do Cudnowa. Kozaczyzna między Rzecząpospolitą a Moskwą w latach 1658–1660* [From the Treaty of Hadiach to Chudniv. The Cossacks between the Commonwealth and Moscow in the Years 1658–1660], Warszawa: Wydawnictwa UW, 2008.

Kuklo, C., *Demografia Rzeczypospolitej przedrozbiorowej* [The Demography of the Pre-Partition Commonwealth], Warszawa: DiG, 2009.

Litwin, H., *Napływ szlachty polskiej na Ukrainę 1569–1648* [The Influx of Polish Nobles to Ukraine, 1569–1648], Warszawa: Semper, 2000.

Mazur, K., *W stronę integracji z Koroną. Sejmiki Wołynia i Ukrainy w latach 1569–1648* [Toward Integration with the Crown. The Local Assemblies of Volhynia and Ukraine in the Years 1569–1648], Warszawa: Neriton, 2006.

Radziwiłł, A. S., *Pamiętnik o dziejach w Polsce* [Memoir of the History of Poland], Vol. 1: 1632–1636, ed. A. Przyboś, R. Żelewski, Warszawa: PIW, 1980.

Serczyk, W. A., *Na dalekiej Ukrainie. Dzieje Kozaczyzny do1648 roku* [In Far Ukraine. The History of the Cossacks to 1648], Kraków: Wydawnictwo Literackie, 1984.

Sysyn, F., *Between Poland and the Ukraine: The Dilemma of Adam Kysil, 1600–1653*, Cambridge: Harvard University Press, 1985.

98

Sysyn, F. and Plokhy, S., *Religion and Nation in Modern Ukraine*, Edmonton–Toronto: Canadian Institute of Ukrainian Studies Press, 2003.

Wijaczka J. (ed.), *Z dziejów Europy wczesnonowożytnej* [From the History of Early Modern Europe], Kielce: Takt, 1997.

Wojtasik J. (ed.), *Od Żółkiewskiego i Kosińskiego do Piłsudskiego i Petlury. Z dziejów stosunków polsko-ukraińskich od xvi do xx wieku* [From Żółkiewski and Kosiński to Piłsudski and Petliura. From the History of Polish-Ukrainian Relations from the 16th to the 20th Centuries], Warszawa: AON, 2000.

Wójcik, Z., *Dzikie pola w ogniu* [The Wild Fields Aflame], Warszawa: Wiedza Powszechna, 1960.

THE
ASSIMILATED

GERMANS

⤜

IGOR KĄKOLEWSKI

—

In the Polish language, as in many other Slavic languages, the inhabitants of the regions between the Rhine and Elbe are called *Niemcy* [Germans]. The etymology of this word goes back to the distant Middle Ages, when Germanic peoples had just begun to conquer the lands west of the Elbe from the Slavs there. In the early Middle Ages *Niemiec* meant *niemy* [mute, dumb], that is, a stranger speaking an incomprehensible language, which meant a non-Slavic language. After all, even into the 19th century, some poorly educated Poles would include under the name "Germans" all immigrants or people from northern and western Europe: Dutchmen, Swedes, Danes, Englishmen, even Frenchmen (for example, *"niemcy paryscy"* [Parisian Germans]). Equally imprecise was the colloquial term *szwab*, with a tinge of contempt (the term *szkop* derives from it). In fact, that was how peasants from the region of Swabia who settled in Poland long ago referred to themselves, and their Polish neighbors adopted the term to designate the foreignness of the colonists from a neighboring village.

The first Germans began to arrive in the territory of the Polish state and settle there as early as the times of Mieszko I and his successors. They can be divided into three groups: German clergy arriving in Polish lands in order to Christianize them; knights offering their services to the new dynasty; and also wives of Polish princes and kings. One need only look at the marriage statistics for the Piasts who occupied the Polish throne from the mid-10th to the mid-14th centuries: alliances with the daughters of various rulers of German states predominate. These marriages not only played a political role, but they also made possible what today might be called "cultural transfer." Thanks to them, bridges were built connecting the Polish court with other regions of Germany, for instance, with far-off Lotharingia, thanks to the marriage of Mieszko II with Richeza, the daughter of the Rhine palatine. In the historical memory of Poles, she does not enjoy a good reputation, as a result of a chain of unfavorable political events. In the eyes of her contemporaries, on the other hand, she was regarded as one of the best educated women in Europe at the time. Moreover, she made the Piasts relatives of the Imperial house. Due to Richeza's family connections, her son and the future Duke of Poland, Casimir the Restorer, received his education in the Rhineland; later, based on support from clerics from the Rhineland and Lotharingia whom the uncle of this ruler, Herman, Bishop of Cologne, sent to Poland, it was possible to rebuild the Polish church, which had been devastated during the so-called pagan reaction and the Czech invasion of the 1030s. At that time, many eminent clerics made their way to Poland from that part of Germany, for example, Aron, bishop of Kraków, as well as Benedictines who went to the monastery in Mogilno. These clerics introduced in Polish lands the germ of the Gregorian reform, inculcated a cult of Cologne saints (Geron and Leonard), brought valuable books along with them (the Tyniec manuscript, one of the best known works of the Cologne school from the 11th century), as well as models of Meuse-Cologne architecture (the collegiate church in Tum near Łęczyca, the cathedral church in Płock). This Rhineland influence in the sphere of material culture may have been even more substantial. It is possible that Kraków during the reign of Casimir the Restorer was an architectural copy of Imperial Aachen, which his grandfather, Bolesław the Brave, could have seen earlier with his own eyes while traveling alongside his official "friend," Holy Roman Emperor Otto III. Links between the Piast state and distant Rhineland must have been really long-lasting, since over a century after the death of Casimir the Restorer, Konrad, a goldsmith from the Rhineland, was active at the court of Casimir's great-grandson Mieszko III.

Before we turn our attention to the ordinary emigrants from Germany, that is, peasants, craftsmen, and merchants, let us consider one more point concerning crowned heads. It seems like a paradox that the Piast dynasty, which introduced Christianity in Poland, has not had a single canonized or even beatified representative—unlike, for example, the Czech Přemyslids, the Ruthenian Rurykids, and the Hungarian Árpáds. The honor of the first Polish dynasty is saved by a German, St. Hedwig of Silesia, born at Andechs castle in Bavaria and married to the Silesian Piast, Henry I the Bearded. Her son, the Silesian Duke Henry II the Pious, attained glory by leading Polish and German knights (among whom were members of clans already having settled in Silesia, as well as loyal Teutonic Knights) and finding death in the battle of Legnica in 1241 in defense of Latin Christianity from the Mongols. The grandson of Hedwig, Duke Henry III the White, as well as her great-grandson, Henry IV Probus (Duke of Kraków and pretender to the Polish throne, who wrote poetry in German), introduced to the Wrocław court the Central High German language and fashionable German knightly customs, including the court poetry of the Minnesingers, so highly prized in Europe at the time. By the way, one should note that the Polish words *rycerz* ("knight") and *szlachta* ("nobility") are both borrowed from German: *Ritter*, "knight," and *Geschlecht*, "family, clan," respectively. From the 13th century, German culture began its triumphant march in Silesia, supported by grants for the German knights, clergy, and especially the townsmen and peasants, who settled there in large numbers. Additionally, as a result of a complicated chain of political events, from the 14th century on, the fortunes of that province become inextricably linked with those of Bohemia and the German Reich, rather than with Poland. The last representatives of the Silesian line of the Piasts die out at the turn of the 17th century, completely Germanized in both language and culture, yet conscious and proud of the role their ancestors played in the history of Poland, as is attested to by the Piasts' mausoleum (the so-called *Monumentum Piasteum*) erected by the German mother of the last of the Silesian Piasts, Georg Wilhem, Duke of Legnica and Brieg (died 1675). The Latin inscription placed there reminds us that: "Louise, Duchess of Anhalt, last mother of the Piasts, built this monument to her ancestors and forefathers as well as to her descendants, her husband, son, herself, and her surviving daughter, Karolina, Duchess of Holstein, in the year of our Lord 1679."

During the reign of St. Hedwig's husband, Henry I the Bearded, Duke of Silesia, and on his initiative, one of the most important and long-term modernizing processes in the history of Poland began—colonization on terms of so-called German law, which over the next five hundred years and more gave more western characteristics to Polish lands. The role of Henry the Bearded—often perceived during the 19th and 20th centuries in both Polish and German publications as a "Germanizer," but in reality the most eminent Silesian Piast, and one who did, after all, sit on the throne of Kraków as well—is difficult to overestimate. Colonization on terms of German law caused not only an influx of settlers, mainly peasants and townsmen, from German lands, but especially the adoption of legal models, including those offices and institutions created on the basis of Magdeburg and Lübeck law (the town council and aldermen, the mayor, *wójt, sołtys,* the "village bench" or council); architectural and town-planning solutions (recognizable to this day in the old towns of Polish cities from Gdańsk to Kraków); models of rural development (linear villages); implements (the popularization of the plow); and organization of work and production (in towns, the system of guild crafts; in rural areas, three-field crop rotation). The German influence from this period on the Polish language (in addition to the names of offices and municipal and rural institutions already mentioned: *rada* [council], *burmistrz* [mayor], *wójt, sołtys*) can be seen today in such basic loan-words from German as *mur* [wall, masonry], *cegła* [brick], or *taniec* [dance].

It is estimated that around 100,000 emigrants from Germany may have settled in Polish territory in the 13th century (the population of those areas at the time being some two million); and colonization on terms of German law is thought to have increased in the following century—at that time, however, largely due to settlement activity undertaken by the native population.

Such a large influx of a foreign population led to ethincity- and language-related conflicts. Polish-German conflict on that basis first appeared at the turn of the 13th century, that is, about 700 years ago. Statements by some 20th-century Polish and German historians about a thousand-year record of Polish-German animosity should be included among the patriotic and ideological fairy tales spawned under the influence of 19th- and 20th-century nationalism. At the end of the period of feudal fragmentation (1138–1320), this conflict was intensified by unification efforts on the part of the Polish Church, which in the words of Gniezno Archbishop Jakub Świnka, in a 1285 letter to the Curia of Rome, rebuked the influx of German settlers and the German clergy who followed them to provide pastoral care, often usurping higher Church offices or monopolizing monasteries for German monks: "Much evil has proliferated in our country due to the influx of Germans," the archbishop wrote, "as they oppress the Polish people, hold them in contempt, torment them with attacks [...] snatching them from their own beds in the dead of night." Marek Zybura—author of the well-written book *Niemcy w Polsce* [Germans in Poland], from which I have taken many of the examples cited here—rightly comments with a dose of mockery on the xenophobic scenario of Świnka (probably a reaction to a similar xenophobia on the part of prominent churchmen of German descent settled in Poland at the time): "In this letter the archbishop was the first in history to formulate the thesis, still popular as an ideological tool today, according

—
107
—

to which German immigration to Poland prepares its political annexation." Another phrase of Jakub Świnka—one of the chief architects of the unification of the Kingdom of Poland—has gone down in history, an anti-German slur attested for the first time in this form: "psi łeb niemiecki" [German dog-head].

The anti-German sentiments smoldering at that time in Polish society—especially in large cities such as Kraków or Poznań, where Germans were numerous, predominating in the cities' local government and patrician elite—were used by another architect of the unification of the Kingdom of Poland, Władysław I Łokietek, to further his political goals. In the years 1311 and 1312, assiduously playing upon the anti-German phobia among inhabitants of the capital city and its vicinity, he suppressed in bloody fashion the rebellion of Kraków *wójt* Albert, who led the German townsmen of Kraków in supporting the right of the Czech king of the German dynasty of the Luxembourgs to the Polish crown. During the bloody massacre, Łokietek's supporters murdered every townsman of Kraków who could not repeat in Polish the words *"soczewica, koło miele młyn"* [lentil, wheel grinds mill]. Even so, as late as the 15th and early 16th centuries, the language heard on the streets of Kraków, besides Polish, was German, especially in the wealthiest quarters of that city, that is, around the Main Market Square and Small Market Square (here, in the 14th century, lived, among others, Nikolaus Wirsing, in Polish called Mikołaj Wierzynek). The dominance of the German-speaking community in the life of Kraków may be shown by the fact that in 1537, services with sermons in German were moved from the main altar of St. Mary's Basilica (at that time the altarpiece was already there that had been made by one of the most eminent German sculptors of the late Gothic, from Nuremberg but living for a time in Kraków, Veit Stoß or Wit Stwosz) to the neighboring, smaller Church of St. Barbara.

Let us remain for a time in Kraków, the capital of the Kingdom of Poland and main seat of the royal court. At the turn of the Middle Ages and the Renaissance, the German language was widespread within the walls of the city. In the early 16th century, at least 20 percent of the townsmen used it, and aldermen's registers were kept in German until 1600. It was used not only by successive generations of those citizens of Kraków who came there earlier from Germany and were granted town citizenship. Immigrants from Germany continued arriving in Kraków during the 15th and 16th centuries and left a lasting impression not only on the face of the city but on all of Polish culture. A very important group in the intellectual landscape of the capital city were the lecturers of the Academy of Kraków, which enjoyed a good reputation in Europe at the time (for example, Mateusz of Kraków, Rudolf Agricola, Andreas Schön), but first and foremost the numerous students living in the two academic dormitories designated for the German nation. Mikołaj Kopernik [Nicolaus Copernicus], who studied there in the late 15th century, did not have to use the Polish language at all in Kraków. The language of studies within the walls of the university was Latin; outside his *Alma Mater*, Kopernik—an immigrant from Royal Prussia, at the time dominated by German-language culture, and born into a German-speaking family of Toruń patricians—could rely on being able to communicate in German.

Another group of capital significance for the cultural and technological transfer at the time from western to eastern Europe was that of German families of printers who settled in Kraków at the turn of the 15th century. Thanks to them, the printing press, the invention of which began the greatest media revolution (up until the modern electronic one) in the history of mankind, came to Poland. Printing, often called the "dark art" from the color of printers' ink, could also be called the "German art" in relation to that era, as it was in the German Reich that the largest number of printers were in operation in Europe during the 16th century. It was from there that the first owners of printing presses and publishing houses, as well as the bookstores that often operated alongside them, came to Kraków. We may mention here the itinerant printer from southern

—
109
—

Germany, Kasper Straube, who produced in Kraków the first printed material in Polish lands, a Latin calendar for the year 1474. It is supposed that the publisher of the first book in the Polish language was Kasper Hochfelder, a German printer brought to Kraków. A special place in the annals of Polish printing was secured by representatives of the Kraków printing clans founded by Jan Haller and Florian Ungler. Haller was the publisher of the first illustrated Polish book, which was at the same time the result of one of the most important publishing projects for the political fortunes of the Kingdom of Poland: Jan Łaski's *Statuty i prawa Królestwa Polskiego* [Statutes and Laws of the Kingdom of Poland] (1506). For a time, the status of royal printers was held by the office of the Kraków Szarffenbergs, publishers of, among other things, the first Polish historical romance (1570). This fragmentary enumeration should conclude with the words of another royal typographer and partner of one of the Szarffenbergs, Hieronim Wietor. Born in Silesia, in the area of Hirschberg (Jelenia Góra), a student of the Academy of Kraków, later owner of publishing offices in Vienna and Kraków and publisher of many books in the Polish language, including the first elementary schoolbook, entitled *Polskie książecki ku uczeniu się polskiego* [Polish Booklets for Learning Polish] (reprinted in 1539 as *Wokabularz rozmaitych sentencyi* [Vocabulary of Various Sentences]), he described himself and his efforts within the framework of contemporary Polish culture as follows: "As an assimilated Pole, and not a native, I never cease to be amazed that, while every other nation loves, propagates, polishes, and refines its native tongue, the Polish nation has contempt for and distorts its tongue, which, to my ears, can truly compare with any other in richness and beauty."

Wietor, this "assimilated Pole," was also the owner of a paper mill; it was, once more, immigrants from Germany who were the first and most energetic manufacturers of paper in Poland. The capital brought by German families settling in Poland and Kraków also played a fundamental role in the economic development of the region of Lesser Poland at the

—
110
—

beginning of the modern era. In this context, one must mention the patrician Kraków clan (ennobled at the beginning of the 16th century) of the Boners (from Alsace), engaged in, among other things, salt mining and banking, who financed Sigismund I's war against the Teutonic Knights in the years 1519–1521. Without the capital coming in from Germany and the financiers who controlled it, it is difficult to imagine the development of the mining and metalworking industry in Lesser Poland in the early 16th century, in which Polish landowners also participated.

Let us look finally at the royal court at Wawel during the Renaissance era—a true international crucible in which one easily sees "assimilated Poles" of various provenance, including German. In this case, the Hapsburg wives of Polish monarchs deserve special attention, first from the Jagiellonian dynasty: from the famous Elżbieta Rakuszanka [Elizabeth of Austria], wife of Casimir Jagiellończyk, rightly called "the mother of kings," (she brought into the world three rulers of Poland and Lithuania, as well as a king of Bohemia and Hungary), to the two Hapsburg wives of Sigismund II, unloved by him, of whom the latter, having disappointed the king's hope for successors, was sent away from Kraków to Linz by her husband, causing an uproar in noble public opinion. Similarly, if one considers the marriages of the period of free elections—beginning with the monarch who moved his primary residence to Warsaw, that is, Sigismund III Vasa, and his two Austrian wives, through Władysław IV Vasa, Michał Korybut Wiśniowiecki, to the last married king of Poland, Augustus III the Saxon—it is evident what an important role for the modern politics of the Polish-Lithuanian Commonwealth was played by the alliance with the house of the Catholic Hapsburgs. The Hapsburg wives were followed to the Polish court by their German-speaking servants of various ranks. Renowned figures easily found shelter and upkeep here, for example, Martin Opitz, one of the more eminent poets of the German Baroque, who fled his native Silesia because of the atrocities of the Thirty Years War and came to the court of Władysław IV Vasa, remaining there till his death.

The Assimilated

In the 16th century, a number of distinguished individuals of German descent, who were to be important in Poland's history, passed through the Renaissance court of the Jagiellonians and the royal chancellery, which was at the time a springboard for political, ecclesiastical, and intellectual careers; those men were at the same time eminent diplomats, Humanist scholars, and men of letters, as well as hierarchs of the Church: Jan Dantyszek (Johan Höfen from Gdańsk), Stanisław Hozjusz (born in Kraków to a polonized burgher family coming from Baden), and Marcin Kromer (born in Biecz into a family of German descent). The latter was honored by parliament with special expressions of gratitude for his activity in the field of historiography and popularization of Polish history beyond the country's borders. Apart from the similar course of their careers, diplomatic-political and Humanist-literary, all three men mentioned above had two other things in common: they began their careers at the Academy of Kraków, and finished them as bishops of Warmia, which had been incorporated, along with Royal Prussia, into the Polish Crown after a victorious thirteen-year war (1454–1466) with the Teutonic Knights.

And so we come to one of the most important myths, deeply rooted in the consciousness of Poles (let us refer to the famous paintings by Jan Matejko, *Battle of Grunwald*, 1878, and *The Prussian Homage* from 1882), which equates the Teutonic Knights and Germans. This idea first appeared, however, only during the partition era and the birth of modern national consciousness in the 19th century. It was strengthened additionally by the association, of similar origin, that saw in the Teutonic order a precursor of the Kingdom of Prussia, one of the protagonists of the partitioning of Poland. It is true that even in the Middle Ages, inhabitants of the Kingdom of Poland regarded with dislike, even outright hatred, the Teutonic Knights and their state, which in 1308–1309, during the unification of the Kingdom of Poland, annexed the lands of Gdańsk Pomerania. The statements of witnesses during the 14th-century Poland v. Teutonic Knights trials also attest to this, as well as the descriptions of Polish-Teutonic disputes and wars in Jan Długosz's *Roczniki, czyli kroniki słynnego Królestwa Polskiego* [Annals, or Chronicles of the Famed Kingdom of Poland]. After the 1525 secularization of the Order's state in Prussia, in the 16th and 17th centuries, both in Polish historiography and in various kinds of propaganda pamphlets, for instance, during election campaigns, there were reminders that the Teutonic Knights had presented a mortal danger to Poland in the past; but they were associated not so much with Germans, as with the Hapsburgs, who were putting forward their candidates for the Polish throne. It was in this kind of context—the fierce election campaign during the first interregnum, 1572–1573—that the saying appeared which in later centuries would gain such popularity in the Polish language: "So long as the world exists, Germans and Poles will never be brothers." As concerns the Teutonic Knights themselves, the memory and negative stereotypical images of them in Polish lands had rather limited reach up to the 18th century.

These images were widespread first and foremost in territories formerly under the rule of the Teutonic Knights, that is, in Royal Prussia, with Gdańsk, Toruń, and Elbląg, incorporated into the Kingdom of Poland as a result of the thirteen-year war with the Order. It was there during the early modern era that the demonization of the term *Krzyżak* [Teutonic Knight] occurred. In everyday life, if you wanted to insult someone, you called him a *Krzyżak*. What is more, the local Protestant population—in the cities of Royal Prussia mostly of the Lutheran faith—compared the Teutonic Knights to the Jesuit order, hated for its Counter-reformation activities! In the largest Prussian cities—Gdańsk, Elbląg, and Toruń—the German-speaking town councils organized noisy celebrations for the anniversaries (1654, 1754) of throwing off the yoke of the "Teutonic Knights' Tyranny" *(Creutz-Ritter Tyrannei)* and joining with the Kingdom of Poland voluntarily, as was emphasized in propaganda speeches and writings published in Latin and German. That is also how the matter was presented by the leading historians of Royal Prussia, of German language

113

and culture, who, while faithful to their Prussian Vaterland, were at the same time loyal subjects of the Polish king (like the eminent astronomer and canon of the Warmia chapter mentioned earlier, Mikołaj Kopernik). We are concerned here with such authors as Simon Grunau and Kasper Schütz in the 16th century, Christoph Hartknoch in the 17th, and finally Gottfried Lengnich in the 18th—the latter was, on the one hand, an ardent advocate of Royal Prussia within the framework of the Commonwealth, and on the other hand, a zealous propagator and popularizer of Polish history, about the need for a new image of which he wrote, "We were satisfied with what had already been written about us, paying no mind to whether others had an idea of our deeds, forms of government, and other events."

Let us move on from early modern intellectuals to other groups of the population of Royal Prussia. This region is all the more important for the issue of "Germans under the sky of the old Commonwealth" in that it was home to dense and numerous clusters of German-speaking people, who shaped the culture of that autonomous province, and at the same time generally identified their interests, including economic ones, with the Polish-Lithuanian state. The most eloquent example is Gdańsk, the largest city and Baltic port, called the "eye" of the Commonwealth by contemporaries—and a famous scene from the plafond *Apotheosis of Gdańsk Trade*, by Izaak van den Blocke, from the early 17th century, on the ceiling of the Red Chamber of the Artus Court in Gdańsk. A part of it shows a Gdańsk townsman dressed in German clothes, shaking hands with a Polish nobleman to confirm a deal just made.

In addition, the numerous, large clusters of the German-speaking population in Royal Prussia are important for another reason, namely, their faith, often Protestant, especially in the cities, and more precisely, Lutheran. After the Reformation and the adoption of the Evangelical Augsburg Confession by a large part of the German-speaking population in Poland, the ethnically Polish population swiftly began to identify German language and descent with Lutheranism. This is witnessed by, among other things, the stereotypical, pejorative descriptions used by Catholics to describe the (usually German-speaking) Lutherans, in particular the insult *lutry* [Lutherans], which at times rhymed with another old Polish name for Germans, *pludry*, from the short pants that were an element of the western European clothing they liked to wear, which was foreign to the culture of Polish Sarmatism. The association of *lutry* as tantamount to "Germans," even though not true in relation to Polish Germans or "assimilated Poles" of German origin and Roman Catholic faith, was nonetheless widespread in old Polish culture. From this also came the offensive description in old Polish, *szwabska wiara* [German faith].

During the early modern period, the greatest advances of polonization in Royal Prussia were made among the nobles of German descent, whose ancestors swelled the ranks of lay knighthood in the Teutonic Order's state in the late Middle Ages; perhaps the chief clan of that province was von Baysen, or the Bażyńskis. Likewise, some noble families of German origin from another northern province of the Polish-Lithuanian state, namely, Livonia, such as the Tyzenhauses, were polonized mainly due to the attractiveness of the early modern Polish political system, and also as a result of service in the army of the Polish Crown or of Lithuania. Even in Ducal Prussia, only a Polish vassal state, the noble political model of the old Commonwealth had many adherents among the nobles of German descent and the Lutheran faith, which strengthened their conviction of the necessity for maintaining the closest possible ties with the Crown. One need only cite the words of Otto von Groeben, who, opposing the succession in the Prussian fiefdom being taken over by the Brandenburg electoral branch of the Hohenzollerns, entreated the king and senate at the 1609 Warsaw parliament session not to separate the lands of the duchy "from the body and bosom of its mother and nourisher, the Polish Commonwealth." More than half a century later, there was a similar overtone to the words of another hero of the class opposition in Ducal Prussia, vainly protesting against the abolition of that Duchy's fiefdom

—
115
—

to the Polish Crown (1657–1660), Lt. Colonel Chrystian Ludwik Kalk-stein-Stoliński, of the Crown army. Abducted from Warsaw, held prisoner in the elector's prison in Klaipéda and finally sentenced to death, before the sentence was carried out in 1672, in a letter to his wife, he instructed that the children be educated in "the Lutheran faith" and be taught Latin and Polish, and he ordered his children: "Learn Polish and take shelter in Poland, for there is no place for you in downtrodden Prussia."

A stage of Poland's history that was not overly successful politically, a period of dynastic union with the Electorate of Saxony, lasted from 1697, the year of the the tactical conversion of the Saxon elector of the Wettin dynasty from Lutheranism to Catholicism and his election as king of Poland as Augustus II, up to the death of his son, Augustus III, in 1763. Designated with the gloomy name "the Saxon night" and regarded later as a prelude to the partitioning of the old Commonwealth, this period lives to this day in the sphere of popular sayings, bearing a negative con-notation of anarchy (*"Od Sasa do Lasa"* [From the Saxon to the Forest, the latter interpreted as a reference to the root of Stanisław Leszczyński's name] and loose customs *("Za króla Sasa jedz, pij i popuszczaj pasa")* [While the Saxon is king, eat, drink, and loosen your belt]. This view is, however, decidedly oversimplified. Certainly, both Wettins made many po-litical mistakes, and the first of them made military mistakes as well. In the political sphere, the rule of Augustus II can be regarded as an unsuc-cessful attempt to modernize the Commonwealth for the purpose of im-proving the state's efficiency. In pursuing this goal Wettin tried to follow models of moderate royal absolutism, which tested well in many other European states.

It is hard, however, not to note the positives of the Saxon era as well, such as the beginning of the dynamic development of the capital city of Warsaw, which during the reign of Augustus III began to slowly take on the dimensions of a large city, due to, among other things, the con-struction of a new palace, called "the Saxon," and spatial layouts (the

—
116
—

so-called "Saxon axis"). The influence of Enlightenment culture also begins to appear gradually during this period. One of its pioneers in Poland would be a newcomer from southern Germany (Wirtemberg), later to become an "assimilated" Pole, Wawrzyniec Mitzler de Kolof [also called Lorenz Christoph Mizler], an Enlightenment philosopher, historian, and eminent publisher. The Wettins' court retinue included individuals who do not enjoy the best reputation (such as Heinrich von Brühl, minister and *éminence grise* during the reign of Augustus III), but also some whose record is unambiguously positive, both in the capital and in the whole country (such as the son of the above, Alojzy Fryderyk Brühl [also called Alois Friedrich von Brühl], general and reorganizer of Polish artillery, as well as *starosta* of Warsaw).

The view of the "Saxon night" in the memory of Poles should not completely overshadow the subsequent chapters of Polish-Saxon contacts: the election of the Wettins as hereditary rulers of Poland on the basis of the Constitution of May 3, 1791; the common fates of Saxony and the Duchy of Warsaw under the rule of the Wettins during the Napoleonic era; and finally the tradition of the extraordinary hospitality of Saxony toward Polish emigrants who had to leave the Congress Kingdom as a result of the national uprisings of the 19th century. The Saxon era, like earlier chapters of activity in Poland on the part of newcomers from Germany, many of whom became "assimilated" Poles, may be viewed as an attempt to transfer through them the cultural traits of Western Europe, and therefore an attempt at modernizing Poland—at times more successful, at times less so.

Selected bibliography

Friedrich, K. *The Other Prussia. Royal Prussia, Poland and Liberty, 1569–1772*, Cambridge: Cambridge University Press, 2000.

Friedrich, K., and Pendzich, B. M. (eds.), *Citizenship and Identity in a Multinational Commonwealth: Poland-Lithuania in Context, 1569–1795*, Leiden: Brill, 2009.

Gross, F., *Citizenship and Ethnicity: The Growth and Development of a Democratic Multiethnic Institution*, Westport: Greenwood Press, 1999.

Kąkolewski, I., *Słownik stereotypów polsko-niemieckich* [Dictionary of Polish-German Stereotypes], Warszawa: Federacja Polskich Domów Spotkań, 2001.

Labuda, G., "Geneza przysłowia 'Jak świat światem, nie będzie Niemiec Polakowi bratem'" [Genesis of the Saying "So long as the world exists, Germans and Poles will never be brothers"], *Zeszyty Naukowe Uniwersytetu im. Adama Mickiewicza – Historia*, no. 8 (1968).

Salmonowicz, S., *Polacy i Niemcy wobec siebie. Postawy – opinie – stereotypy (1697–1815). Próba zarysu* [Poles and Germans in Regard to Each Other. Attitudes–opinions–stereotypes (1697–1815). An Attempted Sketch], Olsztyn: OBN, 1993.

Tazbir, J. "Krzyżacy" [The Teutonic Knights], in: Kobylińska, E. (ed.), *Polacy i Niemcy: 100 kluczowych pojęć* [Poles and Germans: 100 Key Concepts], Warszawa: Biblioteka Więzi, 1996.

Zientara, B., "Cudzoziemcy w Polsce w X–XV w.: ich rola w zwierciadle polskiej opinii średniowiecznej" [Foreigners in Poland During the 10th–15th Centuries: Their Role in the Reflection of Polish Medieval Opinion], in: Stefanowska, Z. (ed.), *Swojskość i cudzoziemczyzna w dziejach kultury polskiej* [Familiarity and Foreigners in the History of Polish Culture], Warszawa: PWN, 1973.

Zientara, B., "Z zagadnień terminologii historycznej 'Drang nach Osten'" [Issues of Historical Terminology 'Drang nach Osten'], in: *Społeczeństwo, gospodarka, kultura. Studia ofiarowane Marianowi Małowistowi w 40-lecie pracy naukowej* [Society, Economy, Culture. Studies Offered to Marian Małowist on the 40th Anniversary of Scientific Work], Warszawa: PWN, 1974.

Zybura, M., *Niemcy w Polsce* [Germans in Poland], Wrocław: Wydawnictwo Dolnośląskie, 2001.

JEWS

∾

ANDRZEJ ŻBIKOWSKI

—

The question of when exactly the first Jewish settlers arrived in Polish lands provokes a great deal of discussion among historians. Jews probably arrived in the lands united by the Polan tribe from the late 11th century, from the West and, less often, from the East. There were not many of them, however, because in a sparsely populated country, with few towns, Jewish merchants and craftsmen found no jobs. Jews coming to Poland were called Radhanites. They journeyed along an important trade route linking Western Europe with the Khazar state on the Volga and other countries of the Middle and Far East.

Jews who visited Poland in the early Middle Ages, and then settled there, belonged to the Jewish Mediterranean Diaspora, which numbered no more than one and a half million people circa 1000. The definite majority of Jews lived in the North African (Maghreb) and Middle Eastern Arab countries, in religious communities that enjoyed considerable internal autonomy. On the European continent, most Jews were concentrated on the Iberian Peninsula. There, under Arab influence, a separate Jewish group formed, called the Sephardim. A few scattered Jewish communities existed from Roman times in the larger urban centers of the European part of the Byzantine Empire and on the Apennine Peninsula. At the turn of the 9th and 10th centuries, new, small Jewish communities formed in a dozen or more centers in Western Europe (the area of the Paris Basin,

Champagne, and the Rhineland). From the Rhineland center of Jewish settlement, a branch of Jewish culture formed, different in language, customs, and intellectually, called the Ashkenazim, which in time was to dominate the worldwide Diaspora, both in terms of demographics and civilization. Only a small percentage of the worldwide population of Jews lived in German-speaking countries at the time (it is estimated that circa 1000, their numbers were no more than a few thousand); but as a result of favorable economic and demographic processes for that region, and probably of Jews migrating from the area south of the Alps, this community increased at least fourfold over the course of the next two centuries.

Life in the Diaspora made it easier for Jews to play a special role in international trade, and at the same time, to acquire experience in the exchange and lending of money. Jewish merchants served as middlemen in the great transcontinental trade, traveling from what was then Arabic Spain through Aquitaine, Burgundy, the Rhineland, and Slavic lands, all the way to Khazaria, the eastern fringe of the Islamic world, and from there perhaps to India and China. They were called Radhanites, a term derived perhaps from the Persian word *rahdan*, "knowing the way," or from the French river Rodan.

From the 10th century comes the first information concerning Jews in Bohemia (Prague), Moravia, and Hungary, and their contacts with countries farther north (the account of Ibrahim ibn Yakub, a Jewish merchant from the caliphate of Córdoba, the first European to mention the state of Mieszko I). The presence of Jewish merchants in the territory of the future Poland during the 11th and 12th centuries is confirmed by somewhat more numerous written sources, and also by one of the most valuable relics of early medieval art in Poland: the bas-reliefs from the Gniezno Doors. Based on those, it is possible to state that, among other things, they purchased slaves there, for which there was great demand in the eastern markets (the wars that accompanied the formation and consolidation of early feudal state entitities assured a steady and rich supply).

At the turn of the 12th and 13th centuries, small groups of Jews settled in Silesia, and later in the chief cities of other areas. The first traces of permanent Jewish settlement come from Silesia. The oldest Silesian *matzevah* (Jewish tombstone), dating from 1203, suggests that a Jewish community must have existed in Wrocław at the time, with at least some of the institutions typical for a Jewish community (the inscription implies that the deceased was a cantor; one can therefore assume the existence of a house of prayer or even a synagogue; the tombstone attests to the existence of a cemetery; etc.). The first Jewish settlers came primarily straight from a German-speaking region (the Rhine) or via Moravia and Bohemia, bringing with them an Ashkenazi community structure similar to the one we know from Worms, for example, and other German cities. Evidence of the existence of organized Jewish communities in Poland in the early 13th century is also provided by a letter of Rabbi Eliezer ben Isaac of Prague.

Jewish merchants and craftsmen, primarily coiners, worked for regional Piast dukes, including Mieszko III the Old. In the second half of the 13th century, after Tatar invasions had devastated the country, the influx of settlers from German territories gained momentum, and in the following century, turned into a true settling fever. Jews decided to leave Germany and Bohemia mainly due to restrictions placed on them by the local Christian urban patriciate (for example, a ban on retail business, or restrictions on the interest that could be charged on loans). In economic conflict, townsmen resorted to religion as a weapon, and anti-Semitic riots broke out, especially during the period of the Crusades, and later at the time of the plague, the so-called Black Death, in 1348. Church authorities also issued various decrees ordering the separation of Christians and Jews, as, for instance, during the 1267 synod in Wrocław.

By the end of the 14th century, Jewish communities had developed in the majority of Silesian cities and in the more important Polish cities (including Warsaw, in Mazovia, which did not belong to the Piast

—
—

state). The presence of Jews in Warsaw is noted as early as the 13th century, although more information on them comes from the15[th] century (district records from the years 1423–1437). In the second half of the 14th century, Jewish settlement began to spread to Red Ruthenia (Lviv), incorporated by Casimir the Great and rapidly becoming polonized.

In Polish lands, thanks to the hospitality of the rulers, Jews could live and work in peace. The first charter of immunity was issued to Jewish settlers from Bohemia in 1264 by Bolesław the Pious, Duke of Kalisz. Like the majority of European legal documents of this kind, the Statute of Kalisz gave Jews the privileged status of "servants of the ducal treasury," which meant that their persons and possessions were given special legal protection as "property" of the ruler, and their community enjoyed broad internal autonomy. Jews were granted almost complete freedom to practice lending and trade; they had their own judiciary in internal affairs, particular protection and an array of special provisions that sheltered them from enmity on the part of the Christian populace. The ruler also guaranteed the safety of their synagogue and cemetery, and forbade kidnapping Jewish children and forcing them to be baptized.

Political transformations in Poland in the subsequent centuries changed the legal status of Jews to some extent. Although they continued to remain directly dependent on the ruler, his decisions were gradually limited by the nobles' representative body. Jews continued, however (at least until 1538) to be a group explicitly set apart legally as a unit (independently from location, place of residence, and financial status), which to a certain extent made their status similar to that of the knightly and clerical estates, although formally, they were never an estate. The townsmen, among whom the majority of Jews lived, never acquired such status in Poland.

The Statute of Kalisz was extended to all of Poland in 1334 by Casimir the Great, and it was confirmed later, with only minor changes, by successive monarchs, and also by Vytautas, Grand Duke of Lithuania (1388).

—
122
—

The Catholic Church displayed a clear antipathy to Jews, especially since the Lateran Council of 1215, at which a resolution was passed on the separation of Jews from Christians (a ban on feasting together and on employing Christian servants) as well as a special mark for Jews' clothes. It was emphasized in Church teaching that the Jews were Christ-killers who consciously rejected the true faith. In Western and Central Europe (with the exception of Spain), Jews were the most visible non-Christian group, even though they were scattered. Catholic clerics often intervened with the rulers to limit Jews' participation in Christian social life, which resulted in expelling them from certain fields and territories, and even distinguishing them with special badges on their clothing.

Beginning with the Wrocław synod in 1267, the Polish Church systematically renewed injunctions and appeals to Christians to keep the Jews as distant as possible, not to eat with them, nor buy provisions from them, nor seek employment as their servants, and so forth (which seems to indicate that these regulations were not respected in practice). The religious and cultural separateness of both communities, however, favored the monopolization of lending by Jewish merchants. Both Judaism and Christianity looked with disfavor on lending money on interest to coreligionists, but allowed it in dealings with representatives of other religions; for this reason, among others, loaning money to Christians became one of the main occupations of the first generations of Polish Jews.

Economic conflicts were the source of frequent anti-Semitic incidents. Especially active were preaching orders, deeply rooted in urban centers, who gave the economic rivalry a religious dimension. The clashes took the form of violent riots under the pretext of accusations of desecrating hosts, as for example in Poznań in 1399; bloody pogroms, as in Kraków in 1407 and 1463; and fierce agitation, such as that of the Italian Franciscan, John of Capistrano, in Kraków in 1454, who accused Jews of collaborating with Ottoman Turks. Under this pretext, in 1463, Jews of Kazimierz near Kraków were robbed by mercenaries of the papal legate Fregen who were

—
123
—

setting out for war against the Turks; in 1499, the levee en masse of King John I Albert did much the same thing during preparations for the expedition to Muntenia. Anti-Semitic activity, however, was not as common as in Western Europe during the plague period of 1348–1349.

In the 14th and 15th centuries, Kraków's Jews conducted money lending on an impressive scale (of 120 Jewish families living in Kraków at the turn of the 14th century, 20 were employed in usury), becoming the main creditors of the Crown and of a significant part of the nobility. The latter, feeling threatened in their most vital economic interests, in 1423 successfully pressured the king to forbid Jews from making loans secured with real estate (the Warta Statute), which, by that time, had become one of the most important sources of income for Jewish financiers. This prohibition was definitively confirmed by an act of the Piotrków parliament in 1496. At the 1538 parliamentary session in Piotrków, the nobles demanded a prohibition on entrusting to Jewish entrepreneurs the leases of royal estates, as well as other state revenues, such as minting, salterns, duties, and tolls. At most, they could sublease these enterprises from leaseholders remunerated in this way by monarchs. This was consistent with the general line of the nobles' policy, because a year later, Jewish residents of privately-owned villages and towns were put under the administrative and judicial authority of the estate owners—on a par, after all, with the Christian residents of these towns (patrimonial judiciary). At the same time, many smaller royally-owned towns received, at the request of the Christian patriciate, a special law of privilege *de non tolerandis Judeis*, a prohibition on Jews' settling within town walls.

The process of Jewish settlement expansion to the east, which began in the mid-15th century, was accompanied by the phenomenon of settling in smaller towns, more and more often privately owned. Jews were also increasingly involved in the manorial farmstead economy conducted by the nobility; they took leases on inns, breweries, and distilleries; they provided credit for trade in grain, lumber, as well as potash and potassium carbonate, produced from charcoal and used in the production of glass, soap, and dyes, among other things. This was accompanied by further growth in the Jewish population. It is estimated that by the end of the 15th century that population reached about 30,000, which was several percent of the total Jewish Diaspora. According to the poll tax register of 1588, at least 75,000 Jews lived in the Commonwealth. The influx from abroad continued, mainly due to the persecution and expulsion of Jews from neighboring countries; but natural growth began to play an increasing role. In the Crown, in addition to the two oldest Jewish communities— those of Kraków and Poznań, still the most dynamic and mobile Jewish communities in Poland—the Jewish community of Lviv grew substantially, engaged in Levantine trade. This process increased after 1495, when Jews were driven from Kraków to the nearby community of Kazimierz.

At the end of the 15th century, the "golden age" in the history of Polish Jews began, and it lasted up to the period of mass pogroms during the Cossack uprising of Bohdan Khmelnytsky and the Swedish "deluge" in the mid-17th century. Growing wealth was accompanied by growth in the numbers of the Jewish population. The influx of immigrants from German states did not end until the late 16th century, and at the same time, families were larger and larger, for Jews married at a young age and gave their children an exceptional amount of care for those times. By the mid-17th century, the number of Jewish inhabitants of the Polish-Lithuanian state had grown more than tenfold, to as many as 400,000. At that time, Jews made up over one third of all inhabitants of cities; the largest communities were in Kazimierz near Kraków, in Poznań, Leszno, Lviv, and Lublin. From the early 16th century, Jews settled also in private towns in the eastern Commonwealth, attracted by the favorable situation in Red Ruthenia and Lithuania, and later also in Ukraine and Podolia. By the end of the 18th century, their number had grown to between 750,000 and a million.

In time, Jews became irreplaceable intermediaries between village, town, and noble manor. The less enterprising among them became craftsmen, who worked at first mainly for the needs of their own community, or itinerant peddlers.

The Jewish community, large in numbers, diverse in terms of religion, language, and customs, needed its own institutions to defend its interests. Their existence was also advantageous for the state, due to the weakness of the tax and judicial systems. Established around 1580 by Stefan Batory, regular conferences of representatives of Jewish communities *(ziemstwa)* from the main sections of the country, called *sejmy żydowskie* [Jewish parliaments], were to settle tax questions, but after several decades, they began to take decisions affecting all Polish Jews. In the late 16th century, these conferences of representatives from Jewish *ziemstwa* began to be called the Council of Four Lands *(Va'ad Arba Aratzot)*. Lithuanian Jews began to organize separate conferences from 1623 on. At the Va'ad, however, there was also a functioning tribunal, the highest court of appeal in the separate Jewish judicial system. The Council also adopted resolutions regarding social life: it banned certain kinds of financial activities, usually those banned earlier by the authorities (the leasing of state property, mortgaging noble estates); issued so called "anti-luxury laws"; organized collections on behalf of victims of fires, the poor, or Jews living in Palestine; and censored Hebrew books coming in from abroad. The Va'ad had at its disposal a separate fund for syndics, or special delegates who were to seek the favor of the parliaments and local assemblies and to settle various disputes with state officials. Traditional gifts presented to the latter were called *kozubalce*. The best known syndic was the servitor and factor (broker) of Kings John III Sobieski and Augustus II, Fiszel Lewkowicz. The Va'ad met every year until 1764, most often during markets in Lublin or Jarosław. Jewish self-rule was modeled after the Commonwealth's three-tier system; leaders of local denominational communities (kahals, in Hebrew *kehillot*) chose their representatives for regional conferences *(ziemstwa)*, where delegates to the Va'ad were elected in turn. During its proceedings, a lump-sum tax was divided among the *ziemstwa*, and further broken down to the individual communities during the report sessions of the *ziemstwo* council.

The favorable economic situation was conducive to the development of learning and culture. One of the first religious schools or yeshivas was founded in Kraków in 1503 by Jacob Polak, an immigrant from Bohemia, related by marriage to the wealthy and influential Fiszel family. Jacob is universally recognized as the inventor of the *pilpul* (Hebrew "pepper"), a kind of dialectic debate on subjects from the Jewish legal code, the Talmud, and at the same time, a teaching method. Participants were taught to select appropriate quotations from the Talmud, by which they then supported their arguments in the current discussion. From the mid-16th century, a famous academy founded by Salomon Szachno operated in Lublin; Poznań and Lviv also had eminent Talmudists. The rites and customs of Ashkenazic Jews were described by Rabbi Moses Isserles of Kazimierz in the treatise *ha-Mapah* (the Tablecloth), a commentary on the religious code *Shulkhan Arukh* (The Set Table) of the Sephardic scholar Yosef Karo. The successors of Issereles were eminent Talmudists of Kazimierz, Solomon Luria, Mordecai Jaffe [or Yoffe], and Joshua Falk. The 16th century also saw the beginning of writing in the everyday language of Polish Jews, Yiddish, based on southern German dialects with numerous loan words from Hebrew and the Slavic languages. In 1534, Asher Anchel published in Kraków the popular Biblical handbook *Mirkevet ha-Mishneh*, and around 1620, one of the most popular books in Yiddish appeared for the first time in print, *Tse'nah u-Re'nah*, the so-called "Women's Bible," the work of Jacob ben Isaac Ashkenazi of Janów Lubelski. Popular knightly romances were also translated into Yiddish, for example, the story of the adventures of Theodoric of Verona. As early as the 1530s, the Helicz brothers printed books in Hebrew in Kraków, and their work was carried on by two eminent families of publishers, the Prostnitzes and Jaffes (Lublin). Somewhat later, the first cabalistic works written in Polish lands by Joseph of Dubno and Hirsch Kaidanover were published.

—
127
—

Polish-Jewish relations during the period of the nobles' Commonwealth were not always the best. As royal authority weakened, Jews were more and more often accused of the crime of desecrating the host and suspected of the ritual murder of Christian children. A great deal of misfortune was caused by the best known trial for desecration of a host, in Sochaczew in 1556, inspired by Apostolic Nuncio Aloisio Lippomano. While Jews were accused of the crime itself, however, the main target were Protestants, who denied the Catholic dogma of the actual presence of the body and blood of Christ in the host during the service. This charge was directed at Jews at least a dozen times or more up to the mid-17th century. They were more often accused, however, of ritual murder to acquire Christian blood for secret, magical practices. Despite the protective bull of Pope Paul III in 1540, trials took place in Rawa Mazowiecka in 1547, and later in Osocz, Narew, Punia near Vilnius (1574), and Łęczyca (1639). By the middle of the 17th century, there were at least 60 such accusations, most of which ended in the death of the accused. Many Christian writers had successful careers exploiting these accusations, particularly Sebastian Miczyński and Jan Achacy Kmita.

Constant wars and worsening relations with the Christian populace, especially in the Eastern Borderlands after the Khmelnytsky Uprising, favored the development of mysticism among the Jewish populace. Assistance in discovering signs from God foretelling changes for the better was supposedly provided by the "secret science," the Kabbalah, referring to a 13th-century work by Moshe Baal Shem-Tov of León, Spain, entitled *The Book of Splendor (Sefer ha-Zohar)*. This method of reasoning was further developed by the scholar Isaac Luria Ashkenazi, who lived in Safed, Palestine in the 16th century. He urged his fellow-citizens to live a life of asceticism, in a continuous mystical rapture, in prayer and strict compliance with ritual rules. This was a condition for the swift coming of the Messiah. One false Messiah, who had crowds of followers in the Commonwealth (carrying his image in processions was forbidden by

King John Casimir in 1666) was Sabbatai Zevi, who declared he was the Messiah in 1665 in Turkish Smyrna. His conversion to Islam a year later in Adrianople shook the faith of some of his followers; but the hopes he had awakened persisted. An environment of unwavering belief in Sabbatai's mission was created in the Balkans by Jacob Querido of Thessaloniki. Jewish *maggids*, popular teachers practicing Kabbalah, journeyed to him from Podolia, which was occupied by the Turks from 1672 to 1699.

Another pseudo-Messiah, Jacob Frank, son of Leiba, an opponent of the traditional Jewish teaching contained in the Talmud who was prepared to reach an understanding with Catholicism, was the next to try to take advantage of Messianic hopes. He, too, was raised in the milieu of Sabbatai, practicing Kabbalah. He called his sect "Anti-Talmudic," and in order to come nearer to Christianity, he recognized the trinity of the divine person. After being excommunicated by the rabbis of Sataniv and Brody, he accepted the protection of the bishop of Kamianets-Podilskyi, Mikołaj Dembowski, and subsequently of King Augustus III, who was later his godfather. Several thousand Jews followed him and were rewarded with the title of noble; in the course of two generations, they became completely polonized.

Social unrest and the growth of religious zealotry found an outlet in a mass movement, Hasidism, founded in Podolia by Israel ben Eliezer, called the Master of the Good Name (*Baal Shem Tov*, abbreviated *Besht*). The movement initiated by Besht was simpler doctrinally than the Frankist heresy; he taught that the most important thing for every Jew was constant and complete union with God, possible both through prayer leading to ecstasy and through everyday activities, if they are also devoted to Him. Essential, however, was the mediation of the *tzadik* [righteous one], a wonder-worker who reveals the divine intentions as well as the mystery of the divine work of creation. The *tzadik's* prestige was not a consequence of his social position or family connections; he was directly chosen by God. After Besht's death, the movement rapidly gained hundreds of thousands of followers. Only Lithuania resisted it actively, mainly due to the persistence of another eminent Jewish rabbi, Elijah Zalman, called the "Vilna *gaon*" (honorable sage of Vilnius). During the 19th century, Hasidism drew into its orbit almost half of Polish Jews; the rest persisted in traditional Talmudic studies, and only a few were attracted by Jewish rationalism, Haskalah, an intellectual movement founded in Berlin by Moses Mendelssohn.

Jewish daily life during the period of the nobles' Commonwealth went on mainly within the framework of the local community (*kahal*). Its members jointly maintained synagogues, religious schools, a cemetery, baths, and a ritual slaughterhouse. *Kahals* were governed autonomously, and their leaders were elected by all adult males paying a tax for the community's purposes. The poorer strata were organized from the 16th century on, after the model of the Christian townsfolk, into guilds and religious brotherhoods, such as Chevra Kadisha, which cared for the community cemetery, and Talmud Torah, which maintained a school for children from poor families. The pride of each *kahal* was its synagogue. In large communities there were several of them; Kazimierz near Kraków boasted as many as five, the 15th-century Old Synagogue, rebuilt in Renaissance style from a design by Mateo Gucci in 1557 taking pride of place. In small towns, wooden synagogues, characteristic of the Polish territories, were built, and from the 17th century richly adorned in Baroque style.

Jews were distinguished from the rest of society by language, customs, and dress. In the nobles' Commonwealth, the "badge of shame" (a special kind of cap or band, or colored patch on the clothing), ordered by bishops' synods, was never accepted, although the nobility supported this requirement at the Piotrków parliament in 1538. From the 17th century on, however, Jews almost always lived in separate quarters of the towns, sometimes possessing, as in Kazimierz near Kraków, a separate privilege *de non tolerandis Christianis* (1608). They did not shave their facial hair, and wore the tallit (a white prayer shawl with dark stripes and

130

with fringes) on holy days; in the synagogue, they also wore phylacteries or *tefillin* (small leather boxes containing Bible verses and attached to the upper arm and forehead with straps) and ornamental headwear (the flat yarmulke or, among the Hasidim, a *shtreimel*, a hat with a brim of 13 sable skins). Jewish women often shaved their heads after marrying and wore wigs. Men spent a lot of time in the synagogue, studying the Torah and Talmud. Their Christian neighbors were most intrigued by—aside from the incomprehensible Yiddish language—the special customs connected with food (kosher kitchen) and their completely different calendar of holy days and ceremonies of family life, particularly circumcision, confirmation (bar mitzvah upon reaching the age of 13) and marriage, usually at a very early age.

Polish society began to take more interest in the Jewish minority during the era of the Great Parliament (1788–1792), the last great attempt to repair the Commonwealth. The Jewish population was more or less unanimously regarded at the time as a backward, self-absorbed group that effectively avoided burdens involving the benefit of the state. From the point of view both of the nobles and the townspeople, the Jews were the support of the magnates and were parasites on the noble brotherhood. During parliamentary sessions, many reform plans were proposed regarding the political situation and social organization of Polish Jews. An occasion for presenting the various reform ideas was created by the June 1790 appointment of a special committee of the Great Parliament, the Deputation for the Reform of the Jews. Among other things, bringing Jews closer to Polish culture was demanded during the deliberations of this body, in accordance with the title of the pamphlet *Myśli stosowne do sposobu uformowania Żydów polskich w pożytecznych krajowi obywatelów* [Thoughts on the Means of Forming Polish Jews into Useful Citizens for the Country], by the Chełm rabbi, Herszel Józefowicz. The Jewish proposals were rather cautious, but the Polish side demanded rapid and deep assimilation (1792 proposal with the title *Urządzenie ludu żydowskiego w całym narodzie* [Arranging the Jewish People in the Whole Nation]).

This purpose was to be achieved by obligatory education in Polish elementary schools, forced change of dress to European style, and doing work on Saturdays (which would make it impossible to celebrate the Sabbath). There were also plans to eliminate the position of some occupations as distinctly Jewish, forbidding the leasing of inns, and the production of alcohol. Nothing was proposed in return, however, because the Christian townspeople effectively blocked plans to recognize full town rights for the entire Jewish population, including specifically voting rights for municipal bodies.

The partitions rendered impossible the implementation of many legitimate ideas. The laws of the partitioning powers greatly reduced the autonomy of religious communities, and from the 1820s on, they were reduced to the status of strictly religious groups. Jews were subjected to tight administrative and fiscal control aimed at compelling them to assimilate. The Prussian authorities, in particular, followed an active and effective germanization policy accompanied by the gradual introduction of equal civil and political rights. In the Austrian and Russian partitions, segregational legal restrictions continued until the 1860s.

Advancing modernization, secularization, and assimilation of Jews into other communities, primarily under the influence of military service and public schools, changed the structure of the Jewish community. New groups arose within it—the bourgeoisie, the intelligentsia, the petty bourgeoisie—and assimilation to the dominant nation in a given territory facilitated closer relations of related professional groups.

Selected bibliography

Buber, M., *Tales of the Hasidim*, translated by O. Marx, New York: Shocken, 1947–1948.

Eisenbach, A., *Emancypacja Żydów na ziemiach polskich 1785–1870 na tle porównawczym* [The Emancipation of Jews in Polish Territory, 1785–1870 – a Comparative Study], Warszawa: PIW, 1988.

Unterman, A., *The Jews: Their Religious Beliefs and Practises*, Brighton–Portland: Sussex Academic Press, 1996.

Kameraz-Kos, N., *Święta i obyczaje żydowskie* [Jewish Holy Days and Customs], Warszawa: Cyklady, 1997.

Żbikowski, A., *Żydzi* [The Jews], Wrocław: Wydawnictwo Dolnośląskie, 1997.

Haumann, H., *Historia Żydów w Europie Środkowej i Wschodniej* [The History of Eastern European Jews], translated by C. Jenne, Warszawa: Adamantan, 2000.

ARMENIANS

~❧~

KRZYSZTOF STOPKA

—
134
—

In the late 16th century, fierce disputes on economic grounds arose in Lviv between Catholic and Armenian townsmen. Poles and Germans reminded the Armenians that they should not push their way ahead of everyone else, because after all, they had been taken in by Catholic Lviv during the days of Casimir the Great, toward the end of the first half of the 14th century, as "vagabonds and petty peddlers." This produced agitation and outrage among the Armenians. In protest against the insult, their elders produced a document in the Ruthenian language, allegedly dating from 1062, in which a certain Prince Theodore Dymitrowicz invited Armenians to his castle, promising them liberty for three years. This act of privilege, issued in times no one recalled and by a ruler whom the chronicles did not mention, was a forgery. As often happens, the end justified the means, and the end for the wealthy Armenian community was to gain prestige in the eyes of the city's other residents. The forged document made the Poles and Germans appear to have arrived later. From the second half of the 17th century, it served as proof of the 11th-century origins of Armenians not only in Lviv, but in Ruthenia as a whole. To this day it has remained in social memory, which, as it turns out, may not always be strictly true. Unlike earlier historiography, which distinguished phases of Armenian settlement in Poland, today it is considered that this was a long, continuous process, even if marked by greater intensity in certain historical periods.

The Assimilated

There are many similar myths regarding the subject of Polish Armenians. Every community creates its own myths. Sometimes they have little in common with historical fact; but for various reasons, people believe in them and repeat them uncritically. Among these myths is the conviction, popular among Armenians, that their ancestors descended from the great knightly clans of Armenia and were summoned by rulers in Eastern Europe to help as warriors or "crusaders." There is no document that would confirm this descent, and belief in it is most often motivated by human vanity. Yes, many Polish Armenians were ennobled—but only by Polish kings or by the rulers of Austria, after the partitioning of Poland.

Armenians are a Christian nation that has lived since ancient times in eastern Asia Minor and at the foot of the Caucasus. The Armenian state, annihilated by Rome and Persia in the fourth and fifth centuries, was reborn four centuries later. In the 10th century there even existed several Armenian kingdoms. Located at the crossroads of civilizations, a place where important trade routes met, Armenia has always been at risk of invasion, and the Armenian people of massacres or expulsion. From the seventh century, rulers of the Eastern Roman Empire (Byzantium) moved recruits from Armenia to their military garrisons in Thrace (today's Bulgaria), treating them as an uncertain political and religious element. In the 11th century, after the invasion of the Seljuk Turks, Byzantium resettled Armenian kings, aristocratic clans, and peasants to Cappadocia, from which they wandered to neighboring Cilicia (where they created the Kingdom of Armenia, 1199–1375), Syria, Palestine, Egypt, Italy, and Hungary. These migrations of the peasants and elite were an extraordinary and marginal phenomenon. These classes held tight to their ancient residences and properties. It was first and foremost the free urban population, employed in crafts and trade, that left Armenia.

In the second half of the 13th century, after the collapse of the Mongol Empire, we already encounter Armenians in the immediate neighborhood of Poland, in areas dominated by Tatars—in Ruthenia and Crimea, and also at the mouth of the Dniester, Seret, and Danube rivers, where the duchies of Moldavia and Wallachia would form in the next century. The earliest Armenian immigrants wandered into Ruthenian lands not directly from Armenia, but from there, and later also from the Byzantine Empire, and subsequently from the Ottoman Empire founded on its ruins, which controlled the duchies on the Danube, Cilicia, the Near East, and Egypt. Later, Armenians also arrived from Armenia, which was under Persian rule.

The seizure of Galician and Lodomerian Ruthenia by King Casimir the Great during the years 1340–1366 pushed the borders of the Polish state to the southeast. Even though trade routes linking western European countries with the East ran through these regions, the regions were sparsely populated and underdeveloped. The Polish king initiated a large-scale policy of founding towns and villages in Ruthenia and granting them charters under Magdeburg law, attracting settlers from other provinces of Poland, from Silesia, and from German lands. In the 1356 municipal charter of Lviv, King Casimir mentioned Armenians among the local peoples *(gentes)*, alongside Jews, Saracens (that is, Muslim Tatars), Tatars, and Ruthenians. During the times of Władysław Jogaila, Kamianets-Podilskyi and Kyiv were also in the Polish-Lithuanian state, two cities playing an important role on the trade routes of the Orient. Armenian immigrants settled in them, too.

In Poland they found better living and earning conditions, and also broad self-rule, as well as an opportunity to preserve and develop their own culture. These last two elements were particularly important in times of persecution of the Armenian faith in the lands of Islam and Orthodoxy, and of economic collapse in their own country. At first, Armenians settled mainly in royal towns, creating their own emporia situated along international trade routes. From the 16th century on, encouragement from owners of large estates played an increasing role in the process of migration to the Polish state. Polish magnates brought Armenians to their own towns to promote economic prosperity and stability in depopulated border regions. Armenians came not only from the East, but also moved between urban centers already existing in the country.

In the 14th century, we see large concentrations of Armenians in Lviv, Kamianets-Podilskyi, Lutsk, Volodymyr-Volynskyi, and Kyiv; in the 15th century, in Belz and Kremenets as well. In the 16th century, the Armenian centers in Volodymyr-Volynskyi, Belz, and Kremenets died out, while those in Lutsk and Kyiv encountered a serious crisis, because the towns in which they were located lost their importance as trading centers. New concentrations developed, on the other hand, in more attractive places. In the 1520s, Armenians received privileges from

Map 8: Armenian communities and churches in the 14th–18th centuries.

King Sigismund I in Ostrozhets, Volhynia; in the 1530s, attempts were made to settle them in Zolochiv in Ruthenia province, as well as in Bar in Podolia, on the initiative of Queen Bona. Jerzy Jazłowiecki, starosta of Kamianets, attracted them to Yazlovets, which lay on the trade route from Lviv to Kamianets-Podilskyi, and toward the end of that century, the grand *hetman* of the Crown, Jan Zamoyski, settled them in Zamość. In 1628, Armenians from Sniatyn, on the Polish-Moldavian border, acquired privileges from King Sigismund III. In the 17th century other magnates followed in Zamoyski's footsteps: Stanisław Koniecpolski brought Armenians to Brody and Buchach, Stanisław and Andrzej Potocki to Stanisławów (Ivano-Frankivsk), and Stanisław Lanckoroński to Zhvanets. In the 1660s, they also appeared in Lysets in Pokuttia, and subsequently in Horodenka. In that same century, as a result of Cossack wars and uprisings, many other centers declined, including Kyiv, which was then outside the borders of Poland. The Turkish occupation of Podolia in the years 1672–1699 caused Armenians to move to other Polish towns—Berezhany, Olesko, Tysmenytsia, Variazh, and Warsaw. In the first half of the 18th century, during the economic reconstruction of areas devastated by occupations and wars, Armenians were considered desirable settlers, and they appeared on the estates of many magnates—in Raşcov, Sataniv, Obertyn, Mohyliv-Podilskyi, Kuty, Horodenka, and Józefgród (Balta). They also lived in many other localities, including Kraków and Vilnius, but did not form separate legal and political communities there. The main concentration of Armenian settlement in the Commonwealth was in towns located in the southeastern provinces of the Crown, Ruthenia, and Podolia. The Armenian population in Poland is estimated at three to six thousand.

The Armenians' position in trade and crafts was guaranteed by royal privileges obtained in the 14th century. The source of their wealth was far-reaching trade that linked Moldavia, Wallachia, Turkey (along with Egypt), Persia, India, and Moscow with the trade centers of Poland

—
138
—

(Kraków, Vilnius, Lublin, Jarosław, Poznań, Toruń, Gdańsk, and many smaller ones). The eastern markets were easy to exploit for Armenians from Poland because of their language skills and highly-developed family and ethnic connections.

The range of goods the Armenians traded in was extensive: textile raw materials (raw silk, cotton, thread), textiles (silk products, cotton scarves and veils, belts, towels, tablecloths, precious damasks and brocades, or materials interwoven with gold, carpets, rugs, tents, tapestries, and hides), ornaments of various kinds (pearls, diamonds), wine, dried fruit and nuts, tropical fruits, and spices (pepper, ginger, cinnamon, nutmeg, saffron, cloves, thyme, cumin, Tatar herbs or sweet flag, etc.) and weapons (including Persian shields, gear for horses), tobacco, and various Oriental medicines. These goods were called "Turkish" or "Armenian," and their range did not change much up to the 18th century. At Polish markets, Armenians also traded in wool and linen products, hides, wax, honey, fox pelts, horses, oxen, and so on. They took special orders for magnate manors and were suppliers to Polish kings. Armenian trade required highly-developed organization. Large amounts of capital were required in order to use risky and distant routes, and that capital was acquired by forming business groups with non-Armenian credit. Merchant companies of Polish Armenians had their own proxies in various European and Asiatic countries. Thanks to this, they could count on rapid and easy loans as needed. Caravans of Armenian merchants led by an elected leader (the so-called *karavanbasha*) set out for the Orient from Kamianets-Podilskyi. On the way, they followed complex security procedures (marking carts with white coverings, banning access to strangers, and so on). As the expeditions were import-oriented, they had to carry large amounts of coins. Those were concealed in barrels underneath a layer of iron axes. Export played a lesser role in Armenian trade, especially after the 15th century. From that time on, Armenians took money instead of goods out of Poland, which had a negative impact on the state's trade balance. They violated the interests

—
139
—

of the state in another way as well. To avoid paying tolls, they did not go by the routes designated in international treaties, which led to tension in Poland's relations with the Ottoman Empire.

Crafts were a secondary but still important source of income for Armenians, who worked as furriers, shoemakers, butchers, tanners, bakers, goldsmiths, blacksmiths, weavers, embroiderers, and painters. In addition, like all townsmen, Armenians made use of gardens, fields, and manorial farmsteads just outside the towns. In the 18th century, when Polish magnates started creating production facilities (manufactures), those that specialized in weaving were directed by Armenians (Dominik Madżarski, Paschalis Jakubowicz). The so-called *persjarnie* produced mainly *kontusz* sashes (Stanisławów, Slutsk, Brody, Warsaw, Lipków, Buchach, Olesko, and Kuty).

By importing oriental wares or producing them on-site, Armenians contributed a great deal to the orientalization of old Polish culture. This phenomenon was already noticeable by the end of the 1560s. Not everyone approved of it. Grzegorz of Sambor, a professor at the Academy of Kraków, said in his poetic composition *Częstochowa* (1568, translated from Latin to Polish by Wincenty Stroka): "What kind of dress is yours, Poles, what sort of weapons? / Poland seems almost wholly Turkish today. / Faithless, you abandon the way of Christ, / Passing for Saracens in dress, thought, and head. / Why, cruel Turk, do you shake your shining armor? / The rabble similar to you wants to be yours."

Because of their knowledge of Oriental languages, Armenians filled an important auxiliary role in the state's diplomacy in the East. They were interpreters, translators, secretaries, diplomatic agents, and sometimes even minor envoys. They performed reconnaissance service in Turkish and Tatar countries, and also counterintelligence, making sure that spies did not hide in merchants' caravans headed to Poland. The post of royal interpreter of the Turkish language residing in Lviv was in the hands of one Armenian family for generation after generation. The city inter-

—
140
—

preter of Lviv was always an Armenian. Kyiv Armenians played a similar role in relations with the Crimean Khanate.

Thanks to these functions, they gained personal and group advantages: connections and protection at court, customs facilitation in trade, and in some instances, ennoblement. Some of the wealthiest Armenians tried to enter the noble estate, to acquire landed estates and hold office. In the 18th century, during the Enlightenment, ennoblement could be granted for contributions to the development of industry and national culture. At this time, we see Armenians in the professions of the intelligentsia: as teachers, officials, lawyers, and clergymen. Among intellectuals of Armenian origin one may mention Grzegorz Piramowicz, secretary of the Society for Elementary Books, functioning with the National Education Commission, as well as Jan Jaśkiewicz, professor of natural history at the university of Kraków (called the Main Crown School at the time).

The Armenian communities in the Kingdom of Poland had their own governing bodies. It was a part of a broader system of Polish liberties for various estates, regions, and communities. The purpose for the existence of individual communities was legal security and preservation of culture. In the multiethnic towns of the Polish Crown, Armenian autonomy was limited, however, by town councils in which there was no representation of non-Catholic nations. The model for the Armenian governing structure in privately-owned towns was the Kamianets community, headed by a separate *wójt* of Armenian law. In Lviv, the Armenian *wójt's* office was abolished in 1469 as a result of persistent efforts on the part of the local Catholic town council.

— 141 —

At the head of the governing structure of an Armenian community was the council of elders, the number of its members ranging from a few to more than a dozen. During the course of a year, half of its members held office and were exempt from taxes for that period. Members of the council of elders came from the wealthiest families. As a rule, their positions were for life, although formal elections were held annually. The council's most important officials were the *wójt*, clerk, deputies (*ierespokhani*, or administrators of church property), stewards, and tax collectors. In Kamianets and Zamość, *wójts* were chosen from among the council of elders (or aldermen). New members of the council of elders (or *collegium* of aldermen) were chosen by the councils and the so-called "commonalty of the community" *(communitas Armenorum)*. The Armenian court was recruited from the councilmen, and met usually in a group of two to four sworn jurors. The court bailiffs and clerks did not have to be Armenians. The judgments of this court could be appealed to the whole council of elders, to the *starosta*, and finally to the king himself (later, also, to the Crown Tribunal) or to a court established by the town's private owner. The jurisdiction of the Armenian courts in Kamianets-Podilskyi and Zamość extended to all civil and criminal matters, while the Lviv court did not rule on matters of rape, murder, injury, theft, and real estate transactions. This court, unlike that of Kamianets, also had no right to judge foreign Armenians (so-called guests). In cases where one party was not an Armenian, the principle of *actor sequitur forum rei* was generally applied, that is, the case was heard by the court proper to the defendant. In criminal cases in Kamianets, a compromise was worked out according to which cases would be heard by two jurisdictions, priority being granted to authorities of Magdeburg law.

Armenian courts issued judgments on the basis of statutes of Armenian law confirmed at the Piotrków parliament by King Sigismund I in 1519. Those were a reworking of the legal code *(Datastanagirk)* formulated in the late 12th century in Great Armenia by the monk Mkhitar Gosh. This was not religious law, although Armenians called it *tora*. Although the statutes contained regulations of a religious nature, they mainly regulated secular affairs and rarely invoked the authority of Scripture or church canons. With time, many solutions were adopted from the law in force in Poland. In 1604 the statutes were supplemented with procedural regulations, the so-called *Porządek sądów i spraw prawa ormiańskiego* [Order

142

of courts and matters of Armenian law]. Armenians themselves at first did not regard preserving their native law as a *sine qua non* condition of group life in the Diaspora. In Vilnius, Lutsk, Volodymyr-Volynskyi, Kyiv, and Kremenets, or in towns located in Lithuania (until the change in its borders by virtue of the Union of Lublin), Armenian communities functioned on the basis of Magdeburg law. Armenians were also admitted to this law in Bar in Podole. We find in sources frequent cases of Armenians fleeing from their own law to Magdeburg law without relinquishing their participation in the religious life of their own community. From the late 16th century, the communities' authorities tried to counteract this phenomenon, because such "runaways" stopped participating in their fiscal obligations. Groups of followers of the Armenian faith also lived under the jurisdiction of *starostas* near royal castles (Lviv, Kyiv), where obviously no Armenian law was in force. All Armenian courts issued judgments in the king's name.

In addition to secular courts, clerical (ecclesiastical) courts existed as well in the more important centers, dealing with cases connected with premarital agreements, testaments, and other matters relevant to the functioning of churches and liturgy. Armenian elders, the bishop, or his official *(avakarets)* as well as clergymen also had seats in this type of court. Appeals of this court's judgments were made to the superior of the Armenian Church.

According to tradition, Christianity became the state religion of the Kingdom of Armenia as early as 301. The conversion of the king and people was accomplished through the mediation of Saint Gregory the Illuminator, who became the first patriarch of the Armenian Church. In the early fifth century, the monk Mesrob Mashtots created the Armenian alphabet. Thanks to it, the Bible was translated into Armenian, as were philosophical and theological works and the liturgy. The language of that era (Old Armenian, also called Grabar) is used to this day in church rites. The Armenian Church did not accept the decrees of the Fourth Ecumenical Council in Chalcedon (451), rejecting the doctrine adopted there of the two natures

—

143

—

in Christ. Because of these views, it was numbered among the family of Monophysitic churches. It formed its own liturgy (its characteristics included the custom of not mixing water with wine in the Eucharistic chalice, and the addition of the words "who was crucified for us" to the hymn *Holy God*, the so-called Trisagion). The Armenian Church was headed from the Middle Ages by the Catholicoi, with sees in Etchmiadzin, Akdamar (Great Armenia), and Sis (Cilicia), as well as two patriarchs, in Constantinople and Jerusalem. Only the Catholicoi had the right to consecrate bishops and distribute *myron* (chrism). Although some bishops bore the titles of metropolitan and archbishop, all bishops were equal and independent. Independent from the bishops' authority were the jurisdictions of the *vardapets*, monks learned in Scripture, who could even excommunicate hierarchs and temporarily administer dioceses.

The migration of Armenians to lands far from their ancient homeland produced many changes. At times it even led to adopting a new language. The majority of Armenian immigrants to Poland, whose ancestors had lived for a long time in Tatar lands, used the Kipchak tongue, belonging to the Turkish group of languages. A minority, who arrived later from the Far East (Persia, Turkey) or from the principalities on the Danube, spoke Armenian, so-called Ashkharhabar (the Western version of that language). Armenians wrote their books in Kipchak as well as Armenian, using letters of the Armenian alphabet. They also used the local languages, Polish and Ruthenian.

In Poland, Armenians gradually yielded to the influence of the local culture. Their churches erected from the 16th century on no longer hearken back to the architectural and painting models of their old homeland. In wealthy Armenian townhouses one could see numerous creations of Western culture: Dutch paintings, Latin and Polish books, Gdańsk furniture, and Nuremberg silver. Their customs connected with celebration and amusement were also polonized. Armenian women adopted the fashions of Polish women of the noble and burgher classes, and the men did not differ from Polish nobles wearing *żupany* and *kontusze*. These were signs of acculturation, that is, the process of cultural changes arising during contacts between communities with different traditions. The acculturation processes grew stronger from generation to generation. It was not only a matter of adopting the language and tastes of the majority, but also of a more fundamental change in worldview. Martin Gruneweg, a native of Gdańsk who stayed among Lviv Armenians for several years at the end of the 16ᵗʰ century, recorded a significant statement by a culturally integrated Armenian woman about her traditional father: "It is amazing, noble Father, that you have lived in Poland so long and still keep up Turkish manners. It were better if you locked me up for your heart's peace in the Turkish manner, and ordered me to go about with my face veiled." Acculturation processes involving Armenians also worked the other way. One must remember that the great Armenian trade intensified Poland's relations with the Orient. Undoubtedly, Armenians made their own contribution to the cultural transformation of their new homeland.

—

145

—

Despite advancing acculturation, Armenians tried to preserve everything that was valuable, important, and their own. Most important was religion. The Armenian diocese in Lviv was created in the 14ᵗʰ century, and all Armenians living in Poland and Lithuania were under its authority, as well as those of Moldavia, for a time. The first bishop referred to in sources, Gregory, was confirmed in 1367 by King Casimir the Great. The Armenian bishops of Lviv were selected by the Lviv council of elders and clergy, and confirmed by the kings of Poland. For Armenians, orthodoxy meant unity with the Catholicos and preserving their own liturgical rite. This demanded maintaining regular contacts with Church centers in the East. Polish Armenians recognized the authority of the Catholicoi of Etchmiadzin from the mid-15ᵗʰ century on. Every nominee for bishop of Lviv had to go to the Catholicos for consecration. The Catholicoi or patriarchs appeared at times in Polish cities; two of them, Stepanos V Salmastetsy (died 1552) and Melchisedek (died 1627) found thier final resting places there: in Lviv and Kamianets-Podilskyi, respectively. Special representatives of foreign hierarchs, or *nevirags*, visited Poland regularly; they collected donations and alms, and sometimes officiated at courts of law. An Armenian community maintained many church institutions that were essential for its full functioning: a temple, a clerical court, a school, monasteries, and charitable organizations. Most highly developed in this regard were communities in Lviv and Kamianets; others formed only the most essential religious organs. The bishop exercised his authority in close connection with the whole community. Making church structures dependent on the laity was a characteristic feature of the Armenian Church. The source of this domination of the *profanum* over the *sacrum* in Armenian communities was the way in which religious institutions were financed. In contrast to the Catholic and Orthodox Churches, the Armenian religious community was financed not by land revenues, but from capital funds, the primary source of which were community donations. The generosity of the faithful to the Church was considerable; it showed itself in the founding of churches and bequests in wills. Monasteries played an important role. Monks often came from faraway places. In addition to prayer and work on the monastery farm, they served community guests and managed the hospital and school. Monasteries were the places where handwritten books were preserved and copied. In the library of the Lviv monastery, many valuable manuscripts were kept that had been brought from various parts of the Orient. In addition, books were copied and collected at all Armenian churches. Numerous scribes and illustrators copied and decorated books. In 1616, an Armenian printing house was established in Lviv, but it only remained open for a short time, because Armenians were attached to traditional handwritten books. The church provided Polish Armenians with a complementary cultural offering in a national version: education, literature (in Grabar and in Kipchak), music, various forms of popular culture, and aesthetic experience. Clergymen were depositaries of group memory. In Kamianets and in Lviv, chronicles of Armenian life were created in connection with the histories of two homelands: the old one, Oriental, and the new one, Polish.

In addition to the Church, matrimonial strategy also contributed to the preservation of identity; marriages were contracted exclusively within the Armenian community. Armenians did not willingly make family alliances with followers of other religions. In 1572, the Lviv community asked Catholicos Michael of Sebastia for a permanent dispensation on marrying close relatives in order to avoid the necessity of marrying Catholics or members of the Orthodox Church, for that would lead to a "division in faith."

Religious union with the Roman Catholic Church was a powerful impulse influencing changes in Armenian identity. It was initiated by disputes within the Lviv community over the election of a new bishop. In 1627, Catholicos Melchisedek consecrated a young monk, Mikołaj Torosowicz, to that office against the will of the majority. As he struggled with his opponents, the young bishop decided to take a radical step—he made a profession of the Catholic faith, putting himself under the protection of the local Catholic clergy (mainly Jesuits) and the Papal nunciature in Warsaw (1630). He then went to Rome, where he was confirmed as a Catholic hierarch and the archbishop of Armenians in Lviv (1635). The archbishop's bitter fight with the faithful lasted for decades. When the community elders deprived him of revenues, he seized the cemetery and all churches in Lviv, and squandered the treasures and valuables collected there on a lavish and luxurious life. This scandalized his compatriots, and for many years, they boycotted him and would not go to the cathedral. Not until 1653 did Torosowicz make his peace with the Catholicos, and that reconciled him with the majority of the faithful, because for many Armenians, union was tantamount to treason. They even preferred to leave the country rather than accept it. The union was not well established until the 1667 founding in Lviv of a Papal collegium or seminary for Armenian clergymen, run by the Theatine order. The Theatines succeeded

—
147
—

in persuading the archbishop to carry out liturgical reforms in the Catholic spirit. Furthermore, in Rome in 1675, Torosowicz consecrated Rev. Vartan Hunian as his coadjutor (successor). He did so under pressure from the Apostolic See, which trusted the new bishop more than him. The latter, however, could not remain in Poland due to the hatred of Torosowicz and Polish Armenians, and went on a mission to the East, assuming authority in the Lviv diocese only after the death of Torosowicz in 1681.

The activities of the Theatine seminary, the formation of the Order of Armenian Benedectine nuns (1690), and the pastoral zeal of subsequent archbishops strengthened the union in following generations. Until the partitions, the Lviv Armenian archbishops were selected only by the Armenian clergy while their predecessors were still alive, after which they were confirmed in Rome. The point was not to allow the Etchmiadzin Catholicoi to install their own nominees as bishops of Lviv. One consequence of the union was the narrowing of horizons of the Armenians in Poland to the Catholic community, which led to a rupture with the Armenian world faithful to the traditional Church. The union also removed a barrier separating Armenians from Poles, but it did not automatically result in polonization. The separate Armenian rite remained an ethnic characteristic for Armenians within Polish society. Marriages within their own ethnic group also continued to be the practice.

As a result of the multi-century presence of Armenians in Poland and the influence of Polish culture upon them, they developed a special and unusual identity: a strong attachment to their own traditions (especially religious) combined with a strong emotional connection with the Polish fatherland. That is why a separate word exists in the Armenian language, *Lehahayer*, or Armenian Poles (from *Leh*, "Pole" and *Hai*, "Armenian, with the plural ending *–er*). For many generations, they were involved in all Polish issues, political, cultural, and economic. In the 19th century they took part in the uprisings and struggles for independence; their last archbishop in independent Poland, Józef Teodorowicz, was a recognized national authority; and during World War II, they became the victims of persecutions aimed at Poles. The lands where Polish Armenians lived for many centuries no longer belong to Poland today, but to Ukraine. That is why they are sometimes erroneously called Ukrainian Armenians; but that was never how they regarded themselves.

Selected bibliography

Adel-Golobi, E., "Armenians and Jews in Medieval Lvov: Their Role in Oriental Trade, 1400–1600," *Cahiers du Monde Russe et Soviétique*, vol. 20 N°3–4. Juillet–Décembre 1979, pp. 345–388.

Balzer, O., *Statut ormiański w zatwierdzeniu Zygmunta I z r. 1519* [The Armenian Statute from 1519 Approved by Sigismund I], Lwów: Towarzystwo dla Popierania Nauki Polskiej, 1910.

Barącz, S., *Rys dziejów ormiańskich* [A Sketch of Armenian History], Tarnopol: Komitet Budowy Kościoła Ormiańskiego w Czerniowcach, 1869 (reprinted in 1989).

Lechicki, C., *Kościół ormiański w Polsce* [The Armenian Church in Poland], Lwów, 1928.

Oleś, M., *The Armenian Law in the Polish Kingdom (1356–1519)*, Roma: Hosianum, 1966.

Stopka, K., *Ormianie w Polsce dawnej i dzisiejszej* [Armenians in Ancient Poland and Today's], Kraków: Księgarnia Akademicka, 2000.

Stopka, K., "Origins of Armenian Church Organization in Ruthenia," *Armenian Review*, vol. 38 (1985), pp. 1–12.

Stopka, K., "The Religious Culture of Polish Armenians (Church-Public Structures and Relations)," *Acta Poloniae Historica*, vol. 101 (2010), pp. 163–205.

Tryjarski, E., "The History of Armenian Professional Groups in Poland," *Armenian Review* 40, nr 4–60 (Winter 1987), pp. 75–120.

Zakrzewska-Dubasowa, M., *Ormianie w dawnej Polsce* [Armenians in Ancient Poland], Lublin: Wydawnictwo Lubelskie, 1982.

TATARS

୶

JAN TYSZKIEWICZ

—

—

The Mongols united various tribes of nomads. By the year 1240, they had overcome the resistance of Ruthenia, and in 1245 they subjugated the Duchies of Halych and Volodymyr-Volynskyi, adjacent to Polish territory. Only the Ruthenian duchies incorporated into the Grand Duchy of Lithuania remained beyond the Tatars' control. Tatar invasions of Poland—in 1241, and at the turn of 1259/1260 and 1287/1288—caused great devastation and abduction of captives. At that time, the attackers did not settle in Polish territory, or even remain there temporarily. The battles of Casimir the Great with the Tatars in Ruthenia (up to 1360) did not change the situation. But in 1358, a long-lasting civil war broke out in the Great Horde. Followers of the defeated khans, with all their families and retinues, sought refuge in the Grand Duchy of Lithuania, with the consent of Grand Duke Algirdas (1345–1377). After the battle of Kulikovo in 1380, won by Dmitri, Prince of Moscow, a subsequent group of Tatars was settled by Jogaila (Jagiełło) near Poltava. When Tokhtamysh Khan was banished from the Horde, he stayed with his followers in Lithuania 1396–1399, assisting in Duke Vytautas's expeditions to Crimea. His sons came to Lithuania circa 1409. His oldest son, Jalal-ad-Din Khan, took part in the Battle of Grunwald. The number of Tatar warriors who fought in the battle, both old and new settlers, proves that at least fifteen hundred Muslims lived in the Grand Duchy of Lithuania at the time. Tatar settlement flourished there during the rule of Duke Vytautas (1401–1430) and Casimir Jagiellończyk (1440–1492).

Kozakłary, Prudziany [Prūdžionys], Mereszlany [Merešlėnai], and Sorok Tatary [Keturiasdešimt Totorių] are probably among the oldest Tatar settlements. In 1414, Trakai, according to the account of the traveler Gilbert de Lannoy, resembled a town on the Volga. In its vicinity lived numerous Tatars (he wrote, "Saracens, i.e., Muslims"), and in the town and castle, one could encounter Lithuanians, Germans, Ruthenians, and Jews. The latter probably refers to Karaites, followers of Judaism, resettled there from Crimea after 1397. In the 15th and 16th centuries, the largest concentrations of Tatars could be found near the larger economic and political centers: Kaunas, Vilnius, Trakai, Hrodna, Slonim, Navahrudak, Krev, and Minsk. By the mid-16th century, changes in the distribution of Tatars occurred as a result of the search for employment and income. The group of Tatar landowners began to diminish. Tatar immigrants came from various tribes. They spoke different languages and dialects of the Turkish group, and brought their own cultural traditions, but they were all Muslims. Because of that, they began to form a new Tatar-Muslim community in Lithuania. Numerous marriages with Ruthenian or Lithuanian women and the observance of monogamy, which were the strongest influences on the Crimean Tatars' culture, led to customs becoming more uniform and to the adoption of the Ruthenian language, so-called Old White Ruthenian. By the late 17th century, groups of East European Muslims from among the Kazakhs, Nogais, Bashkirs, Chuvashes, and the Crimean, Kazan, and Budjak Tatars, had been accepted within the borders of the Polish-Lithuanian state.

Defining the rights of Tatars in the Grand Duchy of Lithuania poses a difficult task. This is due to the complicated socio-legal structure in the Grand Duchy of Lithuania, differences among the Tatars themselves, and ongoing assimilation processes. In addition, the legal situation of Muslim Tatars was not the same in Lithuania and Poland. There is a lack

—
151
—

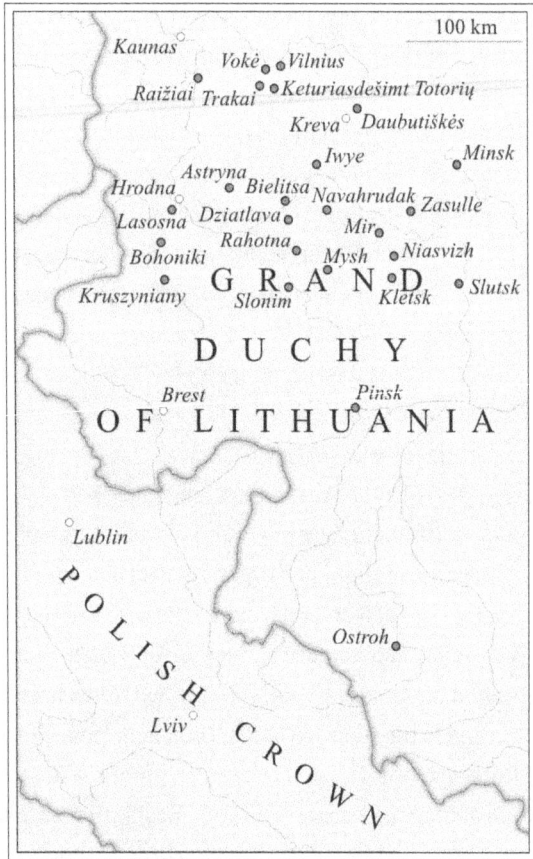

Map 9: Locations of Tatar settlements
in the 16th–17th centuries.

The Assimilated

of sources speaking clearly about the principles on which the earliest groups of Tatar immigrants were settled in the late 14th century. In the early 15th century, free Tatars received land from the *hospodar* or lord (the Grand Duke of Lithuania) in exchange for an obligation to perform military service upon demand. They could receive land along with the dependent populace, or as forest wildernesses, which they could then settle with prisoners of war and people kidnapped from enemy territory. Simple warriors taken prisoner by subjects of the Lithuanian dukes were also settled on land, with military obligations and additional duties to perform. This less privileged group was referred to with the term "Tatar Cossacks."

From the beginning of their residence in the Grand Duchy of Lithuania, the Tatars were divided into four groups. So-called *hospodarski* Tatars, who had large sections of land at their disposal, made up the elite in terms of family and tribe, a group of *mirzas* and *uhlans*. They formed well-equipped units of light cavalry, the Grand Duke's guard. Cossack Tatars had small farms without dependent population. They were relatively numerous, and over the course of the 16th century, they dispersed into the other groups, generally receiving individual or group privileges. This caused their legal position to become significantly closer to that of the first group. At first, they performed various duties, such as repairing roads, transporting building materials, hunting for criminals, filling the role of couriers, and the like. Simple Tatars, plebeians without land who came mainly from among prisoners of war and captives, were settled as subjects of the ruler or of magnates in towns, at castles, and at manors. They occupied the lowest social position, although they enjoyed full religious tolerance on a par with the others. They formed religious groups with nearby clusters of Tatar landowners in some towns. In later times, a separate group was made up of Tatars subordinate to magnates, at first exclusively as servants, craftsmen, or gardeners, but from the mid-16th century on also as subordinate landowners who received their land from a wealthy lord. According to the prevailing model, they were divided into

—
153
—

warriors, who created new villages and were committed to serving in magnates' private militias, or servants at lords' manors or in privately-owned towns (the 17th–18th centuries).

The Tatars' autonomy was recognized in matters of religion, military organization, and administration of justice. Their own social hierarchy was solidified in Lithuania by appropriate grants and privileges. They continued to use traditional titles brought from the Horde and khanates: *sultan* (descendant of a khan), *uhlan*, and *mirza* (noble born). The most distinguished of them in the 16th century were Aziubek Dowleszowicz (died 1514), nephew of the Crimean Khan Menkli Girai, and two families of tsareviches [a term used historically for descendants of Tatar Khans as well as for the sons of Tsars], imperial offspring related to Genghis Khan, the Puńskis and Ostryńskis. In documents from the 16th and 17th centuries, the titles *uhlan* and *mirza* began to be used interchangeably. From the 17th century, all Tatar landowners willingly used the title *kniaź* [prince]. This Ruthenian term represented a formal social advancement for Tatars of various descents, desirable in view of incomplete noble rights. In Lithuania, even wealthy hospodar Tatars belonging to the category of boyars did not have political rights, did not hold state office, could not participate in local assemblies, and could not participate in parliamentary sessions. Religious tolerance did not eliminate the fundamental restriction due to their Islamic faith. The Catholic nobility of Lithuania refused for a long time to grant them rights equal to those of the Orthodox boyars in the Polish-Lithuanian state; and so it is no surprise that up to the end of the 18th century, full noble rights were not granted in the Commonwealth to any Muslims. Non-Christian citizens were not allowed to enjoy full rights, only individual privileges and entitlements that were strictly defined.

The jurisdiction of the *tsareviches* included matters involving genealogy of good birth, some property issues, and command over the Tatar companies in the Lithuanian army. The *tsarevich* also had a seat in the Grand Duke's council in the hospodar's presence. Tatar standard-bearers and marshals holding military command positions were selected from among the Tatar elders. Much like the standard-bearers of the nobility (the boyars), the Tatar standard-bearers also led units to war, gathered them, carried out inspections, kept records, and confirmed participation in service. Each Tatar presented himself in person for the expedition, mounted, and led an appropriate number of warriors in accordance with the size of his property. A widow sent a substitute. The standard-bearer also collected payments from the plebeian Tatar populace exempt from military duty (the so-called poll tax). The standard-bearer gave an accounting of his treasury obligations, swearing on the Koran. Marshals were deputies and assistants of standard-bearers. The ruler confirmed selected standard-bearers and marshals.

An important role was played by the Muslim clergy (imams) called *mullahs*. They were elected by members of their religious group, and performed the functions of leaders and priests in that group. Thus, they kept documentation, performed marriages, named newborns, served as judges, supervised the execution of wills, and took oaths from their coreligionists in court and in the army. From the 17th century on, there were posts for military *mullahs* in the light cavalry corps.

The obligations of military service during the numerous wars caused significant expense, physical disability, and loss of life. Because the requirement of military service was connected with the possession of designated lands (the so-called *tatarszczyzna*), from the mid-16th century on, a process began of abandoning those lands, exchanging them, and selling them off to Christians. Despite prohibitions on this, the majority of Tatar landowners relinquished their old residences, moving to magnate estates, settling elsewhere, or transferring to other professions.

As early as the Thirteen Years War (1454–1466), the king formed mercenary Tatar detachments that fought in the Polish army. Wars waged separately by the Grand Duchy of Lithuania and the Polish Crown against the Teutonic Knights, the Grand Duchy of Moscow, the Crimean Khanate,

155

and Turkey brought about the emergence of a large group of professional soldiers recruited from Lithuanian Muslims. The growing needs of the military in the 17th and 18th century caused enlistment of foreign subjects coming from Crimea and other Khanates, Moldavia, Wallachia, and even Chechnya in the so-called Tatar companies, the light cavalry. Some of them probably remained permanently. In Ukraine, the Ostrogski princes admitted refugees from the Kazan and Astrakhan Khanates to their estates; in 1659, the newcomers gained privileges equivalent to those of Tatars in Lithuania. After the mutiny of Tatar companies due to long delays in receiving pay, new warriors were settled on the royal estates in Podlasie (Hrodna and Brest provinces, 1679–1691). It was then that new Muslim communities, *jamaats*, developed, with mosques that survive to the present day in Bohoniki and Kruszyniany. The majority of those communities were located in the oldest Tatar clusters in Lithuania. In the mid-17th century, their number rose to 20, and there were about 25 mosques at that time. The interior of wooden mosques was modest, covered in rugs and carpets, devoid of all other ornaments and images. On the walls, there hung nothing but tablets with calligraphed verses from the Quran.

Favorable decisions by John III Sobieski, made because he wished to have an excellent light cavalry, were not given sufficient legal authorization by parliament. The review of royal estates begun in 1766, therefore, brought about the removal of Tatar users, extraction of overdue taxes from them, trials, petitions, and negotiations lasting until the end of the Commonwealth. From 1778 to 1786, Tatars were resettled on other lands as compensation. On private latifundia, the majority of Tatars had to purchase the land they used and begin to pay rent. In this way, the wealthiest of them became landowners; the rest moved to the cities or became servants. In the 16th through the 18th centuries, Tatar landowners were entitled to legal protection equal to that of Christian nobles (as evidenced by the number of punishments for murder and injury), and from 1699 on,

—
156
—

they had the right to sell land freely and possess serfs. In this way, resolutions of local assemblies in Lithuania from the early 17ᵗʰ century, which banned Tatars from owning subordinate Christian populations, were nullified. The Muslim commoners in towns had rights equal to those of other townsmen, with the exception of the right to join guilds.

In the towns, Tatars were craftsmen at the manors of magnates, or servants, coachmen, or transport entrepreneurs. They created separate suburbs, the so-called "Tatar streets." In Old Polish times, simple Tatars cultivated gardens, transported food products to market, and worked as tanners. They conducted trade on a small scale. Tatar farmers and landowners raised horses necessary for the army and for transport. They also had a certain reputation as self-trained veterinarians. In magnates' jurisdictions, they were free to earn, paying taxes. In towns and on private estates, they served in militia detachments. In hospodar (state) towns, they were subject to castle or municipal law, under the jurisdiction of the owner's court. Muslim townsmen did not have the privilege of forming their own governing bodies. They were organized exclusively as a religious group.

Throughout the Old Polish period, the Tatars' basic employment was military service. The Tatar light cavalry in the Grand Duchy of Lithuania was an important part of the army, and from the 16ᵗʰ century on, perhaps the most important. Mobile, efficient, swift, well acquainted with the terrain, valiant, and experienced—in the 17ᵗʰ and 18ᵗʰ centuries as a professional army—it took on the main burden of duties for the defense of the country. This army was described in sources as the "Tatar companies." This description was apt, because except for the Christian commanders— Lithuanians, Poles, and Ruthenians—the units were made up of Muslim citizens. In the mid-17ᵗʰ century, kings appointed standard-bearers and captains of Tatar companies, entrusting to them the recruitment of soldiers and the command. In the Grand Duchy of Lithuania, the Tatar companies were the mainstay of the Grand Duke's authority, becoming a counterweight against the armies of the magnates and squads of vassals of regional dukes. From the time of Stefan Batory on, mercenary Tatar regiments also played an important role in the Crown's army. Tatar Muslims of various social classes—landowners, Cossacks, plebeians, and groups of foreigners—took up military service. Many years of service granted them a steady income and social advancement.

Tatar landowners received the most important privileges in the years 1634, 1659, 1669, 1679, 1698, and 1713. The privileges alternated with local assembly resolutions demanding restrictions on their legal and financial liberties. Church doctrine and the constant armed conflicts with Crimea and Turkey influenced the delay in granting full equal rights to Muslims. In 1616, 1617, and 1643, an anti-Tatar lampoon was printed under the title *Alfurkan tatarski*, maliciously describing the customs and entitlements of Tatars in the state. Despite these attacks, full religious tolerance for Muslims continued, at the cost of a ban on mixed marriages and a requirement to obtain bishops' permission to build new mosques. Mullahs conducted the teaching of Islam. They taught how to read and write religious texts in the Arabic alphabet. Muslims made use of various types of handwritten religious books *(kitaby)* from the 16th century on. Most often, these were texts of the Quran, collections of prayers, religious tales, and in some cases, notes on healing. The basic prayers were written in the Arabic language; the other texts were in Old White Ruthenian or Old Polish, but in Arabic letters. In courts, Tatars signed their names in Polish, less often in the Arabic alphabet; military men sometimes signed in Turkish.

From the end of the 15th century, Lithuanian Tatars were slowly becoming polonized; they did, however, preserve their religion, as well as customs associated with Muslim beliefs, holy days, and obligations. The expensive pilgrimage to Mecca was undertaken by a few of the wealthiest men, after many years of military service, and by former mullahs (imams). They were then entitled to the title *hadż* [*hajj*], which was put on their tombstones. Lithuanian-Polish Tatars were and remained Sunni Muslims, belonging to the most numerous branch of Islam. They did not conduct religious disputes with those of other faiths; they accepted all rules based on the Ten Commandments and the Quran. From their arrival in Lithuania, they observed the principle of monogamy. Cemeteries were established in the vicinity of the oldest mosques. The dead were buried in shrouds directly in the ground, and a single stone was erected with a short religious formula, and name and surname, in Arabic letters. Individual graves from the 17th century have been preserved to this day.

The everyday life of Muslims, their customs, dress, and weaponry, often Oriental, bought or won in wars, as well as carpets, eastern sashes and fabrics, differed little from those of the nobles or the wealthiest townsmen. The fashion called "Sarmatian" assured the popularity and influx of products from the East, through Crimea and Turkey, to the whole Polish-Lithuanian state. In addition to folk practices that were universal, Muslims practiced the wearing of small pouches with Quranic verses, while the women carried silver coins with verses in Arabic script. Tatars differed from the average group of nobles in their restraint in drinking alcohol and their observance of a long and strict fast (*Ramadan*). They celebrated Muslim holy days, but those were not very numerous in comparison with those of Christians.

Tatar Muslims and Armenians rendered much service to the diplomacy of Lithuanian and Polish rulers. Knowing the Oriental languages—Turkish and Crimean Tatar, and in some cases, Arabic, Persian, and Greek (the Armenians)—they were valued workers in the Grand Ducal and Crown chancelleries. As early as circa 1401, Duke Vytautas, son of Kęstutis, employed so-called Tatar translators/interpreters. They drew up letters in Oriental languages and took part in embassies and exchanges of correspondence, traveling to Crimea to the Great Horde. Casimir Jagiellończyk and his sons, Aleksander and Sigismund I, and also Stefan Batory and Sigismund Vasa, while conducting separate Lithuanian diplomacy, made use of trusted officials supported by experienced and able Muslims. Tatars or Armenians were sent from the royal chancellery as diplomatic couriers and envoys to conduct preliminary talks. Large legations used the services of interpreters, armed guards, and transportation organized on the model of merchants' caravans. Large wagons carrying supplies, equipment, and numerous gifts for a succession of Turkish officials and functionaries were led by Ruthenian and Tatar citizens of the Commonwealth. The lively international trade with the East, both crossing the Polish-Lithuanian state and aimed for destinations in Poland, was served to a large degree by Tatars and Armenians. In the 17th century, Turkey issued business licenses to its subjects, thus limiting the participation of subjects of the Commonwealth. The Polish side responded with similar limitations. Polish Tatars, Armenians, and Jews could operate on the long roads within the state from the Crimean Steppes and Moldavia to Ducal Prussia and Gdańsk, to Poznań and Mahilyoŭ, and sometimes to Smolensk. Contacts with Crimea were interrupted by Bohdan Khmelnytskyi's uprising in 1648 and later wars in Ukraine.

During Saxon times and the rule of Stanisław August Poniatowski (1764–1795), the situation changed. Eastern diplomacy and trade died out. Lithuanian and Polish Tatars began to serve in foreign armies as well, especially in Saxony. During the Cossack wars in Ukraine (1648–1652), fifteen Tatar companies served in the Crown's military, averaging 120 horses each. During the long war with Turkey (1683–1699), the most famous episode is the participation of Polish Tatar units in the Battle of Vienna (1683). Tatar regiments of Gen. Józef Bielak, Col. Aleksander Korycki, and Col. Czymbaj Rudnicki, recruited in Podlasie, joined the Confederation of Bar (1768–1772) to defend independence from Russian rule. In the 1792 armed conflict with Russia and the battles of the Kościuszko Insurrection in 1794, Tatar regiments played an important role, recognized as a good, regular army and commanded by Gen. Józef Bielak, Col. Jakub Azulewicz, and Col. Mustafa Achmatowicz. They fought in the field at Maciejowice and in defense of Warsaw. In the final years of the Commonwealth, there was not enough money to maintain all posts in the regiments, and Tatar soldiers received modern rifles only after 1790; before then, they fought mainly with sword and lance. After the first two Partitions, the Tatars continued to serve in the military but on a smaller scale. Tatars were a minority of several thousand people. Fairly complete censuses from the late 18th century covered only some voivodeships—Navahrudak, Vilnius, and Minsk—that included their main settlement clusters, and found fewer than 2,000 Muslims. The Tatar group adapted to earning opportunities, specializing in several trades (tanning, transport, gardening) as well as traditional service in the military. There are no entries in the sources about crimes and criminal misdemeanors by Tatars. Several hundred years of military service, from the late 14th century to the late 17th, formed their patriotism and readiness to fight for independence, which later Polish Tatars proved during the Napoleonic Wars, in the Uprisings of 1830 and 1863, and later in the illegal activity of the Polish Socialist Party up to the year 1918.

—

161

—

Selected bibliography

Bohdanowicz, L., Chazbijewicz, S., and Tyszkiewicz, J., *Tatarzy muzułmanie w Polsce* [Tatar Muslims in Poland], Gdańsk: Rocznik Tatarów Polskich, 1997.

Borawski, P., Dubiński, A., *Tatarzy polscy. Dzieje, obrzędy, legendy, tradycje* [Polish Tatars. History, Rituals, Legends, Traditions], Warszawa: Iskry, 1986.

Dziadulewicz, S., *Herbarz rodzin tatarskich w Polsce* [Armorial of Tatar Families in Poland], Wilno: Lux, 1929.

Kryczyński, S., *Tatarzy litewscy. Próba monografii historyczno-etnograficznej* [Lithuanian Tatars. An Attempt at a Historical and Ethnographical Monograph], Warszawa: Rocznik Tatarski, 1938.

Podhorodecki, L., *Chanat Krymski i jego stosunki z Polską w xv–xviii w.* [The Crimean Khanate and Its Relations with Poland in the 15th–18th Centuries], Warszawa: Książka i Wiedza, 1987.

The Assimilated

Sobczak, J., *Położenie prawne ludności tatarskiej w Wielkim Księstwie Litewskim* [The Legal Situation of the Tatar Populace in the Grand Duchy of Lithuania], Warszawa–Poznań: PWN, 1984.

Tyszkiewicz, J., *Tatarzy na Litwie i w Polsce. Studia z dziejów XIII–XVIII w.* [Tatars in Lithuania and in Poland. Studies from the History of the 13th–18th Centuries], Warszawa: PWN, 1989.

Tyszkiewicz, J., *Z historii Tatarów polskich: 1794–1944* [From the History of Polish Tatars: 1794–1944], Pułtusk: Wyższa Szkoła Humanistyczna, 1998.

Tyszkiewicz, J., *Tatarzy w Polsce i Europie. Fragmenty dziejów* [*Tatars in Poland and Europe. Fragments of History*], Pułtusk: Akademia Humanistyczna im. Aleksandra Gieysztora, 2008.

KARAITES

ক্ক

ANNA SULIMOWICZ

—

One of the smallest pebbles in the colorful ethnic and religious mosaic of the Commonwealth was the Karaites, immigrants from Crimea and followers of a religion that had grown out of Judaism on the grounds of anti-Talmudic opposition. "Bringing with them the Pentateuch of Moses and the Prophets, they preserved upon themselves the unblemished mark of the people of God," Władysław Syrokomla wrote of them in his *Wycieczki po Litwie [Excursions in Lithuania]*. Karaism, which recognizes only the Torah, rejects all additions to it, especially the oral tradition written down in the form of the Talmud. The codifier of the doctrine was Anan ben David of Basra, who lived in the eighth century and gathered around himself an anti-rabbinical opposition, calling for rejection of oral tradition and relying on the orders and prohibitions contained in Scripture, interpreted literally. Anan's followers were initially called Ananites, from his name. Later, more or less from the ninth century, the term karaim began to be used for them, deriving from a Semitic root meaning "to read" (the same root appears in the Arab word *kur'ân*, Quran). Hebrew *qara'im* means "readers." This name refers, therefore, to the basic command of the Karaite religion, that is, reading and studying Scripture.

The ideas proclaimed by Anan and his successors found followers throughout the Near East. Already in its leader's lifetime, the main center of Karaism moved from Mesopotamia to Jerusalem, where the oldest

Karaite temple or *kenesa* was built. Thanks to active missionary work, Karaite communities sprang up in Persia, Syria, Egypt, and Byzantium.

From the territory of Persia and Asia Minor, Karaite emissaries moved to the Black Sea and on to Crimea, where they met the Khazars. This nomadic people of Turkish origin had come from Asia, following in the footsteps of the Huns, and after the downfall of the Western Turkic Khaganate in the mid-seventh century, they formed their own state, the territory of which stretched between the Caspian and Black Seas and to the northern shores of the latter (the Azov-Black Sea steppes, and part of Crimea). The Khazar state, a sort of loose federation of tribes under the authority of the Khazar leader, the *khagan*, included peoples of various ethnic origins: Alans, Goths, and Caucasian, Finno-Ugric, and Slavic tribes. Their lands were also inhabited by an immigrant population drawn both by the trade routes that led through the khaganate's territory, and by religious tolerance. The Khazar state reached the apogee of its might in the eighth century, becoming a force to reckon with for its greatest rivals, Christian Byzantium and Muslim Persia. Its location between mighty neighbors representing two of the three great monotheistic religions lay at the foundation of an unprecedented event that continues to create controversy—the so-called Judaization of the Khazars in the mid-ninth century. Sources mention a dispute between representatives of the three great monotheistic religions that is said to have taken place at the khagan's court. After familiarizing himself with the principles of Judaism, Christianity, and Islam, the ruler decided to embrace the first of these religions. It should be noted that this event was not a state-wide or nation-wide conversion; it affected only the ruler and his immediate retinue. A question still not fully settled is which version of Judaism the Khazars are supposed to have embraced. Some researchers favor the view that it may have been not rabbinical Judaism, but Karaism. There is no doubt that after the downfall of the khaganate—which gradually lost power and finally collapsed in the mid-10th century due to decentralizing tendencies and the growing importance of Kyivan Ruś—a group of people remained in Crimea who spoke a language belonging to the Kipchak branch of the Turkish language family and professed the Karaite religion. Even if they are not direct descendants of the Khazars, the Karaites—for it is them we are speaking of—have a Khazar substratum in their genealogy, as is evidenced by relics of ancient beliefs and culture preserved in their language.

The main settlement points of the Karaites on the Crimean Peninsula were the towns of Qirq Yer (now Chufut-Kale) near Bakhchysarai, Mangup, Solkhat (Staryi Krym) and Kaffa (Feodosiya). Under Tatar rule, the Karaites, who were employed in trade and crafts, enjoyed a great many liberties and a high social status for non-Muslims.

Karaite tradition connects their arrival in Lithuania with the person of the Grand Duke of Lithuania, Vytautas. He is said to have brought Karaite settlers from Crimea (the legend says it was 383 families, which would be some 1,500 people, more or less) and settled them in Trakai, as well as localities such as Saločiai, Biržai, Panevėžys, Upytė, among others. They were to man fortresses there, as is indicated by the distribution of historical Karaite settlements along the border of the Grand Duchy and that of the Livonian Brothers of the Sword.

Although tradition may overstate the number of settlers, it holds the proverbial kernel of truth. Jan Długosz states in his *Annales* that in 1397, Duke Vytautas, during an expedition to Crimea, "took prisoner many thousands of Tatars and their wives, children, and cattle, and brought them back to Lithuania." There may have been Karaites as well in this group, especially since Vytautas went as far as Kaffa and Qirq Yer, and perhaps also to Mangup and Solkhat, where clusters of them were located. It seems probable that they were not taken prisoner by the duke, but rather that they voluntarily agreed to resettle farther north. This would be confirmed by the fact of their retaining their faith—if they had been slaves, they would probably have been forced to convert to Christianity. The situation prevailing in the Crimean Peninsula could have inclined

—
165
—

them toward making the decision to resettle. The second half of the 14th century was a stormy period in the history of the khanate. Fratricidal battles between the Girays, the invasion by Mongols under the leadership of Timur, and the devastation of Crimean towns induced some of the inhabitants to seek less dangerous dwelling places. One may assume that at that point, the Karaites began to settle in the territories of southern Ruthenia, and encouraged by the liberties guaranteed by privileges of both King (the charter of Casimir the Great that established the town of Lviv in 1357, confirmed by subsequent rulers) and Grand Duke (the general grant of privilege for Jewish communities issued by Vytautas in 1388), agreed to move to Lithuania in the years 1397–1398. Their appearance in the Grand Duchy was undoubtedly in the interest of Vytautas. On the one hand, the Karaite population of craftsmen and merchants contributed to economic recovery and development; on the other hand, an influx of immigrants from the East (first and foremost the Armenians and Jews, but also the less numerous Karaites) restricted opportunities for Polish and German colonization. The oldest Karaite clusters, settled in the Middle Ages, were in Trakai and perhaps Kaunas.

—
166
—

Karaites probably appeared in Volhynia at more or less the same time. Here, too, tradition has it that they were brought there by Vytautas. The Karaite scholar Mordechai Sułtański says that the duke supposedly settled them on the right bank of the Styr River, opposite a fortress. The oldest preserved document that mentions them–an appeal for the abolition of the tax on houses of prayer, made jointly by Jews and Karaites to the Grand Duke of Lithuania, Sigismund I—dates from as late as 1506; but references in documents from the early 16th century to land used by Karaites, called *"dworzyszcza karaimowskie"* and *"pola karaimowskie"* ("Karaite manors and fields"), indicate their presence in the town before 1495, when Jews (and Karaites, who were not distinguished from them) were expelled from the Grand Duchy of Lithuania, although they were allowed to return a few years later.

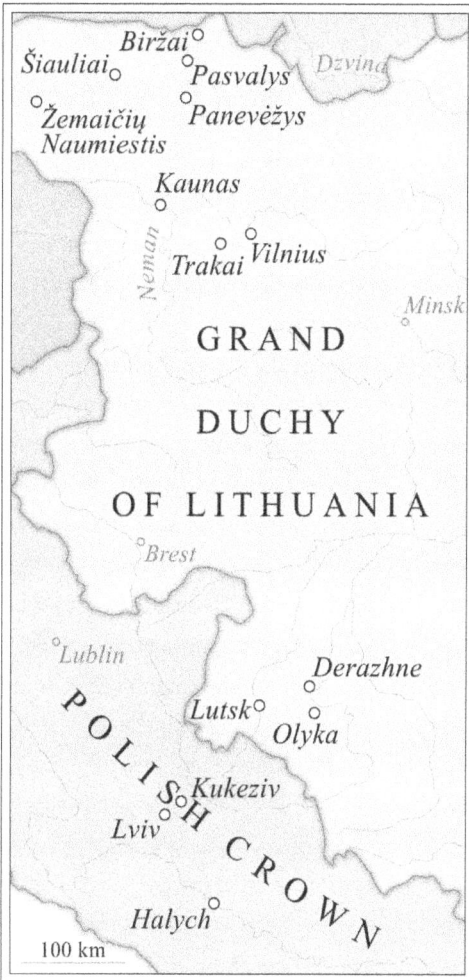

Map 10: Karaite settlements
in the Commonwealth.

Besides Lutsk, Karaite clusters existed in Volhynia at Derazhne and Olyka. In the first half of the 17th century, the community in Derazhne was one of the four most important communities, alongside Halych, Lutsk, and Trakai; but it was almost completely destroyed during Khmelnytskyi's uprising. It was rebuilt, however, probably due to arrivals from Lutsk, and lasted until 1768, when the Massacre of Uman put an end to its existence.

Karaites also lived in lands belonging to the Crown. A 1475 document dealing with a settlement between them and Jews indicates the existence in Lviv of an organized Karaite community, which proves that they must have appeared in that city at some earlier point. It is difficult, however, to establish when that happened and how the Karaites came to be there. The Lviv community was certainly not very numerous and was connected with the Jewish one (they shared a common cemetery, for instance); and after the mid-15th century it is no longer mentioned.

Although evidence of the presence of Karaites in Halych dates only from the 16th century, some scholars are of the opinion that they could have arrived there as early as the mid-13th century. A prayer book that was preserved in the local kenesa, and had been brought there from Crimea, was said to have included notes on the community's origins that point to the year 1246. According to them, Danylo, Duke of Halych, asked the Tatar leader to send him 100 Karaite families; 80 came from Solkhat, Mangup, and Kaffa to Halych, where the duke bestowed land upon them, as well as the right to free trade and to sell liquor. Unfortunately, the prayer book was destroyed in an 1830 fire, and so it is difficult to assess the reliability of this account. Danylo visited Batu Khan in 1245 (*Latopis halicko-wołyński* gives the date of this event as 1250) and recognized his authority; the next year, Danylo received from Batu confirmation of his rule over the Duchy of Lodomeria-Halych, along with, perhaps, a group of Karaite settlers. The presence of this merchant community in the 13th century in Halych, located on an important trade route, seems, therefore, completely plausible.

A significantly more recent Karaite cluster was Kukeziv near Lviv, belonging to the Sobieski family, to which six Karaite families moved from Trakai in 1688. Favorable grants of privilege to the new settlement in 1692 from John III Sobieski induced three more families to move there, this time from Halych. The Kukeziv community ceased to exist in the early 19th century, when its members moved to Halych and Lutsk.

There is no doubt that the Karaites were one of the least numerous ethno-religious groups living in the old Commonwealth; defining precisely the extent and numbers of their settlement, however, presents many difficulties. Obstacles include the scarcity of preserved sources and their failure to distinguish between Karaites and Talmudist Jews, and even the occasional confusion of Karaites with Tatars. In view of the lack of precise religious information, the Old Testament names used by the Karaites do not allow us to establish whether we are dealing with representatives of Karaism or rabbinical Judaism. Furthermore, the Karaite population was characterized by substantial mobility, which, as has already been mentioned, played an essential role in the arrival of Karaites in the Commonwealth. While they lived in relatively compact clusters in Trakai, Halych, and Lutsk as late as the 16th century, they dispersed in subsequent centuries, settling in fairly small groups, families, or even individually in different localities, where their numbers and sometimes their very presence often went unnoted in the sources. Their numbers were reckoned in hundreds rather than in thousands. The historian Stefan Gąsiorowski estimates the total number of Karaites as of the Commonwealth's end at around 700 people, perhaps a little more. In the 17th and 18th centuries the Karaite population decreased significantly. In Lithuania, the plague epidemic that devastated the country in 1710 particularly contributed to this. The mournful elegy "Oyanhyn yuragim" (Awake, my heart) by Salomon of Pasvalys (1650–1715), commemorating plague victims, is sung to this day during prayers for the deceased at the cemetery on the occasion of the summer fast.

The legal status of Karaites in the Commonwealth was defined above all by privileges granted by the King and Grand Duke, which assured Karaites freedom to practice their religion (including the right to possess temples and cemeteries), the right to possess their own community organization and judiciary, and also to engage in trade and crafts. At the beginning of their presence in the Commonwealth, Karaites probably enjoyed the same rights as Jews. By virtue of a grant of privilege of Vytautas dated 24 June 1388 that referred to Jews living in the Grand Duchy, Trakai Karaites as well could freely conduct money lending; and when traveling on business, they were exempt from tolls other than those which they were obliged to pay as residents of their towns. They were also excluded from the jurisdiction of castle courts (*sądy starościńskie*) and were judged by their own magistrate; cases dealing with their most important matters were decided by the court of the *starosta* or even the Grand Duke. Their possessions, houses of prayer, and cemeteries were under the protection of the Grand Duke. Karaites alone were affected by another, extraordinarily important act; in 1441, Grand Duke Casimir Jagiellończyk granted Karaite residents of Trakai (described as "Trakai Jews") Magdeburg law. From then on, they had their own *wójt*, who answered only to the duke and his court; he administered the community and settled disputes among his coreligionists. By the same grant, the duke assigned Karaites half the income from the town scales and from wax melting. This grant was confirmed and sometimes also expanded by subsequent rulers: Aleksander Jagiellończyk in 1492, Sigismund I in 1507, Stefan Batory in 1579, and Władysław IV in 1646. In 1576, Karaites of Lutsk and other localities in Volhynia (along with the Jews) received from Stefan Batory a grant of privilege that assured them, among other things, their own judiciary and just treatment in case of a trial before the assistant voivode or *starosta*. A grant of privilege issued by the same king two years later included the Halych Karaites (again, along with the Jews).

The Karaite communities in Volhynia and Ruthenia were independent units, headed by a clergyman or *hazzan*. Not much information has survived as to their structure and activities. Population clusters in Lithuania were under the authority of the Trakai community, which was headed, as Magdeburg law provided, by a *wójt* who resided in Trakai, was elected by the community, and was directly answerable to the duke (later the king and his representative, the voivode). Among his duties were representing the community, settling disputes among his coreligionists, and collecting taxes (especially the poll tax). He was compensated for performing these duties with a pound of pepper from the bridge toll on Lake Galvė, threescore *grosz* from the town scales, and part of payments made to the court. All Karaites were to render him obedience. A dynasty of *wójts* of the Łobanos family is known to have administered the community for almost all of the 18ᵗʰ century.

The spiritual leadership of the community rested in the hands of the *hazzan*, who led prayers in the kenesa, saw to the observation of holy days, celebrated marriages, and officiated at funerals and at the ceremonies connected with circumcision. He was consulted for explanation and interpretation of Biblical law, and also took part in deliberations before the community court. The *hazzan*'s assistant was the so-called *shkolnik*, the steward of the kenesa, called the *shamash* in Hebrew, who, in addition to assisting in religious service and taking care of the temple, also filled the functions of court bailiff, community clerk, herald, and the like. The treasurer, *gabbai* in Hebrew, dealt with the finances of the larger communities.

The legislative, executive, and judicial authority was exercised in communities in Lithuania, as well as Volhynia and Ruthenia, by a board of several persons made up of the most respected members of the community, the so-called elders. It included the *hazzan* and his assistant by virtue of their office, and in Trakai, the *wójt* as well. In Trakai, the *wójt* also appointed committees, the so-called *kahalny*, whose task was to deal with

—
—

specific activities in the community (for example, collecting tolls or payments from the scales).

In Lithuania, conferences of community representatives were held to pass resolutions in matters of particular importance, including the choice of *wójt*. One of the first was held in 1553 in Trakai.

Karaite tradition says that the first occupation of the Karaites was warcraft. Until they were decimated by the 1710 plague mentioned earlier, they were required to produce two companies through recruitment of volunteers, one to serve as the castle guard in Trakai, the other in the service of the Radziwiłłs. The Orientalist Gustav Geringer, an envoy of the Swedish king Charles XI, writes of them in his account of his journey in Lithuania in 1690: "This nation is not very numerous, because from childhood they enlist for war." King John Casimir mentioned their military services in a 1665 grant authorizing them to rebuild a kenesa and a school in Trakai. The Karaites of Halych and Volhynia, in turn, served in the units of the Registered Cossacks.

The Karaites proved to be enterprising merchants, enjoying a reputation as sound and fair business partners. Liberties guaranteed by grants of privilege, as well as exemptions from duties and bridge tolls and also from the duties of providing transport, service in the fire brigade, and work on royal estates, enabled them to travel freely for business purposes throughout the country and also beyond its borders, to Silesia, Prussia, and the Netherlands. They also conducted business locally—from 1516, Karaite and Christian merchants from Trakai had the right to set up two-week markets twice a year. (The Kukeziv Karaites, horse traders, had a similar grant.) In 1646, King Władysław IV forbade Jews to live and do business in Trakai, and as a result, local merchants rid themselves of their most important competitors.

Extensive business contacts, constantly maintained ties with relatives from Crimea, and knowledge of the language made the Karaites effective intermediaries in the ransom of Polish prisoners of war from Tatar enslavement. As they themselves emphasized in a petition to the Four-Year Parliament (1788–1792), they also served the Commonwealth as interpreters, guides, and scouts during the wars with Turkey.

Besides trade, Karaites were employed in leasing taxes, land, and property (for example, ponds, fields, gardens, taverns, mills), and also lent money on interest and worked as pawnbrokers. They owned fields and other farmland, cultivated gardens, but began to engage in agriculture only in the 17th and 18th centuries. Karaite craftsmen offered their services as butchers, bakers, brewers, cobblers, and tailors, but as they were not allowed to belong to Christian guilds, they served mainly the needs of their own communities. There were barbers and doctors among them—the most famous was Ezra ha-Rofe, son of Nisan (ca. 1596–1666), the Radziwiłłs' doctor, who is said to have healed Maria Katarzyna, the alleged daughter of John Casimir. It is a noteworthy fact that the numerically small Karaite community produced a significant number of scholars, students of Scripture, and philosophers. A special place among them belongs to Isaac ben Abraham of Trakai (1533–1594), author of the work *Sefer Hizzuk Emunah* (Fortification of Faith), written in Hebrew and containing an apologia for the Mosaic faith and a critical analysis of the dogmas of Christianity. This work, first published only in 1621, was highly regarded by 18th-century freethinkers, including Voltaire himself.

The Karaites, immigrants from Crimea, found a second homeland in the Commonwealth, to which they remained loyal, serving it initially as soldiers, later doing their part, albeit small, as merchants for its economic development. Although they were few in number, surrounded by a foreign element, they were able to survive and preserve their faith, language, traditions, and customs intact. By virtue of privileges granted by Kings and Grand Dukes, they were assured the economic means of making a living, and guarantees of religious freedom allowed them to develop spiritually—the days of the old Commonwealth were a "golden age" for Karaite learning.

The partitions meant the end of an era also for the Karaites. The communities in Halych and Kukeziv were divided by the border from the communities in Lithuania and Volhynia, and Karaites lost the status they had enjoyed in the Commonwealth and were forced to make efforts to restore it. This induced them to seek an answer to the question "Who are we?" and as a result initiated the change that would occur during the next century, from a religious community to a nation.

Selected bibliography

Abkowicz, M., and Sulimowicz, A. (eds.), *Almanach karaimski 2007* [2007 Karaite Almanac], Wrocław: Bitik, 2007.

Abkowicz, M., and Jankowski, H. (eds.), *Karaj kiuńlari. Dziedzictwo narodu karaimskiego we współczesnej Europie* [Karaj Kiuńlari. The Heritage of the Karaite Nation in Contemporary Europe], with the collaboration of I. Jaroszyńska, Wrocław: Bitik, 2004.

Dubiński, A., *Caraimica. Prace karaimoznawcze* [Caraimica. Works on the Karaites], Warszawa: Wydawnictwo Akademickie Dialog, 1994.

Dubiński, A., and Śliwka, E. (eds.), *Karaimi. (Materiały z sesji naukowej)* [Karaites. (Materials from a Scholarly Session)], Pieniężno: Muzeum Misyjno-Etnograficzne, 1987.

Gąsiorowski, S., *Karaimi w Koronie i na Litwie w XV–XVIII wieku* [Karaites in the Crown and in Lithuania in the 15th–18th Centuries], Kraków–Budapeszt: Austeria, 2008.

Pełczyński, G., *Karaimi polscy* [Polish Karaites], Poznań: PTPN, 2004.

Pełczyński, G., *Najmniejsza mniejszość. Rzecz o Karaimach polskich* [The Smallest Minority. The Issue of Polish Karaites], Warszawa: Wydawnictwo Stanisław Kryciński, Towarzystwo Karpackie, 1995.

Szyszman, S., *Karaimizm. Doktryna i historia* [Karaite Judaism. History and Doctrine], Wrocław: Bitik, 2005.

Tyszkiewicz, J., *Tatarzy na Litwie i w Polsce. Studia z dziejów XIII–XVIII w.* [Tatars in Lithuania and in Poland. Studies from the History of the 13th–18th Centuries], Warszawa: PWN, 1989.

Zajączkowski, A., *Karaims in Poland. History. Language. Folklore. Science*, Warszawa: PWN, 1961.

GYPSIES — ROMANI

⤸

LECH MRÓZ

—

Gypsies—today most often called *Romowie* [Romani] in Poland—have been a constant element of the country's cultural and ethnic mosaic for six centuries. Their history is little known, however, and few scholars have taken an interest in it. What has attracted attention is the uniqueness and exoticism of the Gypsies, rather than their fortunes in the Commonwealth. It should be emphasized that the Gypsies themselves have never written their history—for centuries, they have been an essentially illiterate people. We must, therefore, recreate their history on the basis of sources created by non-Gypsies, and these are often superficial and biased.

The name *Rom, Romowie* has only been used for a decade or two as a term for the ethnic affiliation of these who historically appear as Gypsies. The milieu in which they live most often uses the terms *Cygan, Cyganie* [Gypsy, Gypsies] (and their equivalents in other languages, *Tsiganes*, *Zigeuner*, and other similar-sounding names). This term has been adopted also by the Romani themselves to the extent that many continue to use it in contact with non-Romani, using *Rom* in contacts within the group. Gypsies are not a uniform community and not all of them in Europe want to be called Romani, because they identify themselves with other names. In old documents they are designated with the term Gypsies; so, in order to avoid correcting the sources (in a situation where we do not know what identification was used by those to whom the documents refer), I consider it justifiable to use the word Gypsies rather than replace it mechanically with the word Romani (even if current political correctness would demand it).

Sources from southern Europe note the presence of Gypsies, also called Egyptians, as early as the second half of the 14th century. Their ancestors had come from India several centuries earlier. When that took place, however, is the subject of dispute among scholars. The oldest mention in Poland is an entry from 1401 in the official records of Kazimierz, now a section of Kraków. The entry tells us that a certain Mikołaj Czigan paid a tax, probably for land leased in Kazimierz, where he probably lived at the time (*Acta consul. Casimir.*, book IV, p. 548, State Archives in Kraków, Section III, signature K 4). We do not know where this Mikołaj came from, but we may suppose it was from the south, from Hungary. The situation was surely the same for Piotr Cygan, who is mentioned in an entry in the books of the city of Lviv from April 1405. Piotr Cygan lived in the most stately part of town, in the Market Square; several entries from subsequent years note that he paid his taxes ([*Leopol.*] *Percepta et expisita civitatis*, 1401–1414, page 55ff., TSDIAL [Central State Historical Archives of Ukraine, Lviv], signature F.52, o. 2, no. 695).

The oldest records in Kazimierz also mention several times a certain Andrzej Cygan, who provided the royal court at Wawel with transport service. This Andrzej Cygan must have been a reliable man, because his services were used often over several years. For example, on 25 April 1419, he was sent with a letter of the king to Wieliczka, and on 17 May of that year "with letters of the queen to the king, in a carriage drawn by two horses, to Wieliczka" (*Acta consul. Casimir.*, *1416–1431*, book II, p. 56v, Jagiellonian Library, Manuscript Section, Kraków, signature 1045/ II). A person carrying royal letters, the correspondence of Elżbieta and Władysław Jagiełło, must have been trusted and worthy.

In the Sanok records for the years 1423–1462 and in the Kraków records from the middle of the century, there are particularly intriguing mentions of Mikołaj Cygan, described as *pallatinus sanocensis*, "voivode of Sanok," and Jan Cygan, *"wójt* of Sandomierz" *(Terr. Sanoc., 1423–1462,* pp. 63–64, TSDIAL, signature F.16, o. 1, no. 1; *Terr. Crac.,* vol. 151, p. 49, State Archives in Kraków, Section I). Holding office and ruling on disputes or charges indicates that Mikołaj Cygan probably belonged to the noble class. The office of *wójt* was even more significant, and Jan Cygan must have been among the eminent figures of Sandomierz, both in terms of property and authority.

Our knowledge of the history of Gypsies in Poland is meager. The picture that emerges from these old documents, however, does not fit with the image that later sources have passed down to us. The oldest records show Gypsies as people who had settled down and become assimilated with the local populace. So these first Gypsies in the Commonwealth were neither poor vagrants nor suspicious persons. Much indicates that they enjoyed trust and belonged to the affluent. Wandering is not mentioned in documents until the 16th century. In these oldest records, the word "Gypsy" is a term of identification, like "Armenian," "Ruthenian," or "Jew." It was most certainly not a word with a pejorative meaning.

Not long after they arrived in the towns of southern Poland, Gypsies began to move to central Poland. This is shown by information from Mazovia, dated 27 October 1427, that tells of the sale of land by Jan, called Cygan *(Metr. Kor.,* Vol. 333, k. 77v, Central Archives of Historical Records, Warsaw).

The geographical distribution of the oldest information allows us to assume that they had come from Hungary, where their presence was noted a dozen or more years earlier.

In the countries of Western Europe, unlike in the Commonwealth, nomadic Gypsies had begun to appear by the early 15th century, moving in groups numbering sometimes several dozen people. The appearance of such large groups sometimes led to conflicts between the newcomers and the local population. The turn of the 15th and 16th centuries, especially

—
177
—

the years of the rule of Emperor Maximilian I, was a time when a number of laws were issued against the Gypsies. As a result, many of them fled repression and headed eastward.

It is not known exactly when the first nomadic Gypsies appeared in the Commonwealth; it is curious that the oldest known documents refer to the territory of the Grand Duchy of Lithuania. It appears they were not treated there as odd and suspicious vagabond strangers, but rather as people with certain skills, mainly connected with horses. From the mid-16th century on, horse trading became the Gypsies' specialty in the Grand Duchy of Lithuania.

For the first time, also, accusations are noted of Gypsies practicing thievery, mainly stealing horses; telling fortunes for a living is also mentioned. In the official records of Kraków from 1564 there is the following entry: "Jadwiga Cyganka [...] testified that Gypsies make a living by telling fortunes, stealing, and trading horses" (*Cas. Act. Malef., 1548–1610*, p. 66, State Archives in Kraków, Section III, signature K 266). There is an interesting report of an investigation from 1577, from the Sanok records, regarding Jan Cygan (*Testam. Furtum Castr. Sanoc.*, Vol. 448, p. 106, TSDIAL, signature F. 15, o. 1, no. 448). He is reported to have been helped in his thievery by non-Gypsies, including local nobility. That is important information, for sometimes it turns out that non-Gypsies had a part in Gypsy offenses; all the blame, however, usually fell on the Gypsies.

Of all the 16th-century documents, a unique piece of evidence of the earliest history of Gypsies in the Commonwealth is an entry on a case dated 8 February 1595, registered in the official records of Minsk (today, the capital of Belarus). This document proves that settled Gypsies formed communities that resolved even serious disputes within the group, according to their own laws; but they must have also recognized the law of the state or local laws, since the decision of their own Gypsy court was entered into the records of the Minsk castle. From the contents of the court entry we learn that on 20 May 1594, in the village of Jarsze-wice, Aleksander Matysowicz, Gypsy, servant of the voivode of Vilnius, Krzysztof Radziwiłł, entered a charge "before all the lords, his brother Gypsies," against his own servant, Kasper Marcinowicz, a Gypsy, of caus-ing a brawl, during the course of which the complainant's wife was injured, and she died as a result. From a further fragment, it turns out that the assembled Gypsies heard the charge, and because the accused denied it, the court decided that the accused had to swear an oath that he had not committed the deed with which he was charged. He defaulted, however; and so the court ruled, "We condemn this Kasper Marcinowicz to death according to the judgment and decree of all our brothers" (*Akty izdavae-mye Vilenskoiu Arkheograficheskoiu Kommisseiu*, Vol. 18, Vilna 1891, pp. 129–130).

Little is known about the internal affairs of Gypsy communities. The above entry is an exceptional document. It shows that before a case was entered in the castle records, it was decided by a Gypsy court. To this day, an oath is an important element in settling disputes and arriving at the truth within groups of Gypsies; and to this day, there is a strong belief in its effectiveness, and also a conviction of the punishment that will befall perjurers.

The most original and complete set of documents regarding a nomadic group in the lands of the Commonwealth and adjacent territory is the set of records connected with the name Piotr of Rotemberg, a knight, a count, a Philistine from Little Egypt—that is how he is named in the documents. It is a unique collection; today it is in Berlin, in the set of doc-uments saved from Königsberg (Kaliningrad) before the Soviet army en-tered. Thanks to these letters, we can follow the wanderings of a group over a period of 19 years and hundreds of kilometers. The collection of documents dates from 1542–1561 and numbers 25 letters. They are all basically letters of reference, but we learn a great deal about the group itself.

—
179
—

The Assimilated

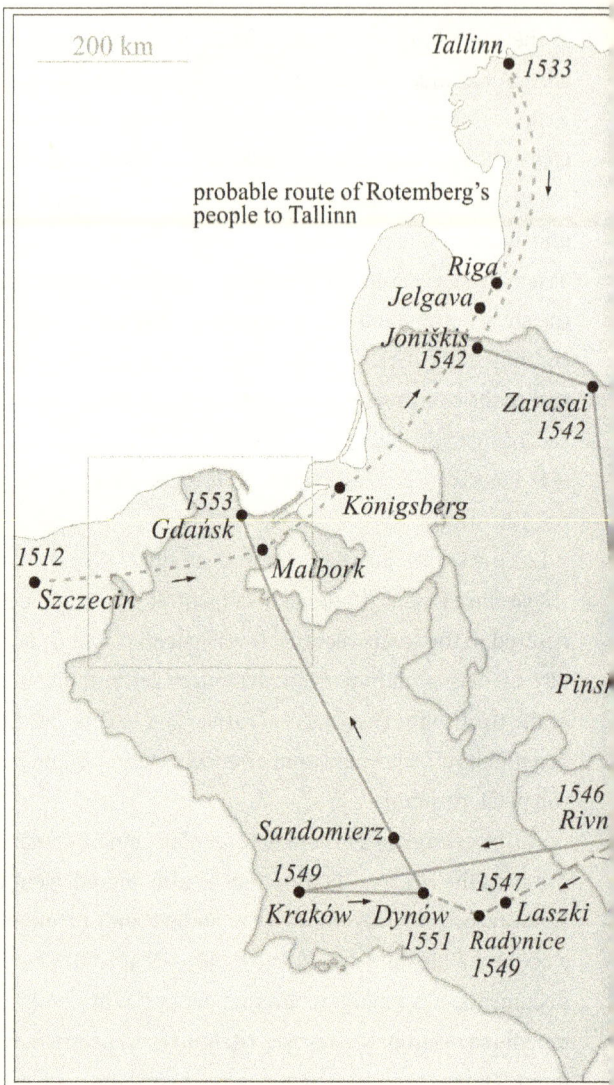

200 km

Tallinn
● 1533

probable route of Rotemberg's
people to Tallinn

Riga
●
Jelgava ●
Joniškis ●
1542
Zarasai
1542

1553   Königsberg
Gdańsk ●
1512   Malbork
●
Szczecin

Pinsk

1546
Rivne

Sandomierz ●
1549   1547
Kraków ● → Dynów   ● Laszki
1551   Radynice
1549

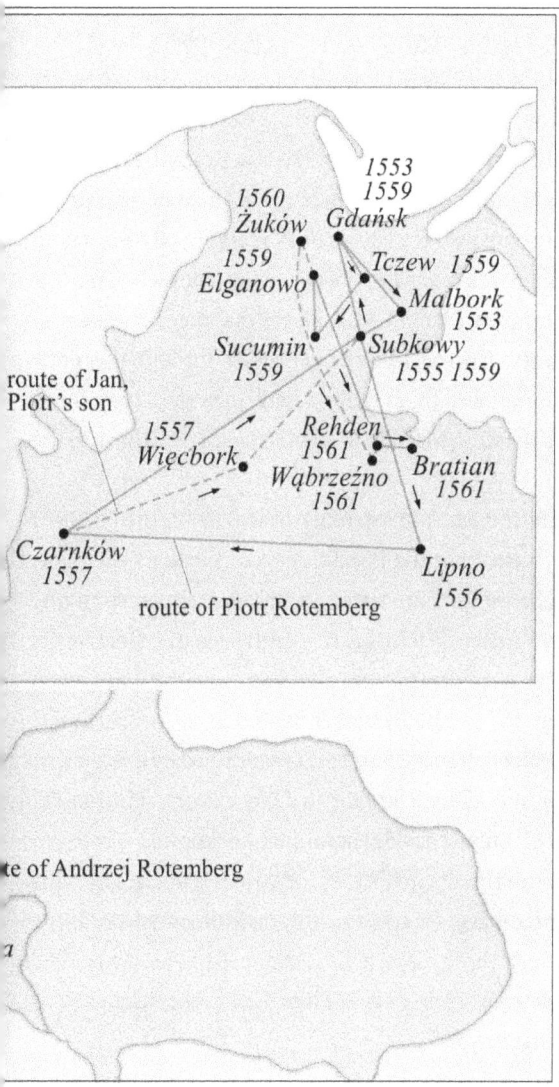

1553
1559
1560
Żuków
Gdańsk

1559
Elganowo
Tczew 1559

Malbork
1553

Sucumin
1559
Subkowy
1555 1559

route of Jan,
Piotr's son

1557
Więcbork
Rehden
1561
Wąbrzeźno
1561
Bratian
1561

Czarnków
1557
Lipno
1556

route of Piotr Rotemberg

te of Andrzej Rotemberg

—

Map 11: The wanderings of Piotr
Rotemberg's group.

The oldest preserved letter regarding Piotr of Rotemberg dates from 1542 and was written in Joniškis (near today's Lithuania-Latvia border), which means the group must have arrived in the Commonwealth much earlier. The last document was drawn up in 1561, in Bratian, Pomerania. The dates and places of their composition present a map of the wanderings of Piotr and his group over the course of 19 years. To be sure, it is an incomplete map—there are many gaps between the dates when individual documents were drawn. Nonetheless, we see that they covered a sizable area of the country. The trail leads from Prussia, through the northern lands of the Commonwealth, to today's Latvian border, then south to Podolia, and on to the west, to Kraków, and then once more back to the east and north.

The first document is a letter of reference drawn up on the bishop's estate—the writer states that the Philistine from Little Egypt, Piotr Rotemberg, "has behaved well, modestly, openly, and virtuously among the inhabitants and subjects." Joniškis was famous at one time for its fairs, to which horses were driven from afar. Fairs and the dates when they took place seem to have had an essential influence on the choice of path by Piotr of Rotemberg's group. This is confirmed by a letter written three years later in Podolia, Ukraine, in a place over a thousand kilometers away. On 14 August 1545, Hieronim Lanckoroński, *starosta* of Skala in Podolia (on the Zbruch River, today in Ukraine), gave this letter to Piotr of Rotemberg. Piotr is not only "a Philistine from Little Egypt"; in the course of three years he has advanced to the status of noble-born. The Lanckoroński letter says of him "nobly born Count Piotr of Rotemberg, of Little Egypt."

The Lanckoroński letter seems to indicate that even at that time, trade (above all, horse-trading) was already an important and profitable occupation for Gypsies. The document was drawn up on the eve of the Feast of the Assumption of the Blessed Virgin Mary; and on the day of the Feast itself, a great fair was held in Skala. The appearance of Piotr and his group in Skala at this time, just as earlier in Joniškis, was certainly no coincidence; most clearly, a great fair and the opportunity for trade were essential in establishing the route of this group's migrations.

We see that by that time, two categories of Gypsies had already emerged. The first consisted of settled individuals and families of descendants of former immigrants; these are designated with the name "Gypsies." The second was made of groups migrating from the west and south who arrived in the 16th century; these are distinguished from the former with the name "Philistines" or "immigrants from Little Egypt."

The word "Philistines" makes it easy to understand the dislike for them, which was not uncommon. It appears in Poland as a name for the Gypsies in the mid-16th century, along with the arrival of the nomadic groups. The Philistines were a non-Semitic people, and armed conflict between them and Jews was frequent. Philistines were foreigners, wanderers, the *Practical Biblical Dictionary* explains. Whereas no hidden, negative associations adhered to the name "Gypsies," the description "Philistines" emphasizes the nomadic character of the group, its foreignness.

—

183

—

Toward the end of that century, there was also migration from the direction of Wallachia. The appearance of Wallachian Gypsies (one may perhaps call them by the name "Romani") became a cause for conflict between them and the Hungarian, Polish, and Lithuanian Gypsies who had already settled down. This is important information that tells us indirectly of the diversity and feeling of separateness of the Gypsy groups. Such descriptions as Wallachian, Hungarian, Lithuanian, and Polish Gypsies show that settlement in different countries had influenced the way they described themselves.

The term Roma, so common today, appears in documents for the first time in 1642. On April 30th of that year, an entry was made in the records of the Lviv city hall about a conflict between Stanisław Gorczyca and Paweł Rom; Gorczyca demanded the return of 20 złotys owed him by Hrycko Cyganik, the stepfather of Paweł Rom (*Protocolli Actorum*

Officii Aduocat Leopol., 1640–1643, p. 1494, TSDIAL, signature F. 52, o. 2, no. 459). This entry is extremely important for the history of Gypsies in Poland. There can be no doubt that the similarity of the words is not coincidental. The word *Rom* is connected with the *Cyganie* or Gypsies—and the stepfather of Paweł Rom is Hrycko Cyganik. We cannot say that a Romani ethnic awareness had already formed and that they had intentionally begun to use this self-description. On the other hand, we have a clear signal that the word *Rom* is applied for identification purposes and definition of affiliation.

In documents from the 17th century we find more than a dozen entries regarding disputes among Gypsies. Through them, we learn of relations among groups. A letter written on the 25th of May 1694 by authorities of the city of Kovel (currently in northern Ukraine) to the authorities of various levels in royal cities informs us that the Wallachian Gypsies Hryhor and Vasyl Mityga made accusations against the Hungarian Gypsies Matyi, Arseni, and others, who had attacked them on a forest road and robbed them. The documents mention among the stolen goods "tools and vessels for the crafts of coppersmiths and smiths" (*Et.-Min., 110b*, no. 2, p. 15, GStAPK Berlng). We have no doubt, therefore, that the professions of smith and coppersmith, the making of gear that they surely traded at fairs and sold at manors along the road, were their specialties, occupations that supported them and were the basis of their prosperity. The Mitygas were Wallachian Gypsies and lived in a family group. This is indicated by the repetition in the documents of the names of three brothers, and also information that three carts had been stolen from them. One may conclude from this that they traveled with their families, and each family had one cart, a horse, and gear at its disposal—but they lived, worked, and traveled together.

From almost the first years when they appeared in Central and Western Europe, we find references to their exhibiting trained bears, snakes, and also monkeys. In some countries, the term "bear-trainer" became

—
184
—

a synonym for "Gypsy." Activities connected with metalworking were also generally associated with Gypsies. Beginning with the 15th century and the appearance of Gypsies in Central Europe, wandering became inseparably bound with their image. Descriptions and iconographic images illustrate the penitential character of Gypsy life—the stick in hand and shells adorning their clothes (hat or some other item) confirm their pilgrim condition.

In Renaissance Europe, the image of the Gypsies becomes more and more unfavorable. It is precisely then that laws and repression against the Gypsies intensified in many countries of Western Europe. The Commonwealth was the natural direction of escape, especially since laws there had not yet been directed against Gypsies. It was not long, however, before the first bill in Poland directed against the Gypsies was passed. *Statuta Seymu Warszawskiego, Roku Pańskiego 1557* decreed, "Gypsies, or unwanted people, will be summoned from the land by us, and thenceforth they will not be allowed into it any more" (*Volumina Legum*, II. p. 13). Much as in Western Europe, an attempt was made to solve the problem of wanderers by driving them out. The resolution of the Warsaw parliament was not heeded, and the Piotrków parliament returned to the matter of Gypsies in 1565, declaring "There are to be no Gypsies in the Crown" and forbidding anyone to give them shelter (*Volumina Legum*, II, p. 52).

It appears there must have been charges of ignoring the law; the fact that the matter of the Gypsies and hiding them was raised again seems to attest to it. The Warsaw parliament convened in the spring of 1578 declared that those giving shelter to Gypsies would be judged as their accomplices (*Volumina Legum*, II, p. 187). The application of this provision of the 1578 parliament sometimes led to accusations and conflicts, as voices began to be raised demanding the act be repealed. Protests came from the nobles of Podlasie, and a dozen or so years later, the enforcement of this law was suspended in regard to that region. We do not know the causes of the exception. We can only surmise various forms of cooperation and

—

185

—

economic links existed—such as using the services of Gypsy craftsmen, and trade in animals, especially horses—because the delegates to the 1607 general parliament recognized the legitimacy of exempting Podlasie province from the obligations of this law.

The fact that numerous Gypsies lived in the Grand Duchy of Lithuania seems to prove that the regulation expelling Gypsies was not rigorously observed there, and the universal tax proclamation of 1589 obligated Gypsies in the Grand Duchy of Lithuania to pay tax, and also set its size (*Volumina Legum*, II, p. 298). The law of the time may probably be understood as requiring those Gypsies who led the life of vagrants to leave the Grand Duchy of Lithuania, but not those who settled down or moved around after having gained permission to do so and were engaged in some sort of occupation (for instance, crafts or trade); those were required to pay tax.

As was already mentioned, hostile attitudes toward Gypsies intensified in almost all of Europe in the 16th century, and the law became more and more repressive. The goal was usually to drive Gypsies out, less often to make them settle down. One of the few ideas going beyond that scheme consisted in attempts to designate a supervisor of Gypsies. In Western Europe, this idea was never widely implemented. In the Commonwealth, on the other hand, plans to appoint a supervisor over the Gypsies and attempts to manage things with his help were carried out from the time of King John Casimir, and perhaps even Władysław IV. The first known document designating a supervisor of the Gypsies in the Commonwealth dates from 1652. On August 12th in Warsaw, the royal chancellery issued a letter of privilege for Matiasz Karolowicz, appointing him to "the office of seniority over all Gypsies who [...] are or will be in the Crown and the states subject to it, with all prerogatives, revenues, and benefits" (*Castr. Sanoc. Ind. Rel.*, vol. 165, pp. 1191–1193, TSDIAL, signature F. 15, o. 1, no. 165). Ten years after the privilege for Karolowicz, in October 1662, John Casimir entrusted "seniority over Gypsies both in the Crown and in Lithuania [...] to the nobly-born Sebastian Gałęzowski" (*Sigillata*, vol.

—

186

—

5, k. 130v, Central Archives of Historical Records, Warsaw). From that time on, those appointed to the office of supervisor of the Gypsies were of noble status.

Some years later, King John III Sobieski granted the privilege of seniority over the Gypsies to Stanisław Węgłowski, nobleman, for "continual military services." The appointment of a new supervisor over those who were described in the act as "the wandering people of the Gypsy nation" bears the date 10 July 1682. In the document there is also a royal order that representatives of city and other authorities were not to cause any difficulties, "and that the Gypsies render him that obedience and duties they owe him of old" (*Castr. Crac. Rel.*, vol. 116, pp. 1015-1018, State Archives in Kraków, Dept. I). For the first time, the statement appears in this grant that the supervisor's duty is to care for the Gypsies and protect them from harm; before, only protecting the non-Gypsy populace was mentioned. One may judge that King John III treated the institution of Gypsy supervisor as an important element of internal policy.

After the death of John III Sobieski, Augustus II was elected king. In December 1697, at the beginning of his long reign, Augustus II granted the privilege of "kingship over the Gypsies" to Łukasz Michał Iwaszkiewicz. The appointment was a reward for services rendered during the election, for Iwaszkiewicz was among those who elected Augustus II to the kingship, and also in view of Iwaszkiewicz's "deteriorating fortune" (*Lit. Metr., e. h. 149,* part 4, pp. 468–469, Lithuanian State Historical Archives, Vilnius). In September 1705, Augustus II appointed a new Gypsy supervisor, Bonawentura Jan Wiera. The document states that Wiera has the right to judge and punish, to appoint his own assistants, judges, and lower-level supervisors, and to see to law and order among the Gypsies, especially during fairs. The institution of elder becomes increasingly important, and the Gypsy supervisor gains a broader scope for his powers; in the grant of privilege, tributes and revenues due to him are also mentioned (*Castr. Sanoc. Ind. Rel.*, vol. 209, pp. 2096–2098, TSDIAL, signature F. 15, o. 1, no. 209).

—
187
—

Augustus issued at least six grants of privilege for the supervisor of the Gypsies. From the time of John III Sobieski on, appointment to that office was treated as a reward for services rendered. Connected with it was the power to collect taxes and thereby hope of enrichment and of improving the condition of "deteriorating fortune"—as it was put in Augustus II's appointment of Łukasz Michał Iwaszkiewicz.

The last known ruler of the Gypsies was Jakub Znamierowski, a landowner from the district of Lida. Stanisław August Poniatowski granted him the privilege of supervision over the Gypsies on 17 August 1780. More is known about the figure of this king of the Gypsies; we know that Znamierowski maintained close contacts with the Gypsies, and traded horses with them. Intimacy and common interests with the Gypsies may prove that King Stanisław August placed the office of supervisor in the right hands. Znamierowski had a relatively long rule, until his death in 1795. That was also the last year of Stanisław August Poniatowski's reign and the year of the Commonwealth's downfall. With the death of Znamierowski ended a program, carried out with exceptional consistency, of subordinating the Gypsies to royal authority and to the rules governing the whole society.

Eighteenth-century records clearly show deepening conflict and increasing distance between Gypsies and the rest of society. Charges against the Gypsies predominate in the documents. This is a surprising change when compared with the tenor of earlier documents, and does not necessarily prove a drastic increase in Gypsy criminality, but rather a clear change in attitude toward them and increased distance between the two communities. Trade contacts between Gypsies and non-Gypsies become more rare; there is no more mention of the situation, not uncommon earlier, when Gypsies turned to non-Gypsy institutions with their affairs, requesting a fair decision and verdict. Increasingly, Gypsies and non-Gypsies began to form clearly separate worlds that were more and more unfriendly toward each other.

Almost all the charges of giving Gypsies hospitality or keeping them on private estates refer to the minor nobility, leaseholders, or owners of one small village. There are, however, many documents which suggest that Gypsies were permanent residents on large private estates in the eastern territories of the Commonwealth. One may get the impression that in those areas, the law's provisions were carried out less rigorously, and the owners of large estates, including those owned by the Church, established their own rules regulating the presence of Gypsies there.

Gypsies probably moved all over the Commonwealth. Only in the eastern regions of the state, however, did they lead settled lives—many lived in towns, and other inhabitants engaged in trade with them, entered into all kinds of contacts, lent them money—in other words, they enjoyed some trust. We know that Gypsies lived permanently on the estates of the Potockis in Podolia; they were also on the properties of the Sanguszkos. Only on the Radziwiłł estates, however, did they form a sizable community and find especially favorable conditions.

The permanent presence of rather large groups of Gypsies, moving to and between fairs and settling down, demanded regulations for how Gypsies were to function on large private properties. For that reason, the owners of some private estates named their own Gypsy supervisors independently of the persons appointed by the king.

A document issued in Iziaslav in January 1727 shows that we are dealing with two different communities living side by side, and not a random group of people: "I give this my charter to the Polish and Wallachian Gypsies; I appoint Bazyli Mikołajewicz *wójt* over the Polish Gypsies, and over the Wallachian Gypsies, Baran of the Gypsy nation" (*Arch. Sanguszków*, manuscript 441/4, p. 319, State Archives in Kraków, Dept. I). This passage is especially significant: "whom I allow to bring Gypsies from everywhere and to settle them in the suburb of Starokostiantyniv." This is an incentive for settlement. The author of the document was most expressly interested in having Gypsies live on his estates. Five years later, in 1732, Paweł Karol Sanguszko named Bartosz Aleksandrowicz supervisor of the Gypsies on his estates in Iziaslav and Starokostiantyniv *(Arch. Sanguszków*, doc. No. 305, State Archives in Kraków, Dept. I). Aleksandrowicz's jurisdiction covered a sizable area, as the towns of Iziaslav and Starokostiantyniv were both under him, and they are separated by over 60 km. The newly-appointed *wójt* was also to see to it that Gypsies did not commit any crimes, either on the Sanguszko estates or beyond them. Like other inhabitants, they were obligated to pay taxes, which it was Aleksandrowicz's duty to collect.

We know more about the Gypsies on the Lithuanian estates of the Radziwiłłs. Documents show that they had the rights due to other subjects, were not treated as a disruptive underclass, and had their own supervisors. It is not clear what caused so many Gypsies to live in the Grand Duchy of Lithuania, many of them non-nomadic; and their stabilization had all the hallmarks of people having settled down and settled into the life generally accepted as proper for middle-class craftsmen. On the Radziwiłł estates, this state of affairs lasted at least until the early 19th century.

The institution of Gypsy supervisor in the town of Mir (now in western Belarus) appointed by the Radziwiłłs persisted until the early 18th century. Documents from 1719 prove that; they are letters signed by the Mir townsman "Józef Marcinkiewicz, Gypsy Elder, with his company" *(Arch. Radziwiłłów*, section XXIII, vol. 150, and section XXIII, file 92 (Mir 3), Central Archives of Historical Records, Warsaw).

We do not known when the Marcinkiewiczes settled in Mir; it may have been as early as the 17th century. A particularly important record connected with the Gypsies on the Radziwiłł estates is the so-called letter of protection issued at the castle in Niasvizh in 1778 by Karol Stanisław Radziwiłł: "I take Jan Marcinkiewicz, Gypsy elder, townsman and citizen of my city of Mir, with all his company settled and having their homes in that same city, under my protection as my own townsmen and subjects"

(*Arch. Radziwiłłów*, section XXIII, file 92 (Mir 3), Central Archives of Historical Records, Warsaw).

This raises the question, how was it possible to support Gypsies so openly, when, formally speaking, the law that required their expulsion and forbade giving them shelter was still in force? An analysis of further cases leads to the conclusion that the law in the Commonwealth was directed chiefly against the wandering groups, the Philistines, as they were often called; the law was not applied in cases involving families or small groups that had settled down (and there were many of those). In the case under discussion here, the matter is obvious—Gypsies from Mir, the Marcinkiewiczes, were settled people; at the same time, there is no doubt as to their ethnic affiliation—perhaps they maintained contacts with nomads, perhaps their means of earning a living was the same as that of other Gypsies on Radziwiłł estates. In any case, the phrase referring to Marcinkiewicz's company leaves no doubt that we are dealing with a settled, organized group that had its own leader.

A sentence crucial to the importance of the office and to Marcinkiewicz himself appears in the final part of the letter: "I permit the said Jan Marcinkiewicz to punish criminals and to bar those not settled in our towns from doing business at fairs and markets, except with the permission of the Gypsy elder, Jan Marcinkiewicz, townsman and citizen of my city of Mir." This is factual confirmation of Jan Marcinkiewicz's sovereignty over Gypsies on the Radziwiłł estates.

More famous than Mir was Smarhoń (now in Belarus), known for the Bears' Academy, a training school from which bear-trainers set forth to wander many countries of Europe. The Academy in Smarhoń was not the Gypsies' idea; it was one of the schools training bears in the Lithuanian and Ruthenian lands of the old Commonwealth. It may have been Karol Radziwiłł who first settled Gypsies there and put the school under the administration of Jan Marcinkiewicz, the Gypsy supervisor of Mir. Bears were trained mainly for the needs of the Radziwiłłs' court in Niasvizh.

—
191
—

The Assimilated

The most interesting descriptions of the school and its training methods date only from the first quarter of the 19th century—the time when the Academy probably had its heyday. It is from this period that we know descriptions of the rides Karol Radziwiłł formerly took in a carriage drawn by four bears. The end of the Academy came with the November Uprising and the confiscation of the Smarhoń estate by the Russian authorities.

Documents show that the Sanguszkos and Radziwiłłs carried out a deliberate policy toward the Gypsies, threatening only swindlers and thieves with punishment, but taking under their protection those who lived peacefully. The mystery of the sizable number of Gypsies living in the Lithuanian-Ruthenian lands of the old Commonwealth is probably due in large part to this.

Selected bibliography

Broda, J., "Przywileje nominacyjne na króla cygańskiego w Polsce z 1731 r. i na wójtostwo cygańskie z 1732 r." [Grants of Privilege Appointing the King of the Gypsies in Poland in 1731 and the Gypsy Wójt in 1732], *Czasopismo Prawno-Historyczne*, vol. 3 (1951), pp. 346–356.

Czacki, T., *O Cyganach* [About the Gypsies], vol. 3, Poznań, 1845.

Daniłowicz, I., *O Cyganach wiadomość historyczna* [Historical Information about the Gypsies], Wilno, 1824.

Ficowski, J., *Cyganie na polskich drogach* [Gypsies on Polish Roads], Kraków: Wydawnictwo Literackie, 1985.

Geremek, B., "Cyganie w Europie średniowiecznej i nowożytnej" [Gypsies in Medieval and Modern Europe], *Przegląd Historyczny*, vol. 75 (1984), pp. 569–594.

Gluziński, J., "Król cygański i Akademia Niedźwiedzia" [King of the Gypsies and the Bears' Academy], in *Kalendarz Polski Ilustrowany J. Jaworskiego* [J. Jaworski's Illustrated Polish Calendar], Warszawa, 1867.

Modelski, T. E., "Przywilej na starszeństwo cygańskie z r. 1703" [Grant of Privilege of Seniority over the Gypsies from 1703], *Ateneum Wileńskie*, 1929, pp. 583–588.

Mróz, L., *Dzieje Cyganów–Romów w Rzeczpospolitej, xv–xviii* [History of the Gypsies—Romani in the Commonwealth, 15th–18th Centuries], Warszawa: DiG, 2001.

Mróz, L., *Od Cyganów do Romów. Z Indii do Unii Europejskiej* [From Gypsies to Romani. From India to the European Union], Warszawa: DiG, 2007.

Narbutt, T., *Rys historyczny ludu cygańskiego* [Historical Sketch of the Gypsy People], Wilno: A. Marcinkowski, 1830.

Prochaska, A., "Przywileje dla cygańskiej starszyzny w Polsce" [Privileges for the Gypsy Elders in Poland], *Kwartalnik Historyczny*, vol. 14 (1900), pp. 453–457.

THE

NEWCOMERS

ITALIANS

‹ß›

WOJCIECH TYGIELSKI

—

"Italian colonies, especially the one in Kraków, were among the wealthiest; in addition to merchants and craftsmen, one quite often encountered representatives of the intelligentsia of the time: doctors and pharmacists, architects, and men of letters. At the lords' courts in the 16th and 17th centuries, the painter, musician, or *kawalkator* (horse trainer) was most often an Italian." These words of Janusz Tazbir aptly describe the most important fields of Italian activity, and at the same time, contain an essential indication of their character as "intelligentsia." The activity of many of the representatives of this ethnic group in the structures of Old Polish society was in fact associated with high intellectual and professional qualifications.

There is no question that in early modern times, newcomers from Italy were a foreign group whose representatives exerted a noticeable influence on the reality of our country. One may even say that Italians in the Commonwealth were model foreigners: coming from far away, different in culture—language, customs, and civilizational background—working and settling in select, identifiable locations, and sometimes even, as in Kraków and Lviv, forming separate clusters.

Italians arrived in the territory of the Polish state as early as the Middle Ages; at that time, however, as far as it is possible to judge on the basis of preserved sources, this phenomenon was individual in nature, even insofar as the missionary activity of the Catholic clergy is concerned. The arrival of Italians in the Commonwealth became a relatively large-scale phenomenon—although there are essentially no sources that allow us to quantify this—in the 16th and 17th centuries. This occurred at the same time that foreign travel, including first and foremost Italian towns, manors, and universities, became an important element of the education of elite young Poles. A flow of people, and therefore also of the ideas they subscribed to or the exemplars they endorsed, took place in both directions.

In a later period, beginning in the late 17th century, the phenomenon gradually lost its intensity, and in the 19th and 20th centuries—much as in ancient times—it took on the dimension of individual decisions to migrate or stay of no great social or economic consequence.

In the early modern period, however, we are dealing both with the apogee of the phenomenon and with the greatest richness of its variants. Italian newcomers are led by different motives, and also present various strategies in terms of their length of stay—from one or several trips on business, through attempts at installing themselves in the Commonwealth for a lengthy period but with the prospect of return, to clearly formulated and effectively realized plans of emigration.

Italians sought in the east outlets for their goods, mainly silk fabrics as well as wines and spices. This phenomenon had already existed in the Middle Ages, but in modern times its intensity increased, because the purchasing power of the Polish consumer rose markedly, and demand for the goods offered along with it. Italian entrepreneurs attempted to do business in Poland as early as the 14th and 15th centuries, leasing duties and tolls and investing their capital as well as their technical and organizational skills in extracting minerals, salt, and lead, as well as the manufacture of glass. Branches of Italian banks, mainly those of Florence and Venice, offered the first banking services in Polish territory. Somewhat later, Italians (Prospero Provana and the Montelupi family) organized the first regular postal system, which connected the most important urban

—
198
—

centers of the Commonwealth with Kraków, and Kraków, by way of Vienna, with Venice.

In the second half of the 17th century, the activities of Italian entrepreneurs expanded to leasing the Crown and Lithuanian mints, which meant obtaining lucrative contracts to mint local coins. Most efficient in this field was Tito Livio Burattini, a merchant, scholar, and journalist combined in one person, who was supported—at least in the initial phase—by Paolo Del Buono, a man of no less versatile interests, thoroughly educated in the fields of physics and mechanics. Also interested in minting was Girolamo Pinocci, the royal secretary, of whom we will speak later. This activity, which was widely associated with the underhanded dealings of "spoiling money," that is, illegally lowering its metal content, was widely criticized and contributed greatly to the deterioration of the image of Italians in influential social circles.

Throughout the period of interest to us Italian artists and craftsmen also came to Poland, foremost among them architects and builders who had received excellent education in Italy but then found no commissions there and came seeking employment in building or rebuilding royal and magnate residences, town halls, and numerous churches. Among the most eminent—and in this field the Italians were unrivalled—was undoubtedly Bartolomeo Berrecci, the creator of Sigismund's Chapel. But in addition to him, one may also mention—by way of example, since this was a group both numerous and varied—Santi Gucci, the architect of, among others, the castles in Łobzów and Baranów, and the famous tomb of Stefan Batory in Wawel; Bernardo Morando, active somewhat later, who worked in Warsaw and Lviv but went down in history associated with a single, unique creation, the building of Zamość (*la città ideale*), commissioned by chancellor Jan Zamoyski; Giovanni Trevano, who rebuilt Wawel Castle after the fire in 1595; and Matteo Castello, who is said to have given final form to the famous Kraków church of Sts. Peter and Paul, partly modelled on the Jesuit *Il Gesù* in Rome, and who later worked in Warsaw

—
199
—

(the Royal Castle, the Ujazdów Castle, *Villa Regia*—the palace later called Kazimierzowski) and in Vilnius (St. Casimir Chapel).

At the royal court, at least from the time of Sigismund III, and also at many magnates' courts, one could encounter Italian musicians, singers and instrumentalists specially brought from Italy and well compensated (Luca Marenzio, Asprilio Pacelli, Marco Scacchi). Also among the Italian "export" specialties was theater, especially opera, in fashion in the 17th and 18th centuries, whose devotees included a series of rulers, beginning with Władysław IV (benefitting from royal patronage were, among others, Virgilio Puccitelli and Agostino Locci, whose specialized in scenography). Among court painters, the names most often mentioned are Bernardo Bellotto Canaletto and Marcello Bacciarelli, who belonged to the artistic entourage of Stanisław August Poniatowski. One should also remember that their famous predecessor was the best known court painter of the Vasas, Tommaso Dolabella.

Italian immigrants also offered high professional skills in many fields, beginning with the sphere of intellect and spirituality. We find Italians among the professors of the Academy of Kraków; the poet and humanist Filippo Buonaccorsi, called Callimachus or Kallimach, held the prestigious position of tutor to the sons of King Casimir Jagiellończyk, and the historian Gianmichele Bruto (Jan Michał Brutus) belonged for a while to the intimate circle of Stefan Batory. Italian religious reformers were also active in the Commonwealth; perhaps the best known among them was Fausto Sozzini (Faust Socyn), a religious thinker and leader of the Polish Anti-Trinitarians. Giorgio Biandrata and Francesco Lismanino were also important and well known figures among religious dissenters.

Various skills with more practical applications also proved attractive to Polish-Lithuanian rulers. A series of rulers valued Italians with chancellery and diplomatic talents, employing them as secretaries. Sebastiano Cefali and Cristoforo Masini worked in the chancellery during the reign of John Casimir; Tommaso Talenti served first Michał Korybut and later

John III, in whose name he sent Pope Innocent XI the Turkish standard taken at Vienna in 1683. Also active in Sobieski's entourage was Agostino Locci, called the younger, as he was the son of the architect and scenographer of the same name already mentioned. Italian immigrants were also entrusted with diplomatic missions, which shows the level of confidence given to specific individuals (Lodovico Fantoni, Domenico Roncalli, Valerio and Francesco Magni) at the Polish court, as well as the appreciation of their experience and competence in this field.

We should add that Domenico Alamani was Stefan Batory's court chef, and that this ruler's health was cared for by Niccolò Bucella and Simone Simoni, who competed fiercely with each other. And so—regardless of the service functions they performed—they ranked relatively high in court hierarchy, and their influence could also be political. Girolamo Pinocci, another royal secretary and diplomat, but also a merchant and journalist, was the publisher of the first Polish newspaper, *Merkuriusz Polski* (1661), which presented information and opinions formed in the circles of the royal court, as well as promoting political solutions and reforms aimed at strengthening the central authority and making it more efficient. This was a conscious attempt to modernize the way of making policy in the Commonwealth—by creating propaganda affecting an influential part of public opinion.

Interesting reform ideas formulated by military men and engineers coming from Italy were connected with the country's defense. Simone Genga was a famous military architect working in Poland during Batory's time. Andrea dell'Aqua, a generation younger and connected at first with the magnate courts of the Sieniawskis, Ostrogskis, Zamoyskis, and Zasławskis, was later in the king's service as head of a school of artillerymen that Sigismund III founded in 1622. Dell'Aqua himself wrote the school's constitution as well as that of an association of gunners, a professional group to which he devoted a particularly large amount of attention; he also wrote a proposal for creating a Knights' Academy at which the art

—
201
—

of artillery and the principles of building fortifications would be taught. Somewhat later, Paolo Del Buono, a physicist, mining entrepreneur, and minter, who was discussed earlier, formulated a proposal for creating a Military Academy. Among the Italian military men in the Polish service during the Swedish Wars, Giovanni Paolo Cellari gained considerable acclaim; Isidoro Affaitati, co-creator of the Kazimierzowski Palace in Warsaw (*Villa Regia*), was also a military engineer.

These are only selected examples of leading figures who demonstrate the range of Italian interests and activities; but they cannot represent to any satisfactory degree the whole population of interest to us. That population was far more numerous, yet its majority remained anonymous, because many Italian craftsmen, chefs, pharmacists, and horse trainers, as well as most of those whose trip to Poland did not turn out successfully, are not included in the sources.

One can, however, attempt to identify the most important spheres of the Italian presence, and the places where that presence was most visible. In view of the number and concentration of the Italian element, it is best to indicate first and foremost urban areas, led by Kraków, where the Italian community was surely most numerous, and in any case best organized and integrated (although that may be an illusion resulting from better preserved sources). We can note fairly large clusters of Italians also in Lviv, Vilnius, and even in Gdańsk. Italian immigrants were active in Poznań, at least as merchants and builders, and in the second half of the 17th century, and especially in the 18th century, they preferred to settle in Warsaw—somewhat belatedly recognizing its status as capital city. Even more sporadic and incomplete is the documentation for smaller towns. It is known that an Italian colony existed in Pińczów, and that Italian merchants operated in Jarosław, Sandomierz, and Zamość; but the exact geography of their presence can no longer be reconstructed.

Certainly smaller in number but incomparably greater in prestige was their presence at the royal court, which for some time functioned in sym-

—
202
—

biosis with the capital in Kraków; here we encounter responsible tasks, the highest qualifications, and appropriately prestigious positions. Later on, the courts of magnates became no less important in that regard; they gradually took on some of the functions of the royal court and began to attract Italians on similar principles. Let us remember, however, that the personnel composition of the vast majority of magnates' courts of the old Commonwealth remains unknown.

The coexistence of such a dynamic group of immigrants with the local populace was no bed of roses, and mutual relations certainly evolved over time. A favorable attitude must have predominated initially; ties of mutual interests were strengthened by a mutual curiosity, a fascination with what was new and exotic; only the burgher class would have felt the effects of Italian competition, and in the Commonwealth at the time, they had no fundamental influence on political reality. Later, the climate for Italian immigrants deteriorated gradually, which can be associated with the economic crisis of the mid-17th century, which all social groups felt. Social irritation must have increased, tolerance for foreigners diminished, as is confirmed by the evolution of stereotypical opinions of Italians that we can reconstruct on the basis of contemporary journalism, correspondence, and even popular sayings and maxims.

— 203 —

At first, positive descriptions and associations were foremost. The features that came to the fore were the Italians' wisdom in how to live and their foresight (Szymon Starowolski urged young nobles "to learn prudence from the Italians"). Their talents, sensuality, and artistic taste were also appreciated. The image of Italy was also positive as a country of high culture, the homeland of poets and thinkers, scholars and theologians, from which the elite branches of Old Polish society tried to benefit personally by visiting the Apennine Peninsula. Less important in this context was the heritage of antiquity; but such figures as Dante Alighieri, Francesco Petrarca, Giovanni Boccaccio, and later Torquato Tasso, Lodovico Ariosto, and Giambattista Marino (as well as Enea Silvio Piccolomini, Giovanni

Botero, and Cesare Baronio) were, however, known and respected in the Commonwealth.

But the relationship with Italian immigrants gradually deteriorated. As early as the 16th century, Queen Bona, the influential wife of Sigismund the Old and the mother of Sigismund August, contributed to this—as a foreigner on the throne, a woman meddling in politics, and also a supporter of strengthening the authority of the monarchy, something that rarely met with approval in the Commonwealth. She was suspected of secret conspiracies, plots, and even the use of poison. The queen's departure from Poland and her return to Italy toward the end of her life added to this negative view the accusation that she had taken great wealth and valuables out of the country.

A conflict of interests already perceived at the time was probably more significant, however. Voices were raised at the 1563 parliament, saying that Italians, "taking over all branches of business, are bringing the common people of the capital to poverty." Economic competition, although not endangering the noble estate directly, was signaled early on. Later, this topic was dominated by the subject of the mints and the coining of money, in which Italians—as we remember—were involved on a large scale, which provoked the largest wave of allegations of an economic nature that were leveled at them.

We may regard the Old Polish opinion of Italian cuisine—which was widely considered in the Commonwealth to be bizarre and of little worth—as a spectacular example of the difficulty in overcoming cultural distance. "A frog is good to an Italian, and with it a salad, / But a piece of meat is always welcome to a Pole," wrote Daniel Naborowski. One may find a similar tone in the work of Wacław Potocki, the author of the statement, "I would not sit down to an Italian banquet with an empty stomach," in whose verses the Italian unused to vodka and having social problems because of it appears again and again. The initially benevolent emphasis on distances and differences, combined with a touch of irony, gradually and barely noticeably changed, however, into a sneer and a demonstration of enmity, so that the innocent subject of cuisine became a pretext for the formulation of fairly serious accusations.

The most serious of them was interference in local politics. "This is bad counsel, o king; be on your guard. / Do not let yourself be ruled in anything by the Italian tribe. / What business does the legate have here? Let him go to Rome, / Let him not increase our great poverty with fire"—read a pamphlet from the period of the Zebrzydowski Rebellion (1606). So the ruler was warned against manipulation by Italians; the immigrants were accused of cynicism and hypocrisy, and in conclusion, their presence was declared unproductive and even bad for the country. "*Via, via* from Poland, little Italian, don't wait for Saturday; / Thanks for your services and Italian work," wrote another anonymous author. The consequences of this sort of statement could be serious, because—as another writer reminded readers—expelling the newcomers would be keeping an earlier promise ("It was sworn that in peace-time we would have no foreigners; no Swedes, no Italians, not even Germans"), which, it is true, affected all foreigners, but the outcries directed against Italians stood out in their harshness.

The image of Italians around the mid-17th century was no longer positive. Except for the qualities of prudence, artistic ability, and skill in making the most of life (if that is to be regarded as a virtue), the traits and descriptions that predominated in the stereotypical image of them were pejorative. Even the wisdom and learning they once exhibited began to be regarded as slyness and deceit, thereby losing their original, positive associations. Otherwise, the picture was all black: cunning and guile, slyness and greed, falseness and religious superficiality. The Italian as a partner and potential neighbor appeared now to be very troublesome! It is true that by their very nature, polemics, as well as popular sayings and maxims, oversimplify, aim to bring out flaws and defects, and use categorical statements; but the change in attitude toward Italian immigrants that took place at that time cannot be doubted. It certainly restricted their field of activity and chances of professional and material success, and probably discouraged some from staying on.

During the period of interest to us—unlike the Jews, Armenians, Scots, and Dutch, each of which ethnic groups possessed formal status that distinguished them within the structure of Old Polish society—the Italians made do without legal distinction as a group. There are discussions among historians as to the nature of social groups of this kind and the criteria for identifying and distinguishing them. In the opinion of some, the question of professional activity and social position, as generally understood, play the greater role in this context; others are inclined to attach more significance to ethnic distinctness and national characteristics. There can be no doubt, though, that immigrants from Italy formed a community that can be defined precisely, and at the same time were a group easily distinguished because they possessed sufficiently clear national characteristics.

One cannot forget, however, that Italians in the Commonwealth were a highly diverse community, not only in social terms but also ethnic and cultural. The Apennine Peninsula was a conglomeration of larger and smaller states that enjoyed longstanding political as well as cultural and economic autonomy. Milan, the Republic of Venice, the Grand Duchy of Tuscany, Rome and the Papal States, and also the Kingdom of Naples—these were the most important political entities in Italy at that time, and also those from which immigrants were most often recruited. A list of city republics and small duchies from which Italian immigrants also came would be much longer. Their mutual relations were complicated, not without some signs of solidarity, but also not without conflicts and distance from each other; there were differences among them of language, culture, and civilization. The term "Italians"—generally used for the sake of simplicity—is therefore very imprecise, at least in regard to the early modern period. It remains an open question whether newcomers from Italy on foreign soil such as the Polish-Lithuanian state had a feeling of community and perhaps solidarity, or whether they more often regarded each other as rivals.

Historians writing about the ethnic groups that existed within Old Polish society try to give some numbers, albeit estimated: from several thousand (Armenians, Tatars) through several tens of thousands (the Dutch, Scots) up to several hundred thousand (Jews). Unfortunately, in the case of the Italians, due to the non-formalized and diverse nature of their presence, there is no basis for estimates of this sort. It is very difficult to acquire reliable data in view of only partial infiltration by Italians of city structures; the enjoyment by some of exceptional status such as that given by royal service; the randomness of sources confirming the presence of Italians at the courts of magnates; the impossibility of documenting a large number of brief stays connected with trading activity; and finally, the various phases and degrees of progressing polonization.

It is difficult to avoid subjectivity. The historian whose attention is directed toward Italian immigrants will notice them while reading various and sundry source materials. The arrivals of Italians may seem more frequent than they actually were, for the presence of representatives of this group was often spectacular or was accompanied by numerous controversies reflected in source documentation that is rather rich by its very nature. The activity of bankers and merchants; the lease of mints that later caused protests; the unique nature of their occupational specialization; their participation in prestigious building projects; their presence at the most renowned courts; all of that—combined with physical and cultural separateness—made representatives of this minority visible and prominent.

In the topography of the Commonwealth's largest cities, we find to this day traces of the Italian presence: street names and elegant townhouses—whether in Lviv or in Kazimierz on the Vistula—are called by the surnames of Italian owners. In Kraków, in the Church of St. Francis of Assisi, there is even the so-called "Italian chapel"—a place of prayer and regular meetings for representatives of this minority, a prominent testimony to their significance and high level of integration.

Although the question of the number of Italian immigrants and of the proportion between that community and other groups of foreigners must remain open, nonetheless, despite all the reservations and restrictions mentioned above, we feel a need to formulate at least some substitute for a hypothesis in that regard. One may perhaps assume that the number of Italian immigrants in Kraków during the probable apogee of their presence at the turn of the 16th century was reckoned in the hundreds rather than thousands. In the whole country, the Italian ethnic group probably numbered several thousand, perhaps ten or more. That would be like the population of a large town—reckoned by the conditions of old Poland—scattered unevenly over the enormous territory of the Polish-Lithuanian state. It is not, however, their numbers but the prominence of specific figures that determined the image of this immigrant group and the significance of its presence.

In conclusion, it is worthwhile to pose some questions: What were the prospects of Italian immigrants in their new environment? Were they able to take advantage of the chance offered by functioning within a different reality? Could they aspire to meaningful advancement within the society of old Poland? Finally, how did their situation appear when contrasted with that of other ethnic and national groups formed as a result of migration?

The main assets that Italian immigrants undoubtedly possessed can be reduced to a few categories: new immigrants drew positive interest that resulted from the attractiveness of the activities in which they engaged, which had the essential virtue of novelty; up to a certain point, the attractiveness of the institutional solutions and cultural models offered by the immigrants, as well as the objective value of their professional skills, were also appreciated. The Polish-Lithuanian state was a peculiar entity—expansive and decentralized, poorly developed economically, with a strong class structure in which the noble class was dominant; it was a state subjected—especially in the 17th century—to powerful political jolts and descending into crisis. Did these conditions offer a chance of effective adaptation and success in life to the Italian immigrants? Would it be easier for them to achieve success in a relatively stable and wealthy state, or in one that was economically backward and descending into crisis and anarchy?

The answer is not simple. On the one hand, a state of wealthy inhabitants, if it accepts foreigners at all, also offers them access to its riches—for example as a trading partner willing to buy the products they offer. An affluent state free from fundamental internal conflict should, therefore, create more possibilities for immigrants, at least in the material sphere; in the politico-social sphere, a stable system often turns out to be closed and hard to penetrate from the outside. A weakly-organized state organism, especially during a period of growing crisis for both its economy and its social and political structures, may, in turn, offer a wide field for activity on the part of individuals able to take advantage of that instability.

This is exactly how we imagine the evolution of the Italians' situation in early modern Poland. A relatively affluent and wealthy Poland in its Golden Age was an avid purchaser of the goods and services offered by Italians at the time, for a rather large part of the noble class, and also the elite of the burgher class, were in a position to take advantage of them. The deteriorating socio-economic realities of the Commonwealth in subsequent centuries drastically limited those possibilities.

The Italians, however, were not ready to give up, because the causes that induced them to emigrate clearly did not go away. They tried to offer their services first and foremost to the magnate elite of the noble class, and at the same time—having gained essential knowledge of Polish-Lithuanian reality—they were able to discover and exploit perceived weaknesses. It is possible to regard their politico-diplomatic activities, and especially the artistic services they offered, and the leasing of mints, in this way.

The position of the Italians and their chances for adaptation depended, therefore, first and foremost on the time at which they arrived, and also on the social context in which they found themselves. Secretaries, court physicians, and horse trainers were not elevated, after all, by their profession, no matter how masterfully practiced, but by the fact of their constant presence at the royal court, or at one of the prestigious magnate centers, and by benefiting from local patronage. The fates of those scholars and intellectuals who came from Italy unfolded in similar fashion; for some, the position of professor at the Academy of Kraków turned out to be attractive; others, perhaps more knowledgeable about the local hierarchy of prestige, tried to gain positions in the court structure.

The relative weakness of the Italian ethnic group resulted above all from the lack of heraldic status of the majority of newcomers, as well as the non-noble character of the professions they practiced, which were not regarded as prestigious for that reason. In the Commonwealth, nobility was the essential condition for aspiring to and being included in elite circles whereas in Italy, this factor—though obviously important—played an incomparably lesser role.

Despite the restrictions described above, Italian trips to the Commonwealth turned out to be a relatively lasting phenomenon; so they must have been attractive to both sides. Representatives of the Italian ethnic group turned out to be effective in many fields, leaving important traces of their presence on the Vistula and the Niemen. The phenomenon we have described should undoubtedly be regarded as an important component of early modern European migrations, the in-depth study of which allows us to reconstruct one of the important phases of the integration of the Old Continent.

Selected bibliography

Barycz, H., *Spojrzenia w przeszłość polsko-włoską* [A Look at the Polish-Italian Past], Wrocław: Zakład Narodowy im. Ossolińskich, 1965.

—
210
—

Białostocki, J., *The Art of the Renaissance in Eastern Europe*, Ithaca: Cornell University Press, 1976.

Burke, P., *The Fortunes of the "Courtier": The European Reception of Castiglione's "Corte-giano,"* University Park: Pennsylvania State University Press, 1996.

Chrościcki, J. A., "Kamieniarze i mafiosi. Zarobkowa emigracja z Włoch do Europy Środkowej i Wschodniej (xv–xvii w.)" [Stonemasons and Mafiosi. Emigration for Wages of Italians to Central and Eastern Europe (15th–17th Centuries)], *Przegląd Humanistyczny*, vol. xl/1 (1996), pp. 69–85.

Hniłko, A., *Włosi w Polsce* [Italians in Poland], vol. 1: *Tytus Liwjusz Boratyni, dworzanin króla Jana Kazimierza, mincarz i uczony* [Tito Livio Burattini, Courtier of King John Casimir, Minter and Scholar], Kraków, 1923.

Karpowicz, M., *Sztuki polskiej drogi dziwne* [The Strange Paths of Polish Art], Bydgoszcz, 1994.

Manikowski, A., "Mercanti italiani in Polonia nel xvi e xvii secolo" [Italian Merchants in Poland in the 16th and 17th Centuries], in *Aspetti della vita economia medievale* [Aspects of Medieval Economic Life], Firenze: Università degli Studi di Firenze, 1985, pp. 359–369.

Mazzei, R., *Itinera Mercatorum. Circolazione di uomini e beni nell'Europa centro-orientale: 1550–1650* [Itinera Mercatorum. Movement of People and Goods in Central and Eastern Europe], Lucca: Pacini Fazzi, 1999.

Ptaśnik, J., *Kultura włoska wieków średnich w Polsce* [Italian Culture of the Middle Ages in Poland], Warszawa: pwn, 1959 (1st edition – Warszawa 1922).

Quirini-Popławska, D., *Działalność Włochów w Polsce w i połowie xvi wieku na dworze królewskim, w dyplomacji i hierarchii kościelnej* [Activities of Italians in Poland in the First Half of the 16th Century at the Royal Court, in Diplomacy, and in the Church Hierarchy], Kraków– Wrocław: Zakład Narodowy im. Ossolińskich 1973.

Sokołowski, J., "Gdańsk (Danzig) – The Polish Window to the World and its Italian Traditions," in *La Via dell'Ambra*, a cura di Riccardo C. Lewanski, Bologna: Università degli Studi di Bologna, 1994.

Stoye, J., *Marsigli's Europe, 1680–1730: The Life and Times of Luigi Ferdinando Marsigli, Soldier and Virtuoso*, New Haven: Yale University Press, 1994.

211

Targosz, K., *Hieronim Pinocci. Studium z dziejów kultury naukowej w Polsce w XVII wieku* [Girolamo Pinocci. A Study from the History of Scientific Culture in Poland in the 17th Century], Wrocław: Zakład Narodowy im. Ossolińskich, 1967.

Tazbir, J., "'Włoszczyzna' w Polsce" ["Italianness" in Poland] in same author, *Sarmaci i świat. Prace wybrane* [Sarmatians and the World. Selected Works], ed. S. Grzybowski, vol. 3, Kraków: Universitas, 2001, pp. 357–365.

Tygielski, W., *Italians in Early Modern Poland. The Lost Opportunity for Modernization?*, translated by K. Popowicz, Frankfurt am Main: Peter Lang, 2015.

Tygielski, W., "The Italian presence in early modern Poland. Its cultural and civilizational consequences," in Huschner, W., Bünz, E., and Lübke, Ch. (eds.), *Italien – Mitteldeutschland – Polen: Geschichte und Kultur im europäischen Kontext vom 10. bis zum 18. Jahrhundert*, Leipzig Leipziger Universitätsverlag, 2013, pp. 761–776.

Tygielski, W., "The Views of Apostolic Nuntios on Poland in the 16th and 17th centuries," in Mączak, A,. and Weber, W. E. J. (eds.), *Der frühmoderne Staat in Ostzentraleuropa I*, Augsburg: Institut für Europäische Kulturgeschichte der Universität Augsburg, 1999, pp. 76–88.

SCOTS

∽

JACEK WIJACZKA

Scotland's first contacts with Poland go back to the 14th century, when Scottish merchants traded with Gdańsk. The first group of Scots settled there in 1380. Relations with them were good, because they did not harm the interests of the major Gdańsk wholesalers. There were not too many ships sailing in from Scotland. During the years 1460–1583, a total of 86 ships from Scotland arrived in the port of Gdańsk, which came to about 1% of all traffic in the port. By the early 15th century, one of the suburbs of Gdańsk was called Stare Szkoty [Old Scots]. The first references to settlement in Stare Szkoty date from the 16th century, when the bishops of Włocławek settled craftsmen in their enclave outside Gdańsk, mostly Dutch Mennonites and Jews, but also some Scots, who, at that time, did not yet have any chance of developing activity in Gdańsk itself.

The immigration of Scots to the territory of the Commonwealth intensified in the second half of the 16th century and lasted until the mid-17th century. It was economic factors above all that determined this, and religious factors to a lesser degree. The emigrants were both Catholics and Protestants. Łukasz Opaliński wrote in 1648, "This nation, tired of its poor and barren homeland, flees from poverty across the sea and seeks work among us." Infertile, mountainous countries such as Scotland and Switzerland occasionally experienced periods of increased emigration. One must also take into account more random and prosaic reasons for emigration—for example, Patrick Gordon left Scotland because of unrequited love, got on a ship, and sailed to Gdańsk.

At first, the Scots settled primarily in Gdańsk and other cities of Royal Prussia. It seems they lived in almost all the cities of that province, with the exceptions of Chełmża and Kurzętnik. Outside of Gdańsk, the earliest we find them was in Chojnice in the mid-16th century. In 1570, there were 15 Scots living in Gniew, three each in Świecie and Starogard. There were eight living in Tuchola in 1651, five in Biały Bór, four in Chojnice, three in Czarne, two in Człuchów, and one each in Debrzno, Gniew, Kościerzyna, Tczew, and Starogard. In Puck, one of the strongest centers of crafts in Royal Prussia, they appeared in the mid-16th century, but played their greatest role in that city in the 1620s and 1630s, when they were among the most economically active residents. At the time, they were engaged in trading timber and shipping.

Some Scots moved from Royal Prussia to other parts of the Commonwealth. We find them in cities in Kujawy. A small but active group of Scots lived in Koronowo. Three Scots were living there in 1597. In the first half of the 17th century, Scots from Koronowo already had positions among the city authorities. In 1630, brothers Jan and Wojciech Kolwin performed the functions of councilors and were among the city's richest residents. Wojciech bought neglected but attractively located properties by the marketplace and sold them at a profit. In general, however, Scots settled in Koronowo had much more modest fortunes, took on various jobs, and also did not avoid work as craftsmen. Wojciech, the son of Jerzy Sykot, was a stove builder.

Many Scots settled in the cities of Greater Poland [Wielkopolska]. They appeared in Borek in 1567 and worked as butchers and brewers. The first representative of this nation arrived in Gostyń in 1572, and 20 Scottish families were living there by the end of the century. They worked in retail trade at first, and after a while had earned fortunes. The Jungs became one of the richest burgher families in Gostyń.

The first mentions of Scots in the cities of Sandomierz province (Lesser Poland, Małopolska] date from the 1570s. Their presence was noted first, in 1576, in Szydłowiec, and subsequently in Sandomierz (1578), Kunów (1592), Tarnów (1599), Koprzywnica, Pińczów, Chęciny, Nowe Miasto Korczyn, Opoczno, Połaniec, Iłża (1600), Secemin (1601), Pacanów (1603), Radom (1603), Kielce (1606), Opatów (1615), Jedlińsk (1619), Raków (1633), Skrzynno (1642), Busko (1619), and Chmielnik (1651). By the mid-17th century, we encounter Scots in 21 cities of Sandomierz province, and there were 114 cities in that province at the time. Only a few mentions of Scots in Sandomierz province are preserved from the second half of the 17th century—by then, they lived only in a few cities.

Scots also settled, among other places, in Węgrów, on the border of Mazovia and Podlasie. The trade route on which Węgrów was located in the 16th–18th centuries played a very important role. Two highways crossed there, the Lithuanian (connecting the Crown with Lithuania) and the Gdańsk (running from Gdańsk to Łuków). In addition to its favorable location, an influx of foreigners contributed to the successful development of Węgrów. On 14 April 1650, Bogusław Radziwiłł gave the town a grant of privilege in which he made equal the rights of all townsmen and allowed foreigners of all faiths to settle there and acquire property. The grant was very favorable to the Scots, whom it not only described as a "fine ornament to the city," but to whom it guaranteed, more importantly, "every freedom and liberty, and protection and defense from outsiders." The town was divided from then on into three separate sections: the Jewish, in the south, the Scottish in the north, and the region of Gdańska street, inhabited by Catholics.

In the mid-17th century, the Scottish (and English) population lived in 119 centers, only seven of which were villages (Lignowy, Miłobądz and Paszulin in Pomerania province, Gniazdowo and Mątowy Wielkie in Malbork province, as well as Jastrowice and Poluczno in Greater Poland). The definite majority of centers populated by the Scots and English were royal properties: 72 royal cities and villages, 34 cities owned by nobles and magnates, and 13 church-owned cities. The largest clusters of Scottish and English population were Gdańsk, Poznań, Warsaw, Kraków, Lublin, Zamość, and Lviv. Sizable Scottish colonies were to be found in Brzeziny, Bydgoszcz, Człopa, Łobżenica, Raciąż, Sieradz, Sierpc, Wałcz, Warka, and Zakroczym.

This is how the division of Scottish (and English) colonies in Poland looked as of 1651: Royal Prussia, 53 clusters; Greater Poland, 31; Lesser Poland, 18; Mazovia and Podlasie, 17.

Scots rarely settled in Lithuania, although a colony of them existed in Kėdainai. However, they undoubtedly conducted business there as peddlers. The noted diarist Jan Antoni Chrapowicki, who lived near Hrodna in Lithuania, wrote under the date 27 October 1665 that on that afternoon "a Scot came by with cloth, of which I bought quite a bit."

It is impossible to give a clear answer to the question of how many Scots lived in the Commonwealth during early modern times. Data on the Scottish population in Polish lands deals almost exclusively with the 16th and first half of the 17th centuries. According to the opinion of the Englishman William Lithgow, who traveled around the Commonwealth in 1616, "And for auspiciousness, I may rather term it to be a mother and nurse for the youth and younglings of Scotland who are yearly sent hither in great numbers, than a proper Dame for her own birth; in clothing, feeding, and enriching them with the fatness of her best things; besides thirty thousand Scots families, that live incorporate in her bowels. And certainly Poland may be termed in this kind to be the mother of our Commons and the first commencement of all our best merchants' wealth, or at least most part of them." Roman Rybarski, on the basis of tax paid in 1651 by Scots living in the Commonwealth, significantly lowered the estimate of the English traveler, for he said that at that time, there were a little over 800 Scottish families living here. This estimate ought to be raised, however, because a group of Scots failed to pay that tax. This included Scots living in Chęciny, Opatów, and Jedlińsk.

According to Anna Biegańska's estimate, made in the 1970s, a total of over 7,400 Scottish families were living in Polish territory during the 16th and 17th centuries. Biegańska assumed that there were five persons in each family, and estimated, therefore, that 37,000 Scots lived in the Commonwealth at that time.

Both Catholic and Protestant Scots emigrated to the Commonwealth from Scotland. It is difficult to state clearly which group predominated. One can only suppose that at the beginning there were somewhat more Protestants, who often converted to Catholicism, however, especially in the second half of the 17th century.

We know that in the early 17th century, Protestant Scots lived in Jedlińsk (Sandomierz province), because in 1619, they endowed a bell for the local Evangelical church. This endowment required considerable financial resources, and the decision must have had a religious basis. In 1630, however, Catholics regained ownership of the church, and with that began the process of the Protestant community's decline. This also had an impact on the assimilation of those Scots who, having to choose between leaving town or accepting Catholicism, chose to convert, not wishing to abandon their homes. In the years 1630–1651, a strong Scottish colony existed in Brody. It numbered over 20 Protestant families.

From 1598 to the mid-17th century, more than a dozen Scottish families were noted in the city records of Szydłowiec. They were generally wealthy townsmen whose main occupation was trade. It appears that the definite majority of Scots in Szydłowiec were Catholics, although a 1617 inspection report mentioned two Scottish heretics, the Calvinists Aleksander and Jan. The wealthiest Scot in Szydłowiec, Aleksander Russell (who died after 1652) was a Catholic. The Catholicism of Szydłowiec Scots is shown by bequests they made on behalf of local churches (among others, the aforementioned Russell bequeathed 100 florins on 5 May 1628), as well as the lives of two sons of Mrs. Zofia Sanxter, one of whom was vicar at the Church of the Blessed Virgin Mary in Kraków, and the other a monk

—
217
—

at the Cistercian monastery in Wąchock. It appears the Scots living in Lublin were Catholics, as a 1651 town ordinance that described precisely the conditions for receiving town citizenship demanded that the recipient profess the Catholic religion. That is certainly how things were in the second half of the 17th century, although in the first half of that century, adherents of other faiths succeeded in getting around that requirement.

Undoubtedly, the Scots living in Iłża (in Małopolska), which belonged to the bishops of Kraków, were Catholics. A large Scottish colony still existed there at the turn of the 16th and 17th centuries. Scots living in Sieradz were also Catholics.

An example of a Catholic Scot may be Jan Jerzy Jonston, born in Warmia around 1617. In 1655, he entered the abbey at Święty Krzyż, where he was the monastery librarian during the years 1685–1703. He wrote a comprehensive chronicle describing the history of the Święty Krzyż monastery to 1704. In 1699, he was the prior and the hospital provost of St. Michael's in Nowa Słupia. He died during a plague in December 1708.

According to a grant of privilege issued to the Scots by King Stefan Batory, the Crown Marshal had supreme jurisdiction over them, but Scots possessed autonomy in the Commonwealth, and organized their own governing structures. There were at least 12 Scottish Brotherhoods in operation, and every Scot had to belong to one of them. The Brotherhoods named judges who settled cases between Scots during fairs. Appeals of their verdicts could be submitted to and reviewed by the "chief Scottish parliament," which took place on the day of the Epiphany fair (January 6th) in Toruń.

The Brotherhoods kept special books in which they recorded all cases and the verdicts given in them. The penalties for individual misdeeds were clearly defined. Every Scot who arrived in the Commonwealth and began to engage in trade was summoned before the presence of the elder of the Brotherhood and induced to join it. He had to sign his name in the Brotherhood's book in his own hand, and take an oath that he would obey the Brotherhood's constitution. The Brotherhoods also collected contributions from their members. In addition to the Brotherhood elders, among Scots there were also clerical elders who collected a contribution each year for building churches and for stipends for the clergy. Every Brotherhood kept its own records.

The Brotherhoods were granted a great deal of power and authority. They were able to excommunicate any of their members, as happened in the early 17th century with Jan Ramsay, living in Poznań, "who left in shame to go back to his homeland" [Scotland]. It appears that every year, four judges were chosen for the entire country; they settled cases and issued verdicts, punishing some with fines, others with imprisonment, and excom- municated yet others, forbidding anyone to speak or share a table with them. Money gained from fines was loaned to other Scots with interest.

One of these Brotherhoods operated in Lublin. It was probably founded in the early 17th century and existed until at least 1732. Its meeting place was the Kramarczykowska townhouse on Dominikańska Street. This Brotherhood kept its records in Polish.

King Sigismund III Vasa attempted to restrict Scottish autonomy; in 1603, he appointed Abraham Young head of the Scottish nation in the Commonwealth. He was supposed to dissolve Scottish autonomy, conduct a census of the Scots, and codify the laws by which they lived. This was meant to lead to total assimilation, but it led instead to rebellion by the Scots. Young was removed from his office in 1607 due to support for the rebellion from the Polish nobility, who saw in Young's appointment a threat to the Polish golden liberty, for they feared that in the future, Sigismund III might also try to limit nobles' rights. Scots retained their governing structures.

Scottish immigrants to the Commonwealth initially worked primarily as stall keepers and peddlers. They dealt mainly in peddlers' wares. These goods were cheap but offered in a broad range, and the peddlers carried them on their backs or on pack-horses. That is how Aleksander and Wojciech Szot of Secemin (in Lesser Poland), among others, earned a living for their families in the early 17th century; in 1601, they paid a duty on "various knives and other peddlers' trifles" which they carried "on themselves" from Kraków. That same year, Gregier Jarnge also carried his merchandise from Kraków, and it consisted of "knives, hooks, needles, and other small items." Like other Scots from that town, they did not avail themselves of any means of transport during their trip to Kraków, and even to Hungary.

This mass participation of Scottish traders in peddling caused that sort of inexpensive merchandise to be called *szocki*, and peddlers in general were *Szoci*. In time, many of these Scottish peddlers came to own sizable fortunes. Łukasz Opaliński writes in 1648, "Formerly, the lowest vendors, whose gear was baskets and hay, sold only needles, knives, buckles, and other trifles of this sort, which they carried in crates and boxes on their backs. Now ... they carry their wares in carts and travel around to town fairs."

Accumulating a fortune was not so easy, however, because the activity of Scottish peddlers came up against action on the part of the state authority and the cities. This can be seen in royal edicts issued against Scottish merchants in Royal Prussia (1531, 1580) and the whole territory of the Crown (1551, 1594). The policy of city authorities toward the Scottish newcomers differed greatly. Scots were forbidden to stay in some cities (Kościan, 1578); in others they were not allowed to appear at the weekly markets (Kcynia, 1495). In Bydgoszcz, by virtue of a 1581 grant from Stefan Batory, only four Scots could belong to the brotherhood of stall-keepers, and in addition, they had to own property in the city. In many cities, however, they were enabled to acquire local citizenship (in, among others, Chęciny, Gdańsk, Kraków, Lublin, Sandomierz, and Szydłowiec). From 1537 to 1709, 135 Scots were admitted to city law in Gdańsk; they came to it most often through marriage with the daughters or widows of wealthy and influential Gdańsk townsmen. In Kraków, 74 Scots acquired citizenship during the years 1573–1702.

Scottish merchants were also accepted to city law in Chęciny. Information from the year 1638 says that some years earlier (1633), Chęciny Scots signed (under compulsion, it seems) the so-called Scottish charter, by virtue of which they were to pay eight *złotys* each on St. Jadwiga's feast day (25 August). The sums collected were designated for the needs of the city. If any of the Scots did not pay, he lost his property and privileges. It may be that these excessive financial obligations led to several Scots' renouncing city law during the years 1639–1644 and returning to city authorities their certificates of duty exemptions. It appears that just before the Swedish "Deluge" (1655–1660), only one Scot lived in Chęciny.

Despite all restrictions, some Scots succeeded in acquiring significant fortunes. One Scottish merchant who had a spectacular career, beyond any doubt, was Robert Wojciech Portius [Robert Gilbert Porteous Lanxeth]. He came to Krosno at the beginning of the 1620s. By the midpoint of that century, he had monopolized the trade in Hungarian wine. He rebuilt the Krosno parish church after a fire and endowed it with pictures at his own expense. He built over 300 meters of new defensive city walls, repaired the Hungarian Gate, and paid for many investments that served the city's defense. In 1658, he designated significant financial means for the teaching of Krosno's children by a teacher from the Academy of Kraków.

—
221
—

Scots are mentioned in universal tax proclamations for the first time in 1563, when a tax was imposed on them in the amount of 12–15 *groszy* [pence]. A year later, however, these obligations were increased; Scots "who carry their things for sale on their person" had to pay a *złoty* each, while those Scottish merchants "who transport their goods with horses" paid 60 *groszy* per horse (at that time, a *złoty* was worth 30 *groszy*).

The activities of Scottish peddlers and merchants provoked criticism from their Polish competitors. For example, in 1668, in Nowe on the Vistula, they were accused of causing a rise in the prices of olive oil and pepper, with the charge "You, Scots, are worse than Jews and Gypsies, because for a shilling one cannot get as much olive oil and pepper from you as one can from a Jew." Two years later, the Nowe merchant Dobran demanded that the city council ban Scottish merchants from selling herbs, and promised he would obligate himself to sell them "much cheaper" than the Scots did. The poet Stanisław Orzelski (circa 1581–1626) placed Jews in first place in hell, and after them, monks who did not observe celibacy, harlots, Poznań merchants, and Scots.

Scots who came to the Commonwealth worked, in addition to trade, primarily as soldiers. In 1577, Gdańsk, which at the time was fighting against the Polish king Stefan Batory, recruited 600–700 Scottish soldiers in Holland. After the end of the siege of Gdańsk, Stefan Batory proposed to the battle-hardened Scots that they serve him. As a result, a separate unit of Scottish infantry took part in the war for Livonia on the royal side. It distinguished itself at the capture of Koknese fortress, and probably for that reason, on the way to Pskov (1581), Batory ordered another unit of Scottish infantry to be recruited. After initial problems, he succeeded in recruiting 150 Scots. They made a splendid impression, because the king's chronicler noted, "If we only had several thousand like them, we would dare to venture against the walls of Pskov."

In subsequent years, more and more Scots served in Polish units. This resulted primarily from the fact that the basic formation in the Polish army was the cavalry; it lacked infantry, in which nobles did not wish to serve; Scots, on the other hand, were famous as superb marksmen and excellent infantrymen. Scottish soldiers were famous in Western and Northern Europe from the 15th century on, and their numbers grew from the second half of the 16th century. They served in Holland, France, Sweden, and Denmark.

Scottish soldiers were recruited by voluntary enlistment . As Spytko Wawrzyniec Jordan, Stefan Batory's captain of horse, wrote, "Scots ... although they walk about with stalls, they have a custom that once they fold them or sell them, they fasten arms at their sides and take flintlocks on their shoulders, and they make no ordinary infantry." A Scottish infantry company numbered 100–300 soldiers on average, and their cadre included a captain, lieutenant, ensign, two sergeants, two corporals, a quartermaster, a provost, a clerk, a nurse, and two drummers. Every regiment had its own chaplain. As of the late 16th century, the rank and file received pay of four to eight Polish *złotys*, junior officers got 10–14, the ensign 30, and the captain 70. These rates were higher than other infantrymen received.

Scots not only served in the Polish army but also helped modernize it. In the 1620s, Jan Fentun (Wenton), who was a master carpenter and lived in Puck, was one of those building six three-mast warships. Another Scot from Puck, James Murray, directed the building of a fleet in Gdańsk from 1621. Due to his work, the royal fleet in 1627 numbered 10 ships. As commander of the galleon *King David*, which he himself built, he took part in the sea battle at Oliwa (1627) in the rank of rear-admiral. Because of his colorful life, he became the hero of five novels by Jerzy Rychliński (among them, *Galeon kapitana Mory* [Captain Murray's Galleon], Warszawa, 1968).

—
223
—

Besides merchants, craftsmen, and military men, we also find among the Scots men in the learned professions: painters (John Gallison), writers (Albert Ines, Andrew Loech, Lechowicz) and doctors (William Davison). Best known, however, is Jan Jonston (John Johnston, born 1603 in Szamotuły, died 1675 in Składowice), natural scientist, historian, pedagogue, and doctor. He was the son of a Scottish immigrant, Simon Johnston, and a German, Anna Becker. Beginning in 1611, he studied for three years at a school of the Czech Brethren in Ostroróg, from which he transferred to the Evangelical *gimnazjum* in Bytom Odrzański. After five years of study at the Bytom *gimnazjum*, he continued his studies at the *gimnazjum* in Toruń, where he gained an excellent knowledge of the Hebrew language. During the years 1623–1625, he studied Hebrew, philosophy, and theology at the University of St. Andrews in Scotland. In 1632, he received his doctorate in medicine at Leiden University. He returned to Leszno (1632) and soon after became the Leszczyńskis' court physician and the city doctor. Jonston created outstanding encyclopedic works. He made particular contributions in the fields of entomology, botany, and ornithology. Despite his foreign origin, he always regarded himself as a Pole.

The immigration of Scots to the Commonwealth lasted till the mid-17th century. Its restriction was influenced by the fact that in 1624, the English king forbade ship captains to take on board young people whose means of support were not assured, either in the form of a letter of recommendation from families who had settled abroad earlier, or cash sufficient to maintain them for the next year. It appears that the Commonwealth was also losing the power to attract people as a stable country in which a fortune could be earned relatively quickly. This was also influenced by the numerous wars of the first half of the 17th century, as well as the clear and growing dislike for "foreigners" in Polish society.

The slowing down of the influx of immigrants caused Scots in the Commonwealth to begin assimilating quickly as early as the first half of the 17th century. Conducive to this was the Catholic faith of some of them (for example, in Szydłowiec), and above all, numerous Polish-Scottish marriages. As generations passed, the differences between the *Szoci* and the rest of the population, once so clear, gradually disappeared.

—
224
—

Selected bibliography

Bajer, P. P., *Scots in the Polish-Lithuanian Commonwealth, 16th–18th Centuries. The Formation and Disappearance of an Ethnic Group*, Leiden–Boston: Brill, 2012.

Biegańska, A., "Żołnierze szkoccy w dawnej Rzeczypospolitej" [Scottish Soldiers in the Former Commonwealth], *Studia i Materiały do Historii Wojskowości*, vol. 27 (1984), pp. 81–111.

Biegańska, A., "The Learned Scots in Poland (from the Mid-Sixteenth to the Close of the Eighteenth Century)," *Canadian Slavonic Papers*, 3, 2001 (www.ualberta.ca/~csp/).

Borowy, W., "Anglicy, Szkoci i Irlandczycy w wojsku polskim za Zygmunta ɪɪɪ" [Englishmen, Scots, and Irishmen int he Polish Army During the Reign of Sigismund ɪɪɪ] in Barycz, H., and Hulewicz, J. (eds.), *Studia z dziejów kultury* polskiej [Studies from the History of Polish Culture], Warszawa: Gebethner i Wolff, 1949, pp. 293–315.

Feduszka, J., "Szkoci i Anglicy w Zamościu w xvɪ–xvɪɪɪ wieku" [Scots and Englishmen in Zamość in the 16ᵗʰ–18ᵗʰ Centuries], *Czasy Nowożytne*, vol. 22 (2009).

Gierszewski, S., "Szkoci w mniejszych miastach Pomorza Gdańskiego (xvɪ–xvɪɪɪ w.)" [Scots in the Smaller Cities of Gdańsk Pomerania (16ᵗʰ–18ᵗʰ Centuries)], *Zeszyty Naukowe Wyższej Szkoły Pedagogicznej im. Powstańców Śląskich w Opolu, Historia* 26 (1988), pp. 49–59.

Guldon, Z., *Żydzi i Szkoci w Polsce w xvɪ–xvɪɪɪ wieku. Studia i materiały* [Jews and Scots in Poland in the 16ᵗʰ–18ᵗʰ Centuries. Studies and Materials], Kielce: wsᴘ, 1990.

Guldon, Z. and Stępkowski, L., "Ludność szkocka i angielska w Polsce w połowie xvɪɪ wieku" [The Scottish and English Population in Poland in the Mid-17ᵗʰ Century], *Kwartalnik Historii Kultury Materialnej* [Quarterly of the History of Material Culture], vol. 30 (1982), no. 2, pp. 201–214.

Guldon, Z., Krzystanek, K., "Żydzi i Szkoci w Sandomierzu w xvɪ–xvɪɪɪ wieku" [Jews and Scots in Sandomierz in the 16ᵗʰ–18ᵗʰ Centuries], *Studia Historyczne*, vol. 31 (1988), no. 4, pp. 527–542.

W. Kowalski, "'Comunitas geniis scoticae' w Jedlińsku w pierwszej połowie xvɪɪ stulecia" ['Communitas geniis scoticae' in Jedlińsk in the First Half of the 17ᵗʰ Century], *Kieleckie Studia Historyczne*, vol. 9 (1991), pp. 23–33.

Kowalski, W., "Scoti, Cives Cracovienses: Their Ethnic and Social Identity, 1570–1660," in Worthington, D. (ed.), *British and Irish Emigrants and Exiles in Europe, 1603–1688*, Leiden–Boston: Brill, 2010, pp. 67–85.

Kowalski, W., "The Placement of Urbanised Scots in the Polish Crown during the Sixteenth and Seventeenth Centuries," in Grosjean, A. and Murdoch, S. (eds.), *Scottish Communities Abroad in the Early Modern Period*, Leiden: Brill, 2005, pp. 53–103.

Kowalski, W., "The Scotsmen in the Cracow Market in the Mid-17ᵗʰ century," *Zeszyty Wszechnicy Świętokrzyskiej*, no. 23 (2006), pp. 15–38.

MENNONITES

∽

EDMUND KIZIK

———

The Mennonites, who settled in the territory of Royal Prussia belonging to Poland from the mid-16th century to the 1620s, were representatives of Dutch Anabaptism, a faith that developed before the mid-16th century on the fringes of the main trends of the Reformation. This movement, directed by a former Catholic priest, a Frisian, Menno Simons (1496–1561), held that, following Christ's example, the sacrament of baptism should be administered only to adults. Unlike previous armed rebellions of Anabaptists, however, including the followers of the messianic movement of John of Leiden that was brutally suppressed in Münster in 1534, Simons gathered around himself followers of a peaceful path toward building a new religion. They decided to "leave the wicked world" in the hands of Satan and his tools on earth—Catholics, Lutherans, and others—and build a new, truly Christian social alternative in isolation. In his commentary on religion (*Fondamentboek*, 1539), Simons repeated doctrinal elements widely discussed in the circles of early 16th-century European heresiarchs: antipedibaptism (that is, baptism of adults), a ban on swearing oaths, and recognition of the New Testament as the rule for conduct; he added on his own absolute pacifism and a proposal to create a model community organization. The originality of this idea, however, should be sought above all in the total elimination of the clerical estate as a socially distinct caste— from then on, the Mennonite religious community was to become a form of collective and nonhierarchical emancipation of spiritual values from all non-religious, secular ties. Its sources lay in the late-medieval *devotio moderna*, although in their outlook, the Mennonites may remind us both of the noble naivety of the medieval companions of St. Francis of Assisi as well as the uncompromising faith of the modern Jehovah's Witnesses.

Opposing the corruption of the temporal world and the cruelty of religious wars, Mennonites cut themselves off from everything by which that temporal world was directed, i.e., from holding office, dealing with courts, participating in politics, and bearing arms. The simplicity of the Mennonite idea and its application to the needs of the society of the 16th-century Netherlands and northern Germany contributed to the movement's local popularity, above all, among peasants and urban plebeians (craftsmen, retail merchants, and laborers).

Because they were fiercely persecuted for their social radicalism both by Catholics and by Lutherans, and later also by Calvinists, and also for financial reasons individual Mennonites, and sometimes whole settlements, decided to leave the Netherlands, which was gripped in war with Spain, and headed toward, among other places, the "state without stakes," the Commonwealth, the lands on the Vistula, which the great Dutch Baroque poet Joost van den Vondel described in his poetic work *Gijsbrechjt van Amstel* (1637) as if it were the biblical Promised Land. The Prussian cities were joined by many economic ties with the Netherlands, and for that reason, quite naturally became a place for economic migration for many Dutch Calvinists; besides them, Mennonites also came to Gdańsk, Elbląg, and villages of the Vistula Delta (Żuławy, the alluvial region). Mennonite communities created in the Vistula Delta region and the valleys of the lower Vistula continued to exist until the end of World War II.

It is important to find an answer to the question of why Mennonites were permitted to settle in the territory of Royal Prussia at all. It was surely connected with the slow, evolutionary formation of Protestant structures in that province of the Commonwealth, which led to the creation

—
227
—

of a specific religious mosaic in a relatively small area. Despite the actual practice of Lutheran liturgy since the mid-16ᵗʰ century, from a legal point of view, the transition of individual rural parishes in the territories of Gdańsk and Elbląg to the new faith is not seen until 1577, and was accompanied by fairly significant organizational turmoil. The transitional chaos was intensified by the emergence of influential Dutch followers of John Calvin's doctrine and the conversion of many in the circles of the local elite to Calvinism (ca. 1570–1620). The two largest Protestant denominations concentrated on fighting with each other, and subsequently on holding onto what they possessed against attempts to recover it by local Catholic bishops.

In this situation, no one bothered too much about the Mennonites as such. After all, if they encountered excessive pressure in one place, they immediately moved somewhere else where better conditions were offered; and no one wanted to lose the benefits of the Mennonites' labor and taxes. Although in later years there were efforts to identify them with the proscribed Arians, no one was interested in applying radical measures against these peaceful farmers and craftsmen, who went out of their way not to be noticed. For this reason, as a rule, conditional tolerance of their presence was the course of action.

Scholars studying the social history of Royal Prussia are generally aware of the problems with collecting appropriate sources for the history of local Mennonites. The problems result from the fact that, as a peasant-plebeian society with a highly flattened internal stratification—with no separate "intelligentsia class" (for instance, the absence of a priesthood, already mentioned), the Mennonites were not a community that would produce many documents. This is true not only about manuscript sources but also material culture, for their quasi-iconoclasm and restraint in public social behavior effectively eliminated the typical forms of plebeian ludic expression, and inhibited "non-practical" creativity tending towards artistic expression. Unlike other foreign immigrants from Western and Southern

—
228
—

Europe—Scots, Englishmen, Italians, or Frenchmen—who can easily be described through the achievements of prominent personalities within their circle, it is difficult to identify prominent representatives of the Mennonites in the Commonwealth. We find among them no great theologians, explorers, eminent leaders or politicians, or creators of famous artistic, musical, literary, or building accomplishments. Their particular religious principles and community organization, their refusal to marry non-Mennonites (a practical endogamy within a few dozens of families that came from the Netherlands), the virtues of modesty and humility, an ascetic attitude to consumption—all these created strong barriers that isolated the Mennonites from other communities quite effectively. Mennonite taciturnity was proverbial, as was their plebeian good-natured coarseness.

As a result, not much was said about the Mennonites in Old Poland. Captain Tadeusz J. Chamski, a veteran of the November Uprising interned near Elbląg, in 1831 mentioned the Vistula Delta peasants, among whom he had happened to live: "They have kept their ancestral customs of diligence, taste, effort [...], care for their belongings and farm buildings, and particularly the exquisite cleanliness of their houses and living quarters ... You can smell the cleanliness. In a word, there is nowhere in these houses to spit, other than in the face of a disgusting Dutch woman, where neither stench nor filth is lacking due to their intemperate use of fatty foods." Indeed, in old 19th-century photographs, obese, rough-hewn plebeian faces look back at us, striking in their ascetic severity.

It is worthwhile to clarify certain facts regarding the history of settlement in the Vistula Delta. The members of Mennonite society arrived in an area suffering from an inadequate work force and devastated by floods in 1540 and 1543. From the time of the Teutonic Knights, however, these were regions with very intensive peasant settlement, with a stable parish structure and a dense network, preserved to the current time, of Gothic churches, sometimes quite splendid. The State of the Teutonic

— 229 —

Order, whose monumental capital, Malbork, lay in this area, organized drainage work that created an essential network of canals. The socio-economic character of the Vistula Delta village, even before Dutch settlers arrived in that area, greatly resembled agrarian relations in the Netherlands or in the villages of Northern Germany (Lower Saxony). Villages in which Mennonites settled usually were established on the sites of previously inhabited villages, or they were settlements established on the pastures, floodplains, and terrain lying alongside old settlement foundations. This land was leased to the new settlers on the basis of collective or individual emphyteutic contracts (with 30- or 40-year leases). Unlike the old villages settled according to Kulmer Recht, the newly-created emphyteutic settlements often consisted of isolated farms some distance from each other. In the later period, the emphyteusis was defined by so-called *prawo holenderskie* (*olenderskie* or *olęderskie*–i.e., Dutch law), and the villages were called Olendry or Olędry (German *Die Hollönderei*). This basic form spread in the 18th century to other regions of the Commonwealth (for example, to Wielkopolska and Kujawy), but most often these were not Mennonite settlements but those of German colonists, Lutherans, and sometimes Catholics.

Mennonites fit into the existing system perfectly, reclaiming sizable tracts of hitherto unused land. But despite contemporary reports and the opinion of many researchers on the matter, they were not a very numerous group in comparison with other communities in Royal Prussia, and represented a significant percentage only locally in the Vistula Delta area, as well as in some villages in a narrow strip of the lower Vistula (in the vicinity of Świecie and Grudziądz) and in suburban settlements of Gdańsk. The most complete statistical data come only from the first years after the partitioning of Poland (end of 18th c.); but there are no source factors that show the number of Mennonites in Royal Prussia as exceeding 13,000 souls, or about 3% of the population of the whole region. Representative data come from the 1770s, shortly before the beginning of the Mennonite

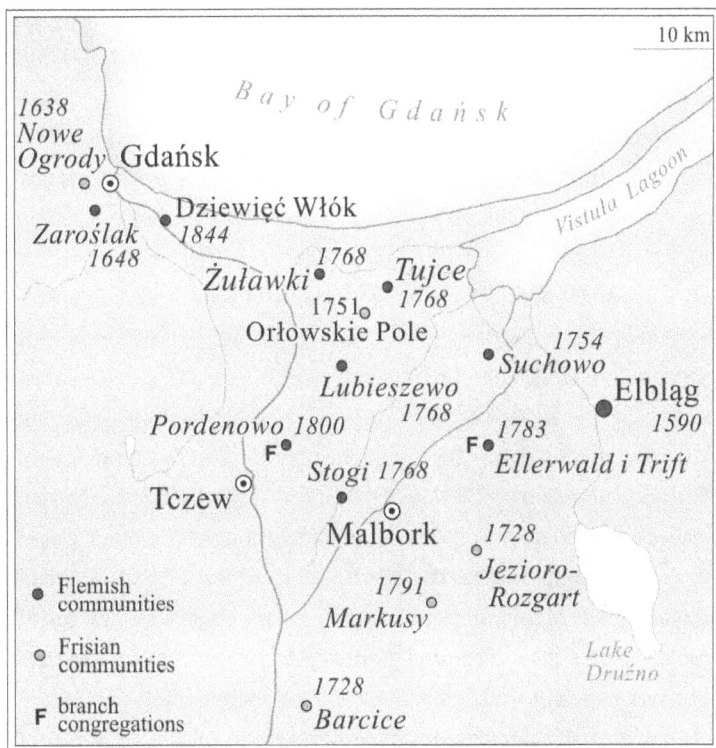

Map 12: Mennonites in the Vistula Delta in the 18th century.

exodus to southern Russia, and suggest numbers between 11,000 and 13,000 people. Although craftsmen in Gdańsk exaggerated the size of the community under discussion (with a bias, indicating financial damage allegedly suffered due to the Mennonites' activity), known sources allow us to estimate the number of Mennonites in Gdańsk and its suburbs at the beginning of the 17th and 18th centuries at about fifteen hundred people. At the time, around 60,000 people lived in the city. The majority of Mennonites did not live in the city itself, but in foreigners' suburban settlements belonging to the Catholic Church: Szkoty, Chełm, Biskupia Górka.

231

The Newcomers

With the gradual decline of Gdańsk's economy in the 18th century, the number of its Mennonite inhabitants also fell gradually. In 1793, 342 persons of this faith were counted in the city (less than half of one percent of its population), while there were 577 persons professing the Mennonite faith living in Gdańsk's rural surroundings. Despite a better legal position, the number of Elbląg's Mennonites probably did not exceed a dozen or more families, or about 100–200 people.

Gdańsk's Mennonites were not admitted to city law, and did not have the right to acquire property. Pushed onto the fringes, they were employed most often in *passementerie* (the making of in-demand textile accessories), the textile and spice trades, retail sale of wine, distilling liquor, and producing quality spiced liqueurs. One may associate with Mennonite distillers widespread production of the famous Gdańsk *Krambambuli* and *Goldwasser*, which the Polish nobles willingly bought and which was exported for foreign markets. This all sufficed for a fairly tolerable standard of living, while Mennonite widows and orphans could count on considerable support from their coreligionists. Only a few families were able to break their way through to join the local economic elite.

Because of the difficulties in acquiring property, relatively few Mennonites lived in villages belonging to the city of Gdańsk (Żuława Gdańska and Szkarpawa). Representatives of this religion were grouped in largest numbers in the Malbork Żuławy and the Elbląg Żuławy, where, according to data from the second decade of the 19th century, they comprised 16.5% in Malbork Żuławy and 10% in Elbląg Żuławy of the total inhabitants, and in a few localities they were the majority. Even assuming the emigration was higher than the 3,500 souls whose departure from Elbląg Żuławy in 1788–1804 is well documented, then Mennonites could have been at most one sixth of the population of the Vistula delta. The percentage of Mennonites participating in the use of local farmland was higher. In many villages, Mennonites leased a large part of the farmland, displaying clear developmental tendencies in the second half of the 18th

—
232
—

century, which were held at the level of 2,100 Chełmno *włóka*s (1 *włóka* equals about 16.8 hectares) due to Prussian administrative restrictions at the end of the century.

In the mid-17th century, Mennonites possessed around 550 *włóka*s of emphyteutic land in the Vistula Delta, and that did not change significantly until the last quarter of the 18th century. In addition to emphyteutic lands, however, Mennonites leased nearly 700 so-called Chełmno *włóka*s in the Malbork Żuławy area—that is, lands which had been farmed as early as the Middle Ages. This data illustrates not only the Mennonites' important participation in the use of local farmland, but also indicates a change in direction in the Mennonite settlement structure from the mid-17th century. Mennonites who bought land in old villages (with *ius culmense*—Chełmno law charters) slowly spread among the local populace and underwent linguistic assimilation, slowly becoming similar to their Lutheran and Catholic neighbors. The processes of quicker assimilation, however, did not set in until the 19th century.

In general, one may say that both the degree of the Mennonites' dispersion and the collective and compulsory nature of the work of draining and securing Vistula Delta farmland usually make it impossible for us to indicate unambiguously their contribution in forming the local cultural landscape. That does not mean, however, that their contribution was minor; the co-creation of Vistula Delta agricultural culture was unspectacular, leaving behind no attractive buildings, "only" well-farmed land and numerous drainage ditches. This guaranteed the local Mennonite peasants considerable wealth, as shown by numerous preserved posthumous property inventories. One must also realize that Vistula Delta farms of several *włóka*s were worth no less than the average manorial farmstead of a Polish nobleman, and the small manors of Kashubian nobles seem rather paltry compared to the Vistula Delta homesteads.

In contrast to many Vistula Delta peasants who owned land on terms of Chełmno law charters, Mennonites were personally free men. As was

—
233
—

mentioned, their legal status during the initial phase of their stay in Polish Prussia was regulated by emphyteutic contracts made with groups of settlers or individual persons. The contracts, usually not specifying the religion of the papers' recipient, influenced the situation of the peasants, the scope of their fiscal burdens, and their obligations toward the locally privileged faith, depending on the particular interests of the issuer of the document. For one settlement there could exist many contracts, concluded in succession, along with progress in draining the land. In 1642, Mennonites acquired a document from King Władysław IV verifying collectively the agreements resulting from emphyteutic contracts confirmed by the chancellery and located on the Żuławy of the Malbork estate. The grant of privilege was confirmed (naturally, for an appropriate sum) by successive Polish kings, and its contents were extended customarily to all Mennonites in Royal Prussia. The royal provisions, however, were respected only in the case of additional verification of their conformity with the particular law of Gdańsk, Elbląg, or church estates.

During the old Polish period, Mennonites did not receive the rights of citizens in Prussian cities, as a rule, and were not admitted into guilds. There was an exception in Elbląg in 1585, when two merchants were admitted to city law, having sworn oaths of loyalty according to specially drawn-up texts. In later times, admission of Mennonites to city law was only sporadic in nature. Mennonites, who balked at military exercises in police units and civil militias, were exempted from this duty in exchange for paying certain fees. Also, in the matter of oaths demanded in business contracts, for example, city authorities were satisfied with rules consistent with the demands of Mennonite doctrine ("yes, yes—no, no"), bypassing the requirement of saying certain formulas or making symbolic gestures, but this was usually connected with certain additional fees. Some forms of the Mennonites' financial activity developed semi-legally (from the point of view of the local majority), thanks to the use of legal loopholes and local social practice. To prevent this and reduce the profitability of farming, Gdańsk and Elbląg Mennonites were burdened with flat-rate "protective" taxes. In Gdańsk as of 1750, the tax came to 5,000 florins, or the value of a small house.

The Mennonite Church had no legal personality, and its adherents were subordinate, both administratively and for tax purposes, to the privileged churches in the territory of a given jurisdiction—the Lutheran Church in Gdańsk and Elbląg, the bishop of Chełmno in Żuławy Malborskie, as well as local pastors. This was manifested primarily in tax matters and in obligatory registration of Mennonite baptisms, weddings, and burials—for a fee—in the Lutheran and Catholic church registers, and in bans on erecting separate worship buildings. Mennonites throughout the Old Polish period did not form a parish network similar to the territorial organization of the local churches, the Catholic and Lutheran. The organization of the Mennonite congregation was flat, restricted to an autonomous congregation—in Vistula Delta conditions, an association of five hundred to about fifteen hundred of the faithful, without clearly defined borders of the territory belonging to a single community (personal parishes). An informal forum coordinating joint policy of the Mennonites in regard to administrative authorities was made up of conferences of elders of individual communities. An elder and his assistants, deacons, were elected by a vote on the part of all the baptized (that is, adult males). In everyday life, these were ordinary peasants or craftsmen, although it was not uncommon for the function to be inherited informally within a single family. The community as an institution was maintained by voluntary collections, periodic taxation of its members, interest from loans of the community's capital, and financial assistance from other Prussian communities or Dutch coreligionists.

Outside of gifts for the local authorities, the religious community did not have too many expenses, and the simplicity of the Mennonites' wooden churches, buildings devoid of any decorations, bells, organs, altars, confessionals, and the like, except for some ornamental carpentry,

—
235
—

to a large extent reflects the spirit of aesthetic asceticism in which the Mennonites lived. They were, after all, forbidden to erect temples that were reminiscent of the churches of the main religions. Unfortunately, the oldest Mennonite churches, dating from the 17th century, have not survived to the present time. As far as is known, these churches were the result of a fusion of the Dutch Calvinist idea of central layout of the church interior, local farm construction, and instructions of the bishops of Włocławek, in which the dimensions, kind of material, and external features of a church were clearly defined. We also know from Abraham Hartwich, author of the famous *Landes Beschreibung derer dreyen im Pohlnischen Preußen liegenden Werdern* [Description of the three parts of the Vistula Delta in Polish Royal Prussia] from 1722, that at the turn of the 17th and 18th centuries, Mennonites still celebrated their services in rebuilt barns and stables that were adorned only with "green boughs." Old barns have been preserved in the Vistula Delta to the present day that are reminiscent in their appearance, size, and construction technique of those churches, with the same practical design banality of Mennonite church construction. Brick Mennonite churches from the second half of the 19th century, in turn, have neo-Gothic features typical of German public buildings from that period in West Prussia. Adopting mainstream architectural models additionally provides a certain evidence of local Mennonites' gradual cultural assimilation, especially as their coreligionists who emigrated to Russia continued to build churches that hearken back to the traditional "Vistula Delta" appearance.

Mennonites in Royal Prussia belonged to two major religious factions, the so-called "Frisians" and "Flemish." During the formative process of Mennonitism in the Netherlands, these names (often replaced with pejorative phrases) lost their ethnic dimension. In Prussian conditions, they described two groups of local Mennonites whose views differed on the degree of isolation from "the world" and on admitting proselytes or offspring of mixed religious marriages into the community. Accord-

—
236
—

ing to contemporary accounts, the Frisians belonged to the more conservative group, which found external expression in modesty of dress and, allegedly, the interior decoration of their dwellings. This did not hamper them, however, in their wealth-accumulation goals, collecting items that were considered luxurious and sumptuous. The more numerous Flemish, on the other hand, were said to be outright "worldly" in their behavior, and their dress was closer to general trends in fashion. The Mennonite community organized not only the forms of religious practices but also the totality of its members' behavior, encroaching deep into their personal lives. Cultural continuity was based mainly on realizing expectations that had their sources in the past, in the experiences of the community's elders and parents. Without doubt, the question of possession and inheriting farms and the frequent need to reach out for neighbors' help additionally deepened dependence on parents and the community hierarchy. Undoubtedly, the deepening of the patriarchal role of the elected individuals of the community administration influenced the custom of dragging out the period of members' initiation through baptism. Often men became members of the community with full rights only in their thirties, after getting married.

Living in a culturally similar environment (the same Vistula Delta dialect of *Plaatdeutsch*, similar forms of material consumption, forms of economic behavior, etc.), Mennonites "fled" from the world of contemporary models of civilization to maintain their own distinctness. By creating group attitudes intended to restrict voluntary contacts with foreigners to essential financial relations only, Mennonites created conditions that made it difficult to integrate into the surrounding society. This escapism, in addition to high self-esteem and self-control, was accompanied by rigorous attachment (although with some differentiation in individual branches of the faith) to their own customs and appearance that arose not only from their dogma but also from the specific nature of the group, which entrenched the habit of the next generation with an almost eschatological sanction.

—
237
—

The characteristic dress of Mennonites was, it seems, normal dress for their surroundings, but a generation or more behind the prevailing fashion. The difference must have been striking, as was observed by travelers who came to Gdańsk. For example, Carl Arndt, a student from Rostock in 1694, wrote after visiting local churches, that the men wore black robes and small collars as well as—to set them apart—short hair. Arndt, who further noted that "the girls are pretty," was clearly surprised that the women did not wear bonnets. How sensitive questions of external appearance could be is demonstrated by the scandal among the Mennonites of Gdańsk in the mid-18th century created by the appearance at services of several Dutch coreligionists in wigs.

In Gdańsk inventories of Mennonite property that I am familiar with, other than religious literature, one can find no trace of any particular items typical only of them. The anachronism of Mennonite dress became striking only on the basis of the increasingly dynamic development of new trends in dress in the second half of the 18th century and the 19th.

—
238
—

We know that some of the religion's rules opposed any use of possessed goods, and inhibited consumption and extravagance in dress, promoting restriction of the forms of social life. Specific forms of asceticism led to establishing the range of morally permissible application of that which one possessed (cash, means of production, etc.) to things that were rational and (from the Mennonite point of view) socially useful, for example, the purchase of land, selfless activity as religious authorities, community charity, enrichment. In order to preserve discipline, punishments were provided in the 17th century for the sins of drunkenness, dancing, making music, gambling, blaspheming, cursing, arguing, and fighting: admonishment in the community church office or reprimand "before the whole community." Recidivism was punished by banishment from the bosom of the community until such time as improvement was clear. Adultery, theft, and crimes ended with absolute exclusion from the religious community. A person who deviated from the religious prohibitions had to deal with strong environmental ostracism and loss of neighborly aid. In rural environments, where one always had to be ready for the threat of flood, fire, or crop failure, selfless assistance from coreligionists was often essential for survival. The famous scene from Peter Weir's popular film *The Witness* (1984), with Harrison Ford in the leading role, presenting communal barn-building among the Amish, one of the offshoots of Mennonitism, very aptly reflects the role of such communality.

Mennonites living in cities and working in freelance professions were often not inclined toward absolute obedience. For example, in 1694, the elders in the Gdańsk Flemish community were not pleased by the rather frivolous paintings of Enoch Seemann, and he was forbidden to attend services, and his wife was ordered not to share table or bed with her husband. Seemann did not submit, and after several years of disputes, he finally left for London, where his son became a famous portrait painter. There were occurrences of running away for love, as well as baptisms, which for Lutherans and Catholics were a clear sign of religious victory over the sectarians. In every case, however, this meant for the convert a complete and irreversible split with his earlier life, community, and family.

The Dutch language, which remained (among the Mennonites of the Vistula Delta) a tongue that was generally understood (partly because of the initially minor differences between the Lower German and Dutch dialects), by the turn of the 17th and 18th centuries played a primarily liturgical function. The text of the service was read in the Dutch and Low German languages until the mid-18th century, and not until the second half of the 19th century was it supplanted by New High German. Those who conducted services quite often used texts taken from Lutheran hymnals and postils, as exemplified by Mennonite hymnals from the late 18th century.

The declining wealth of Gdańsk and its citizens from the mid-17th century on manifested itself, among other things, in a gradual increase in dislike of "foreign" societies, whose financial activity was seen as one of the main factors in the general regression. Mennonites were an easily

—
239
—

identifiable social group, against which it was easy to articulate charges: they were supposedly characterized by their suspicious origin, anti-social business activity, secrecy, "dangerous religious associations," rationally unjustified, and their alleged wealth. But except for fiscal measures, no major restrictions were placed on Mennonite activities. Radical changes did not occur until the elimination of the Polish state.

In the 17th and 18th centuries in the Vistula Delta, certain typical characteristics of the Mennonites' social life developed—their language, a unique mixture of Low German and Dutch, as well as their buildings, dress, and typical furniture design—that left their mark on Mennonite colonists in 19th-century Russia and influenced the historico-symbolic thinking of Mennonite clusters in America. Tracing the subsequent stages of their migration, we discover names of Vistula Delta villages in southern areas of Ukraine, in Canada, and in Paraguay, where radical followers of Mennonitism appear. Even in contemporary meetings, Mennonites from different parts of the world discover common ancestors formerly living in the Vistula Delta, for example, representatives of the families Bestvater, Epp, Jantzen, Kauenhoven, Penner, Wiebe.

After the First Partition of Poland (1772), the Mennonites in West Prussia (not including the Gdańsk community) numbered 13,495 persons farming 2,170 *włókas* (data from 1773). Mennonites regarded King Frederick II as the natural successor to Polish rulers and tried to have their previous religious rights confirmed. The King guaranteed them freedom from recruit conscription in return for a protective tax (by a 1780 grant of privilege). In successive legal acts (1781, 1801), Mennonite freedom from recruitment was connected with an established maximum limit to the increase of farmlands belonging to them, which was set at 2,100 *włókas*. In this way, Mennonites who remained personally exempt from military service took on military obligations at the moment they purchased canton land (from which recruits were chosen). Compliance with these regulations meant breaking one of the religious foundations of Mennonitism, and failure to acquire land was equivalent to inhibiting adequate developmental opportunities from the end of the 18th century. Peasant sons who had no chance to inherit or marry into farms had the choice of either working as farmhands on the farms of firstborn heirs, or leaving the Vistula Delta. The restrictive Prussian policy as well as additional harassment from the Lutheran administration (the introduction of community payments on behalf of pastors) coincided in time with the colonization efforts of Empress Catherine II of Russia. As a result of broad recruiting efforts, in 1789, the first groups of Mennonite settlers began to come to the lands won from Turkey; the monarch is said to have viewed them among the Potemkin villages. Up to 1796, about 2,000 people left former Royal Prussia. In successive waves of emigration that continued until the 1830s, a group of several thousand of the poorer Mennonite peasants and rural craftsmen left the Vistula Delta and the lands on the Vistula. They sought a new "Promised Land" in the steppes of southern Russia. The emigration outflow was equal to the entire current natural growth among Vistula Delta Mennonites, which resulted in a setback to the numerical development of that religious community, causing it to remain at about the level from the end of the Commonwealth, or some 12,000–13,000 souls. The number of Mennonites in that area did not increase until the 20th century.

The war, which swept through the territory of the Vistula Delta in the winter and spring of 1945, destroyed a centuries-old local cultural tradition. Canadian and American Mennonites arriving in the winter of 1945 and in 1946 directed the first convoys of UNRRA aid to devastated Poland, and discovered in the abandoned Vistula Delta only old documents and parish registers, and new, gaunt settlers moving into the abandoned houses. After World War II, Poles settled lands worked for centuries by the Mennonites—people relocated, often against their will, to areas culturally alien to them and symbolically hostile. Despite the close proximity of Kashubian or Polish neighbors, it is difficult to speak of any cultural osmosis between Mennonites and Poles. In the Vistula Delta, in Gdańsk and Elbląg, there was no real coexistence of the new, Polish, postwar culture and the old, German, prewar one. A sudden, brutal, and complete cultural change took place. The habits of the new settlers, often drawn from rural areas lagging in terms of civilization, exacerbated by tragic events during the war, and the situation of the political and mental autarky of the Polish People's Republic (1945–1989) did not create conditions for the respect of local tradition: Mennonite and Lutheran cemeteries, private library collections, furniture, and other objects with which emotions were connected that were rooted deep in tradition, in the past, in generations of use. The sense of loss and the political and legal uncertainty that accompanied the Polish "repatriates" were intensified by various traditions that appealed to newcomers from the Vilnius area, the Grodno area, and Galicia. Furthermore, lack of experience of farming in a geographically difficult area, and the new organization of the agricultural economy, modeled on the Soviet organization (PGR—state-owned collective farms), contributed to the destruction of the old field divisions and the traditional water system. The economic policy of the communists, who kept the local population in the PGR structures for decades at a level of compulsory poverty, led to the irreversible decline of the cultural heritage of the Vistula Delta.

—
242
—

Selected bibliography

Bender, H. S. et al. (eds.), *The Mennonite Encyclopedia. A Comprehensive Reference Work on the Anabaptist-Mennonite Movement*, vol. 1–5, Hillsboro: Mennonite Brethren Publishing House, 1982–1993.

Dyck, C. J., *An Introduction to Mennonite History*, Scottdale: Herald Press, 1993.

Hamilton, A., Voolstra, S., and Visser, P. (eds.), *From Martyr to Muppy. A Historical Introduction to Cultural Assimilation Processes of a Religious Minority in the Netherlands: The Mennonites*, Amsterdam: Amsterdam University Press, 1994.

Kizik, E., "A Radical Attempt to Resolve the Mennonite Question in Danzig in the Mid-Eighteenth Century," *The Mennonite Quarterly Review*, LXVI (1992), 2, pp. 127–151.

Kizik, E., "Inwentarz pośmiertny kramarza gdańskiego, mennonity Hendrika van Dührena z 1694 roku" [Posthumous Inventory of a Gdańsk Stallkeeper, the Mennonite Hendrik von Dühren, from 1694], *Alamanach Historyczny*, no. 2 (2000), pp. 185–208.

Kizik, E., "Religious Freedom and the Limit of the Social Assimilation: The History of the Mennonites in Gdańsk and the Vistula Delta until their Tragic End after World War II," in Hamilton, A., Voolstra, S., and Visser, P. (eds.), *From Martyr to Muppy. A Historical Introduction to Cultural Assimilation Processes of a Religious Minority in the Netherlands: The Mennonites*, pp. 48–64.

Kizik, E., *Mennonici w Gdańsku, Elblągu i na Żuławach Wiślanych w drugiej połowie XVII i w XVIII wieku. Studium z dziejów małej społeczności wyznaniowej* [Mennonites in Gdańsk, Elbląg, and the Vistula Żuławy in the Second Half of the 17th Century and in the 18th Century. A Study from the History of a Small Religious Society], Gdańsk: Wydawnictwo Gdańskie, 1994.

Klassen, P. J., *A Homeland for Strangers. An Introduction to Mennonites in Poland and Prussia*, Fresno: Center for Mennonite Brethren Studies, 1989.

Klassen, P. J., *Mennonites in Early Modern Poland and Prussia*, Baltimore: Johns Hopkins University Press, 2009.

Mennonici na Żuławach. Ocalone dziedzictwo. Katalog wystawy w Muzeum Narodowym w Gdańsku, Oddział Etnografii 30 czerwca – 30 października 2007 [Mennonites in the Żuławy Region. A Surving Heritage. Catalog of an Exhibit in the National Museum in Gdańsk, Ethnography Section, 30 June – 30 October 2007], Gdańsk: Muzeum Narodowe, 2007.

Mężyński, K., "O mennonitach w Polsce" [On the Mennonites in Poland], *Rocznik Gdański*, no. 19/20 (1960–1961), pp. 185–225.

Snyder, C. A., *Anabaptist History and Theology. An Introduction*, Kitchener: Pandora Press, 1995.

UNDER

A COMMON SKY

But where are the Poles?

—

WOJCIECH TYGIELSKI

—

By the end of the Middle Ages, Poles—understood as the inhabitants of Wielkopolska [Greater Poland], Małopolska [Lesser Poland], and Mazowsze [Mazovia], as well as Silesia (which, however, lay outside the borders of the Polish state in the 14th century), formed a community of language, descent, and tradition. The state was also an important integrating factor, and at the same time one that facilitated auto-identification, as all those mentioned above—at least to the end of the reign of Casimir the Great (1333–1370)—were governed only by rulers of the Piast dynasty.

Nonetheless, distinctions persisted as evidence of diversity as well as a remnant of feudal disintegration. Although the Małopolska aristocracy was dominant in the state, those of Wielkopolska tried to defend their position during the disputes over the succession after the death of King Casimir in 1370. Later, in the 16th and 17th centuries, both provinces had separate tribunals (courts of appeal, in Piotrków for Wielkopolska, in Lublin for Małopolska), and there even existed legal differences between them for a time (for example, the Statues of Nieszawa from 1454 were formulated separately for each of the provinces, and the differences were not removed until 1496). We may add that standardization of the law in force was one of the demands of the execution movement, and thus of the most enlightened noble politicians' reform activities, which were undertaken, with various results, around the mid-16th century.

With the passage of time, however, unification, both of law and custom, ensued. Social integration also progressed—more and more often, marriages were contracted between members of the aristocracies of Wielkopolska and Małopolska. There followed the phenomenon of acquiring land in various parts of the state, and even the holding of offices by inhabitants of Wielkopolska and Małopolska—in the neighboring province.

Mazowsze, which remained under the rule of local Piasts, was incorporated into the Crown (formally, into Wielkopolska) in several stages: first the districts of Gostyń and Rawa (1462), then those of Sochaczew (1476) and Płock (1495), and finally, Czersk and Warsaw (1526). For half a century, until 1576, separate law persisted in these territories, too. The process of moving the capital to Warsaw, initiated by Sigismund III Vasa at the end of the 16th century, contributed to the final blurring of Mazowsze particularism—although, interestingly, in other areas, an unflattering stereotype of the inhabitant of Mazowsze continued to operate.

Political and systemic decisions made on the threshold of the modern era fundamentally changed the territorial form of the state, and thus its ethnic structure as well. It is estimated that about the year 1500, in the borders of the Polish state at the time, Poles made up 70% of the inhabitants, Ruthenians 15%, and Germans about 10%; while in Gdańsk Pomerania, the latter could be even half of the population. In the southeastern provinces, meanwhile, Ruthenians constituted about three quarters of the total population; in the lands of central Poland, on the other hand, the Polish element probably accounted for up to 90% of all inhabitants. After the Union of Lublin was completed in 1569, Poles made up about half the inhabitants of the state, and in the mid-17th century—after the borders were shifted further east, as a result of the wars with Moscow in the first half of the 17th century—only 40%.

The "common sky" of the title, and thus the common land and all that it had to offer its inhabitants, was shared by representatives of all the ethnic groups who are represented in our book. The original goal of this

—
248
—

book—which seems clear enough—was to show this diversity, to describe its individual components, with an emphasis on their cultural richness, and thus to paint a portrait of the community that resulted from being long-term neighbors. We must add, however, that the consequence of this kind of closeness can be friendship and cooperation but also conflict—as the experience of many generations confirms, unfortunately.

The texts assembled here document that diversity effectively, not only because of the considerable number of authors invited to contribute and the diversity of their writing ideas and temperaments, but above all in regard to the diversity of the groups and communities described—their internal structures, motivation for migration, and also degree of integration with the local surroundings. For we have received collective portraits both of the groups inhabiting the common or adjoining territories "since time immemorial," and of the immigrant minorities whose representatives decided, for various reasons, to change their place of dwelling, and chose the Commonwealth as the country to settle in.

One must include in the former category, in addition to inhabitants of native Polish provinces, the Lithuanians and Ruthenians (Belarusians and Ukrainians), and perhaps also the Germans and Jews—although in their case, we are dealing with typically migratory phenomena, but with a different character and chronology. It is worth emphasizing—referring to the comments made in the Introduction—that in the context of such diversity, the description "assimilated" immigrants is particularly useful. Igor Kąkolewski used it in his chapter, while Michał Kopczyński and the undersigned recognized this term as a useful category between the "locals" and the "newcomers." This is what finally determined the structure of this book.

For one certainly should regard in a completely different way the presence "under a common sky" of the Italians, Scots, and Dutch (the Olędrzy and the Mennonites) settlers as typical immigrant groups, and—far less obvious—the Armenians and Romani as well. In a dichotomous division that distinguishes the "local" populace and typical immigrants, it would be difficult for Tatars to find their place, as well as Karaites (in their case, let us note, the category "assimilated" also has some justification).

Immigrant groups typically were less numerous, but also differed greatly among themselves. If they had limited influence on the original decisions regarding migration and place of settlement (although it happened that they settled in relatively quickly), others were self-reliant in the this area; some bonded permanently with their new dwelling place, demonstrating assimilative tendencies, while others preferred an itinerant mode of existence, which is generally associated with great care to preserve cultural distinctions. It should be added that representatives of smaller national groups, or rather ethnic groups, often living in peripheral regions, had limited opportunities for articulating their needs as well as making effective efforts on behalf of their group interests, and for this reason often played no significant role in a multinational state, but also posed no real threat to its structures.

A completely different type of grouping should be applied, therefore, when considering the spheres of activity of representatives of individual minorities, the level of their national consciousness, their tendencies toward social or cultural integration with their surroundings, and also—very important—to polonization, broadly understood. A still different division could be made from the viewpoint of material position, professional aptitude, and career opportunities in the structures of the state, or the effectiveness of their efforts on behalf of their group interests.

Whatever perspective one takes, however, the diversity of the entities that made up the multinational Commonwealth remains obvious, with all its positive and negative consequences. Foremost among the former is the cultural richness which results from that diversity, but requires skill to derive benefit from it, and therefore mutual interest, combined with openness and tolerance. The negative consequences, briefly put, are the numerous areas for potential conflict resulting from proximity and differences in customs and religions. As a rule, competition in the economic and social spheres became sharper and fiercer if existing conflicts of interests coincided with ethnic and religious divisions. In the long run, the result of mutual animosity and resentment that could not be mitigated effectively with the aid of systemic reforms was a reduction in the state's cohesiveness, a weakening of its international position, and finally, the loss of its sovereignty. Perhaps the most drastic and, at the same time, most instructive example of this is the history of the Cossacks and the evolution of their status within the Commonwealth, which in the end turned out badly for both sides.

The division mentioned earlier into "newcomers" and "locals" (among whom we would have to include immigrants who had long since become "assimilated") may be useful in attempting to evaluate the mutual relations of ethnic groups, and to perceive their positions within the common state. The situation of the former seems far clearer and easier to describe. For in the case of typical immigrants, we can discern the causes that made them migrate and the motives that led them to choose the Commonwealth as their place of settlement. Subsequently—for purely cognitive reasons— we should be interested in the course of the process of their potential cultural and social assimilation. The successes observed in this area, and also the failures, allow us not only to understand the immigrants' intentions and life strategies but also to come to know better the society that accepted them, that is, the other side of the cultural dialogue. As a result, our knowledge of the social, economic, and political realities in which the newcomers had to function becomes fuller.

In the case of the "locals," who formed a moderately uniform state organism as a result of historical processes as well as concrete decisions of a political character, the research situation is far more complicated. On the one hand, representatives of these groups should be treated as co-hosts of the territory described, while on the other, one must note the obvious asymmetry of the partnership that existed. The level of national consciousness of individual groups as well as whole communities clearly varied. The mutual relationships of the basic segments of society, separated by the criterion of nationality, must here be treated as a central subject of historical debate and—alongside state and religious divisions—a fundamental element of the reality to be studied.

There can be no doubt, therefore, that in the proposed editorial formula, the question of the Poles must appear, because their place in a narrative context so formulated is not at all obvious. For if we speak of "other nations" jointly inhabiting the Commonwealth, we are assuming as obvious in such a conception the domination of the Polish element as well as its "original" character, and therefore its superiority within the state. If we describe that state as "multinational," Poles become only one of its components—perhaps the most important, but still only one of many.

This is not, unfortunately, a purely academic dilemma, nor a solely historiographical one. Decisions of a scholarly and intellectual nature are influenced by contemporary politics, and more specifically, by the current state of our relations with neighboring states, where historical views are constructed differently. We are dealing here with a double dependence. The nature of the coexistence in the past influences the present, while the way of perceiving and describing mutual historical relations can be regarded as a characteristic declaration of worldview. On the other hand, modern relations influence ways of perceiving the past.

The above comments pertain first and foremost to all our neighbors beyond the eastern border, since our neighbors to the west during the period of interest to us—exceptionally—did not create major problems, or generate conflicts. On 18 July 1573, Jan Herburt, castellan of Sanok, one of the Polish delegates on his way to Paris to meet Henry of Valois, said during a stay in Leipzig, "All of Germany is covered by alliances, treaties, and covenants with our Kingdom, and we expect that surely in the future [...] our affairs will find help and shelter in the Reich's princes and not only in matters auspicious and consistent with our desires, but also in all problems."

In these words, which the Polish diplomat directed to Augustus, Duke of Saxony, and his most intimate collaborators, undoubtedly there was a great deal of diplomatic rhetoric; but to a large extent they reflected the real state of affairs as well.

This turning point in the Commonwealth's history certainly encouraged the formulation of innovative visions of international relations. Germany, however—then politically fragmented, weakened by religious wars in the 16th century, and in the next century gravely devastated during the Thirty Years War—for some time displayed no expansionist tendencies, and geopolitical circumstances, including the Turkish threat, inclined both sides toward cooperation and partnership. Undoubtedly, for this reason, the early modern period is neither a subject of fundamental Polish-German historiographical disputes, nor one evoking great emotion. The situation on the eastern border is completely different.

In reference to the comments formulated by Michał Kopczyński in his Introduction, however, let us turn to consideration of the fundamental question of the semantic content of the concept of "nation," a term we try to avoid here—in view of its predominant and completely modern understanding—commenting rather on the subject of ethnic groups, which at that point were in the phase of the nation-making process described.

The formation process of modern nations, let us remember, has been discussed many times, and there is an enormous literature on it. We know that in its contemporary understanding, we relate this term generally to a community inhabiting a specific territory, using a separate language (although, by the latest findings, that is not a *sine qua non* condition), and above all having a sufficiently clear awareness of a common past and cultural achievements. The religious factor was also important in this context, but the decisive issue was one of awareness, or a feeling of belonging to a nation and a cultural community with all the attendant emotional and practical consequences.

This concept, however, cannot be freely applied in relation to times earlier than the 19th century, because preindustrial society—fundamentally divided into the higher strata and the local peasant communities—could not yet form a national community, which is characterized above all by a homogeneous culture. That is formed only in conditions of free flow of information and a uniform educational system (thus Ernest Gellner argued, a quarter century ago).

For the period of the First Commonwealth, on the other hand, the concept of "a political nation" has fundamental significance. The Polish nobility, which formed finally as a distinct estate during the Jagiellonian era, seeking a privileged status in relation to the other social groups, created a quasi-national community. Its essence became a feeling of affiliation with that estate, to which certain rights and privilege accrued, but at the same time duties of a civic nature. This estate, or at least very many representatives of it, felt a responsibility for the fortunes of their common state, the Commonwealth.

—

254

—

It was, however, a highly diverse group ethnically, as its composition—originally limited to descendants of knights of Wielkopolska and Małopolska—included representatives of social elites with different national identifications, above all, Lithuanian and Ruthenian. Their senses of community and collective identity were certainly different; but in voluntarily accepting affiliation with a "political nation," they underwent polonization. This process did not, however, affect all representatives of the noble estate thus formed. Some of its representatives cultivated their religious and cultural diversity, and did not even necessarily use the Polish language, and for this reason belonged primarily to a political community that, at the same time, had its own distinct class dimension.

Ethnic divisions and distinctions, therefore, did not coincide with those of class. "Affiliation with one community," according to the statement of Henryk Litwin, "did not at all preclude affiliation with another," with bonds and group solidarity playing the predominant role, at least within the noble class. "Accessible source material seems to confirm rather unambiguously the thesis that the sense of a noble community definitely took precedence over all displays of ethnic consciousness," is one of the conclusions of Tomasz Kizwalter in reference to the phase of the nation-forming process of interest to us here.

How then—mindful of the specific nature of ethnic divisions at the time—are we to view and describe sensibly the mutual relations of Poles and Lithuanians, Poles and Ukrainians, and Poles and Belarusians, and also, no less essential, those of Lithuanians and Belarusians and of Lithuanians and Ukrainians? Should we rather emphasize the voluntary nature of the existing alliances and the mutual benefits that came from them; or should we look at the inequalities in mutual relations, the domination of one side and the restriction thereby of chances for development of the weaker partner, which, sooner or later, had to bear fruit in fundamental, structural conflict?

Thus, for example, was the Union of Poland and Lithuania primarily the result of a long-lasting process of growing closer, initiated—still during the conflicts with the Teutonic Knights—by the choice of representatives of the Jagiellonian dynasty for the Polish throne; or was it, as some would have it, an obvious manifestation of Polish expansionism? Did Poles, as a result of that historical event, take on themselves the burden of checking Russian westward expansionism, engaging—perhaps needlessly, or too early—in a long-lasting, devastating conflict; or did they simply thus expand their sphere of domination over vast terrains stretching eastward? Did Polish colonization of the borderlands—here we are dealing directly with the Belarusian and Ukrainian question—bring positive effects in the sphere of civilization and economics; or should it be viewed only in terms of expansion and exacerbating social inequalities by force? Should we regard the conflict in Ukraine only through the lens of magnate *latifundia* and Cossack uprisings, and ascribe to the latter—in the spirit of Sienkiewicz—only unjustified aggression, combined with cruelty,

—
255
—

theft, and destruction? Should we rather be interested by the long-lasting impossibility of finding structural solutions that could satisfy both sides and check the process of Ukraine's coming closer to and finally becoming subject to the Russian Empire, which in the not too distant future was to have such fatal consequences for the existence of our state and nation?

Historians are often accused of subjectivity of viewpoint, or of identifying with one side in a conflict. The question is asked, for example, whether scholars should concentrate on studying their own national past, without forgetting the comparative approach, of course; or should they rather study the history of other states and societies, despite the difficulties created by language and cultural barriers? Another doubt of this kind: is the dominance of the clergy among scholars researching and describing the history of the Church (which could be seen as a natural result of the researchers' interest and potential competence) appropriate? But perhaps it would be correct rather to say that such a situation threatens a one-sided point of view? Finally, should the history of colonialism be described by descendants of the colonizers, or rather by people who come from the colonized territories, or perhaps by some third party, that is, historians outside the group of those "directly involved"?

There are no easy answers here, because the necessary competence is generally acquired in an environment vitally interested in the subject, and thus directly and often emotionally involved. The same is true of the potential audience.

It therefore seems more important than decreeing spheres of interest and competence, to contrast different opinions, especially on subjects that produce sharp disputes. This effort, if made in good faith, generally produces positive results. For one must remember that it is not only in the sphere of appraising and evaluating that the historical narrative rarely satisfies all those with a specific interest, but that history, even in that purely factographic part, is fundamentally not "fair." It cannot be. The strong and wealthy have always documented their past better, and created more sources, the reading and subsequent interpretation of which forms the basis of our knowledge about the past. This "unfairness" and disproportion of preserved testimonials concerns social groups as well as ethnic ones.

And thus, Polish historians are in no easy situation in regard to their colleagues beyond the eastern border, broadly conceived; their statements on the subject of political realities, and above all mutual relations between the individual ethnic components that made up the old Commonwealth, are carefully observed and commented on. Recently, in particular, "political correctness" in this area seems more and more assiduously observed, which introduces additional confusion in terminology. For emotions and disputes can be aroused not only by the Union of Lublin in 1569, viewed differently on the Polish side and the Lithuanian side, or by the colonization of the Eastern Borderlands, already mentioned, as well as the failure to find a sensible solution to the Cossack question. Controversy arises, for example, regarding the composition of the army that defeated the Teutonic Knights in 1410 at Grunwald (the Belarusians consider themselves unjustly omitted here), and also, by analogy, the ethnic structure of the expedition that Duke Konstanty Ostrogski led to a famous victory in 1514 over the Muscovite forces at Orsha.

—

257

—

The question returns, therefore, how should one view and correctly define the place of Poles in the state that was traditionally described by the name *Polonia* or *Regnum Poloniae*, as well as *Corona Regni Poloniae*, and therefore, respectively, Poland, the Kingdom of Poland, and the Crown of the Kingdom of Poland?

As we know, beginning in the 16th century, that specific state entity, in which the Polish nobles had primacy, began to be called generally the *Rzeczpospolita (Respublica)*, the Commonwealth, the state of the free citizens who identified themselves with it. Historiography later introduced the term *Rzeczpospolita Obojga Narodów* [Commonwealth of Two Nations], recognizing the equal position of the Lithuanian partner, but thereby diminishing the role of all others—above all, the Ruthenians living in the Grand Duchy. Today, seeking a possibly objective description, we encounter terminological problems; but it does not seem that abandoning the term *Poland* in favor of the obviously more correct *Commonwealth* has been a real solution. The Latin titles of the works of Marcin Kromer and Szymon Starowolski describing this complicated state entity began, after all, with the word *Polonia*.

Returning to the main thread of our reasoning, however, what was the significance of the multicultural neighborhood and the mutual relations within it, and then of the multinational structure of the state, for the development of Polish history? This is a question of fundamental significance which is worth posing even if formulating a thorough, comprehensive answer seems too much of a challenge.

Polish history, if we attempt a maximum of synthesis, was defined by two factors of fundamental significance: affiliation with the Latin civilization originating from Mediterranean culture (which meant openness to cultural and civilizational inspirations coming from there) and location at a physical distance from its main centers—on the border between the Roman-Latin world and the Byzantine-Orthodox one, with all its cultural and political consequences.

A border separates, above all, and serves to emphasize differences. At the same time, however—as Henryk Samsonowicz pointed out not long ago in reference to the considerations of David Abulafia—a border, as a point of contact, can also join; and in any event, a new quality is created in the area along both its sides. For the fabric of social life, and above all for the form of culture of bordering regions, crossing the border and the cultural osmosis that then occurs are of particular importance. It is for this reason that Poland's different neighbors and its multinational internal structure played such an important role in Polish history.

For the period of the Middle Ages, the impact of the West definitely seems more important—political pressure on the part of Germany, both

—
258
—

in modern times and back then, cultural impulses, symbolized by "colonization on German law"—a major settlement movement that revived the local economy and enriched the social fabric. By contrast, on the threshold of the modern era, the dominating political pressure turned out to be from the east, gradually demanding an increasingly firm reaction, especially as it was not accompanied by a stimulating influence in the spheres of economy and culture.

The growing might of the Muscovite state and its consequent westward expansion presented increasingly important problems and dangers which, in the long run, the Commonwealth was unable to deal with effectively. The structures of the Commonwealth of "noble citizens" turned out to be too weak to meet the growing needs of the state, to assure the safety of its inhabitants, to build a modern army and administration. Also lacking was the necessary determination among those social forces that saw the need and could possibly have been in a position to conduct profound modernizing reforms.

At the same time, however, conditions developed in that same state in which a considerable number of its inhabitants felt very well, conditions clearly appreciated by the more and more numerous travelers among whom potential immigrants were recruited. The title of Janusz Tazbir's book, *Państwo bez stosów* [The State Without Stakes (in the sense of burning at the stake)], became an important symbol of our thinking about our Commonwealth, in which freedom and tolerance predominated (although only representatives of the privileged class could fully benefit from them), and about a state of religious peace, a state in principle not oppressive to its citizens, and thereby attractive to its neighbors and thus also to immigrants.

The inhabitants of Prussian towns preferred, after all, to be under Polish rule rather than that of the Teutonic Knights; for that reason, the thirteen-year war with the Order was decided in our favor. Members of the Lithuanian elite desired alliance with the Crown because the privileges enjoyed by the Polish nobles suited them very well. The consequence of this

—
259
—

attitude was the polonization of the most influential families, with the Radziwiłłs at the forefront. The Cossacks were also prepared to "serve the Commonwealth," and the real problems did not begin until they were deprived of that opportunity. Gdańsk, developing and enriching itself with its position as trade intermediary between the Commonwealth and its West European partners, diligently guarded its autonomy for decades; people living at the mouth of the Motława River, however, understood very well that being cut off from the Polish-Lithuanian hinterlands would mean an end to their prosperity. It was for this reason that the Gdańsk patriciate, German by origin, did not voluntarily open their gates to either the Swedish invaders or even the King of Prussia, Frederick II.

The Commonwealth's expanses of territory, which were not called *aurifodina advenarum* [a gold mine for immigrants] by coincidence, undoubtedly created many opportunities for immigrants, while the state, relatively tolerant and disinclined to repress its citizens, additionally attracted those whom repression threatened in their homes. This was true above all for heretics and representatives of ethnic groups that were treated worse somewhere else. It was probably for this reason there were so many of these "assimilated Poles," as—let us remember—Hieronim Wietor, a printer in Kraków who came from Silesia, described himself.

However, especially in situations when the state's existence was in danger or its territorial integrity was challenged, the mutual relations of the "newcomers" and the "locals" could not be and were not idyllic. Megalomania was not, after all, unfamiliar to numerous representatives of Old Polish society. "There is the same rumor both in Germany and in Holland about us Poles, that this is the one nation on earth that is most polite, most handsome, and most humane," Krzysztof Opaliński wrote in 1645 to his brother, Łukasz, referring boastfully to the wide response that his embassy to Paris, to assist Marie Louise Gonzaga as the future Queen of Poland, provoked on his journey. This belief, gladly internalized, was also part of the Sarmatian culture and the noble lords' mentality.

The relationship with foreigners as well as with representatives of other ethnic groups was the result of hospitality and xenophobia, the relative proportions of which are today very difficult to determine. With the gradual deterioration of the economic situation and external conditions, the issue of responsibility for the state and readiness to provide for it was on the daily agenda. Not all representatives of the immigrant groups could pass, and wanted to pass, this "patriotism test" with satisfactory results. At the same time, crisis situations, along with the weakening of the state's structures, occurred more and more often. This provoked understandable criticism of foreigners from the noble citizens; the "hosts" pointed out the "guests'" inappropriate behavior, which further worsened relations.

Spectacular conflicts, let us add, are much more thoroughly and evocatively described in the sources than mutually satisfactory neighborliness in perfect harmony. It may be these conflicts have been exaggerated in our consciousness.

The multinational structure described here briefly, which was essentially founded on a basis of voluntarism, later—during the partitions, and thus during a period of accelerated nation-forming processes—came to operate in neighboring foreign states. The forms of coexistence evolved, therefore, in different circumstances, as did the mutual relations between Poles and other national groups, among whom appeared representatives of the partitioning powers, in appropriately prominent positions. It is worth emphasizing that despite unfavorable circumstances, in many cases the attractiveness of Polish culture was confirmed, although its spread was already made significantly more difficult.

Inevitably, however, new areas of conflict also appeared, which affected the state of relations with neighbors and which were to bear such bloody fruit in the 20th century, a century of totalitarianism, mass deportations and exterminations, and of the cruelest crimes having an ethnic basis. Antagonism was also exacerbated by changes in the territory of the individual states, often made in an arbitrary manner. Poles emerged from that period badly roughed up, undoubtedly, but—one may perhaps express this conviction—wiser for subsequent difficult experiences and lessons flowing from history.

Contemporary thinking about Polish identity in the context of cultural and ethnic pluralism must therefore—and this is probably obvious—take into account the intensive changes that have occurred both in our immediate vicinity and farther away. Their essence seems to be a violent acceleration of European integrational processes, with a simultaneous renaissance of consciousness and local bonds connected with the concept of so-called "small homelands." In a changing Europe, the traditions of the nobles' Commonwealth—wisely interpreted—may prove to be invaluable, becoming one of the cornerstones of building mutual relations.

One should only see to it that the tendency to seek local identities of one's own is devoid of political accents, or at least that they be secondary. If this condition is fulfilled, "small homelands" will not endanger existing national structures in even the slightest degree; thus they will not carry a destructive load, which as a result would minimize the number of their real and potential adversaries. The historical experience of the Commonwealth of many nations and the lessons derived from these experiences should play an important role in the process described.

Selected bibliography

Althoen, D., "'Natione Polonus' and the 'Naród Szlachecki.' Two Myths of National Identity and Noble Solidarity, *Zeitschrift für Ostmitteleuropa-Forschung,* vol. 52, Heft 4 (2003), pp. 475–508.

Fiszman, S. (ed.), *The Polish Renaissance in its European Context*, foreword by Czesław Miłosz, Bloomington: Indiana University Press, 1988.

Hoerder, D., "Metropolitan Migration in the Past: Labour Markets, Commerce, and Cultural Interaction in Europe, 1600–1914," *Journal of International Migration and Integration,* vol. 1/1 (2000), p. 39–58.

Lucassen, J., *Migrant Labour in Europe, 1600–1900*, translated by D. A. Bloch, London: Croom Helm, 1987.

Tazbir, J., *A State without Stakes. Polish Religious Toleration in the Sixteenth and Seventeenth Centuries*, translated by A. T. Jordan, New York: The Kościuszko Foundation, 1973.

Tazbir, J., *Culture of the Baroque in Poland*, in Mączak, A., Samsonowicz, H., and Burke, P. (eds.), *East-Central Europe in Transition*, Cambridge: Cambridge University Press, 1985, pp. 167–180.

IGOR KĄKOLEWSKI, historian, professor at the Institute of Political Sciences, University of Warmia and Mazury in Olsztyn, deputy director at the Center of Historical Research, Polish Academy of Sciences in Berlin. He specializes in the history of early modern Europe, especially in Polish-German relations. His published works include *Nadużycia władzy i korupcja w Prusach Książęcych w połowie XVI w. Narodziny państwa nowożytnego* [Abuse of Authority and Corruption in Ducal Prussia in the Mid-16th Century. The Birth of a Modern State] (2000); *Słownik stereotypów polsko-niemieckich* [Dictionary of Polish-German Stereotypes] (2001); and *Melancholia władzy. Problem tyranii w europejskiej kulturze politycznej XVI stulecia* [The Melancholy of Authority. The Problem of Tyranny in European 16th-Century Political Culture] (2007).

—
265
—

EDMUND KIZIK, historian, professor at the Institute of History of the Polish Academy of Sciences and the University of Gdańsk, specializes in social and cultural history of Gdańsk and the Hanseatic region from the 15th to the early 19th centuries. He is the author and editor of works in the fields of religious history, everyday life, customs, and material culture in the early modern era. His published works include *Mennonici w Gdańsku, Elblągu i na Żuławach Wiślanych w drugiej połowie XVII i w XVIII wieku* [Mennonites in Gdańsk, Elbląg, and the Vistula Żuławy in the Second Half of the 17th Century and in the 18th Century] (1994); *Śmierć w mieście hanzeatyckim w XVI–XVIII wieku. Studium z nowożytnej kultury funeralnej* [Death in a Hanseatic City in the 16th–17th Centuries. A Study of Early Modern Funerary Culture] (1998); *Wesele, kilka chrztów i po-grzebów. Uroczystości rodzinne w mieście hanzeatyckim w XVI–XVIII w.* [Wedding, A Few Baptisms and Funerals. Family Ceremonies in a Hanseatic City in the 16ᵗʰ–18ᵗʰ Centuries] (2001, German edition 2008); and together with Hans-Jürgen Bömelburg: *Altes Reich und Alte Republik Deutsch-polnische Beziehungen und Verflechtungen 1500–1806* (2014).

MICHAŁ KOPCZYŃSKI, historian, professor at the Institute of History, University of Warsaw, research coordinator at the Polish History Museum in Warsaw, specializes in socio-economic history of the 16ᵗʰ–20ᵗʰ centuries. His published works include *Studia nad rodziną chłopską w Koronie w XVII–XVIII wieku* [Studies on the Peasant Family in the Crown in the 17ᵗʰ–18ᵗʰ Centuries] (1998); *Wielka transformacja* [The Great Transformation] (2006); and *Ludzie i technika. Szkice z dziejów cywilizacji przemysłowej* [People and Technology. Sketches from the History of Industrial Civilization] (2009).

OLEG ŁATYSZONEK, historian, professor at the University of Białystok, president of the Belarusian Historical Society, member of the board of the Belarusian Alliance in the Republic of Poland. His published works include *Białoruskie formacje wojskowe 1917–1923* [Belarusian Military Formations, 1917–1923] (1995); *Historia Białorusi od połowy XVIII do końca XX wieku* [History of Belarus from the Mid-18ᵗʰ to the Late 20ᵗʰ Century] (with E. Mironowicz, 2002); and *Od Rusinów Białych do Białorusinów. U źródeł białoruskiej idei narodowej* [From White Ruthenians to Belarusians. At the Sources of the Belarusian National Ideal] (2006). His collected works were translated into Belarusian: *Жаўнеры БНР* [Soldiers of the BPR] (2009, 2010, 2014); *Нацыянальнасьць – Беларус* [Nationality—Belarusian] (2009, 2012); *Гісторыя Беларусі ад сярэдзіны XVIII ст. да пачатку XXI ст.* [History of Belarus from the Mid-18ᵗʰ to the Late 20ᵗʰ Century] (with E. Mironowicz, 2010); *Беласток-Полацак* [Bialystok-Polatsak]

(2010). He is the co-author and co-editor of a manual *Historia Białorusinów Podlasia* [History of Belarusians of Podlasie Region] (2016). Now he is writing a book *Belarus in the Clash of Civilisations*.

LECH MRÓZ, ethnologist, professor at the Institute of Ethnology and Cultural Anthropology, University of Warsaw; from 1999 to 2012 Head of the Institute. Currently professor at the Department of Japanese Culture at the Polish-Japanese Academy of Information Technology in Warsaw; corresponding member of the Polish Academy of Arts and Sciences. He studies the cultures of pastoral and nomadic peoples and has conducted field research in India, Mongolia, Yakutsia, the Balkans, Lithuania and Ukraine. His scholarly interests include in particular conflicts and disputes over symbols, the emergence of national mythology (especially issues of identity in the countries of the former USSR) and ethno-cultural frontiers (he has been studying the Polish-Ukrainian borderland for several years). At present he is leading a joint Polish-Ukrainian team working on the four-year research project "Hutsulia: anthropological areas of memory". He has studied the Gypsies—Romani in Eastern Europe, their history and the processes of cultural change within that ethnic group. His books (as author or co-author) include *Dzieje Cyganów–Romów w Rzeczpospolitej, XV–XVIII w.* [History of the Gypsies—Romani in the Polish-Lithuanian Commonwealth, 15th–18th Centuries] (2001; the Polish Academy of Sciences Prize); *Od Cyganów do Romów. Z Indii do Unii Europejskiej* [From Gypsies to Romani. From India to the European Union] (2007); and *Roma-Gypsy Presence in the Polish-Lithuanian Commonwealth, 15th–18th Centuries*. Budapest–New York: Central European University Press (2015; Honorable Mention for the Kulczycki Book Prize for Polish Studies).

MIROSŁAW NAGIELSKI, historian, professor at the Institute of History, University of Warsaw, specializes in the history of the Polish military and in the general history of the early modern era, and conducts research on the Zaporizhian Cossacks, military biographies, and parliamentarianism in the 17th century. His published works include *Rokosz Jerzego Lubomirskiego w 1665 roku* [Lubomirski's Rebellion of 1665] (1994); as co-author and editor: *Poczet hetmanów Rzeczypospolitej* [List of the Commonwealth's Hetmans] (2005, 2006), *Staropolska sztuka wojenna XVI–XVII wieku* [Old Polish Military Art of the 16th–17th Centuries] (2002); *Druga wojna domowa w Polsce. Z dziejów polityczno-wojskowych Rzeczypospolitej u schyłku rządów Jana Kazimierza Wazy* [The Second Civil War in Poland. Political and Military History at the End of John Casimir's Reign] (2011); as editor of sources: *Relacje wojenne z pierwszych lat walk polsko-kozackich powstania Bohdana Chmielnickiego okresu „Ogniem i mieczem"* *(1648–1651)*[War Accounts from the First Stages of Polish-Cossack War During Bohdan Khmelnystyi's Uprising, the Period of "With Fire and Sword" (1648–1651)] (1999), and *Diariusz kampanii smoleńskiej Władysława IV (1633–1634)* [Diary of the Smolensk Campaign of Władysław IV (1633–1634)] (2006).

ANDRZEJ RACHUBA, historian, professor at the Institute of History of the Polish Academy of Sciences in Warsaw, director of the Editorial Workshop. His interests focus on the history of the Grand Duchy of Lithuania in the early modern period (1569–1732), and especially on political, social, military, legal system, as well as on parliamentary issues. He is the author of around 300 publications, including 25 books (monographs, editions of sources, lists of officials and Tribunal delegates). His published works include *Historia Litwy. Dwugłos polsko-litewski* [The History of Lithuania. The Polish-Lithuanian Dialog] (2009, jointly with J. Kiaupienė, Z. Kiaupa).

KRZYSZTOF STOPKA, historian, professor at the Institute of History of the Jagiellonian University, director of the Museum of the Jagiellonian University. He belongs to the Armenian Cultural Association and chairs the Council of the Foundation of Culture and Heritage of Polish Armenians. He is the author of works on the history and of the Polish Middle Ages. His published works include *Ormianie w Polsce dawnej i dzisiejszej* [Armenians in Ancient and Today's Poland] (2000); *Armenia christiana. Armenian Religious Identity and the Churches of Constantinople and Rome* (English edition 2016); *Pomniki minionej chwały. Ormiański Lwów w opisie Krzysztofa Stopki i w fotografii Andrzeja Płachetki* [Monuments to Past Glory. Armenian Lviv as Described by Krzysztof Stopka and in the Photography of Andrzej Płachetka] (2002); and *Języki oswajane pismem. Alografia kipczacko-ormiańska i polsko-ormiańska w kulturze dawnej Polski* [The Languages Domesticated by Script. Kipchak-Armenian and Polish-Armenian Allographies in the Culture of Ancient Poland] (2013). He translated into Polish the classical work on Armenian Christianity, M. Ormanian, *Kościół ormiański. Historia, doktryna, zarząd, reguły kanoniczne, liturgia, literatura, stan współczesny* [The Armenian Church. History, doctrine, administration, canonical law, liturgy, literature, present state] (2004).

ANNA AKBIKE SULIMOWICZ, Orientalist, lecturer at the Department of Turkish Studies and Inner Asian Peoples, Faculty of Oriental Studies, University of Warsaw, and a member of the board of the Association of Polish Karaites and the editorial board of *Awazymyz*, a Karaite socio-culturo-historical periodical. She is a translator of Turkish literature.

WOJCIECH TYGIELSKI, historian, professor at the Institute of Art History, University of Warsaw, specializes in the social history of Poland and Europe in the 16th–17th centuries, Polish-Italian contacts, the history of travel, and modern diplomacy. He has published sources (including the correspondence of nuncio Francesco Simonetta, 1606–1607, as well as tales from the European journey of Giacomo Fantuzzi, 1652, and Luigi Bevilacqua, 1609). His published works include *Italians*

269

in Early Modern Poland: The Lost Opportunity for Modernization?, translated by K. Popowicz, Frankfurt am Mein: Peter Lang GmbH (2015);
and *Listy – ludzie – władza. Patronat Jana Zamoyskiego w świetle kore-
spondencji* [Letters–People–Authority. The Patronage of Jan Zamoyski
in the Light of Correspondence] (2007).

JAN TYSZKIEWICZ, historian, Professor Emeritus, Institute of History
of the University of Warsaw. He graduated in historical and archaeo-
logical studies, and he works in medieval studies, the auxiliary sciences
of history, historical geography, historical chronology, and demography.
He conducts research in the history of Polish Slavistics, and in the history
of nomadic peoples in Europe, especially the Tatars. His published works
include *Słownik historyczny Europy Środkowo-Wschodniej.* T. 1: *Państwa
Grupy Wyszehradzkiej* [Historical Dictionary of Central and Eastern Europe. Vol. 1: The Visegrad Group Countries] (ed., 2006); *Dawna Rosja
i Rosjanie we współczesnych badaniach polskich* [Ancient Russia and Russians in Contemporary Polish Research] (ed. with Krzysztof Łukawski,
2012, 2014); *Dzieje Mazowsza.* T. 2: *Lata 1527–1794* [History of Mazovia.
Vol. 2: 1527–1794] (ed., 2015); *Brunon z Kwerfurtu w Polsce i krajach
sąsiednich w tysiąclecie śmierci 1009–2009* [Bruno of Querfurt in Poland
and Neighbouring Countries. On his Thousandth Death Anniversary
1009–2009] (2009). Author of 14 books including those about Tatars:
Tatarzy na Litwie i w Polsce. Studia z dziejów XIII–XVIII w. [Tatars in Lithuania and Poland. Studies in 13th–18th Centuries History] (1989); *Ostat-
nia wojna z Zakonem Krzyżackim 1519–1521* [The Last War with the
Teutonic Knights 1519–1521] (1991, 2015); *Z historii Tatarów polskich
1794–1944* [From the History of Polish Tatars 1794–1944] (1998, 2002);
and *Tatarzy w Polsce i Europie* [Tatars in Poland and Europe] (2008).

JACEK WIJACZKA, historian, professor at the Institute of History and
Archival Studies, Nicolaus Copernicus University in Toruń. He researches

the history of Ducal and Royal Prussia in the 16th–18th centuries, Polish-German relations in early modern times, witchcraft trials, and also the history of Jews in the former Commonwealth. His publications include *Stosunki dyplomatyczne Polski z Rzeszą Niemiecką w czasach panowania cesarza Karola v (1519–1556)* [Poland's Diplomatic Relations with the German Empire During the Reign of Emperor Charles V (1519–1556] (1998); *Procesy o czary w Prusach Książęcych (Brandenburskich) w XVI–XVIII wieku* [Witchcraft Trials in Ducal Prussia (Brandenburg) in the 16th–18th Centuries] (2007); and *Kościół wobec czarów w Rzeczypospolitej w XVI–XVIII wieku (na tle europejskim)* [The Attitude of the Church Towards Witchcraft in the Commonwealth in the 16th–18th Centuries (on the European Background)] (2016).

ANDRZEJ ŻBIKOWSKI, historian, professor at the Jewish Historical Institute and in Eastern European Studies at the University of Warsaw. His publications include *U genezy Jedwabnego. Żydzi na Kresach Północno-Wschodnich II Rzeczypospolitej. Wrzesień 1939 – lipiec 1941* [The Genesis of Jedwabne. Jews in the Northeastern Borderlands of the Second Republic. September 1939–July 1941] (2006); *Polacy i Żydzi pod okupacją niemiecką 1939–1945. Studia i materiały* [Poles and Jews under German Occupation, 1939–1945. Studies and Materials] (2006)); *Karski* (2011), and *Sąd Społeczny przy CKŻP* [People's Court affiliated to the Central Committee of Jews in Poland] (2013).

www.ingramcontent.com/pod-product-compliance
Lightning Source LLC
Chambersburg PA
CBHW021221090426
42740CB00006B/315